RESORTS

LAST RESORTS

The Cost of Tourism in the Caribbean

Polly Pattullo

First published in the United Kingdom by
Latin America Bureau
1 Amwell Street
London EC1R 1UL
www.latinamericabureau.org

Latin America Bureau is an independent research and publishing organisation. It works
to broaden public understanding of human rights and social and economic justice in
Latin America and the Caribbean.

ISBN 1 899365 64 8

First published in the United States of America by
Monthly Review Press
122 West 27th Street
New York, NY 10001
www.monthlyreview.org

Library of Congress Cataloging-in-Publication data available from the publisher.
ISBN 1-58367-117X (pbk)

A CIP catalogue record is available from the British Library.

Editing: Jean McNeil
Cover and interior photography: Philip Wolmuth
Cover and interior design: Andy Dark
Printed by Arrowsmith, Bristol, United Kingdom

CONTENTS

Map of The Caribbean
Acknowledgements

1   THE LOCK AND THE KEY: 1
    HISTORY AND POWER

2   LINKAGES AND LEAKAGES: 37
    THE PLANNING FACTOR

3   FROM BANANA FARMER TO BANANA DAIQUIRI: 65
    EMPLOYMENT

4   'LIKE AN ALIEN IN WE OWN LAND':   101
    THE SOCIAL IMPACT

5   GREEN CRIME, GREEN REDEMPTION: 129
    THE ENVIRONMENT AND ECOTOURISM

6   THE HOLIDAY AND ITS MAKERS: 167
    THE TOURISTS

7   SAILING INTO THE SUNSET: 193
    THE CRUISE SHIP INDUSTRY

8   RECLAIMING THE HERITAGE TRAIL: 217
    CULTURE

9   NEW FOOTPRINTS IN THE SAND: 245
    THE FUTURE

Photographs   264
Select Bibliography   265
Index   268

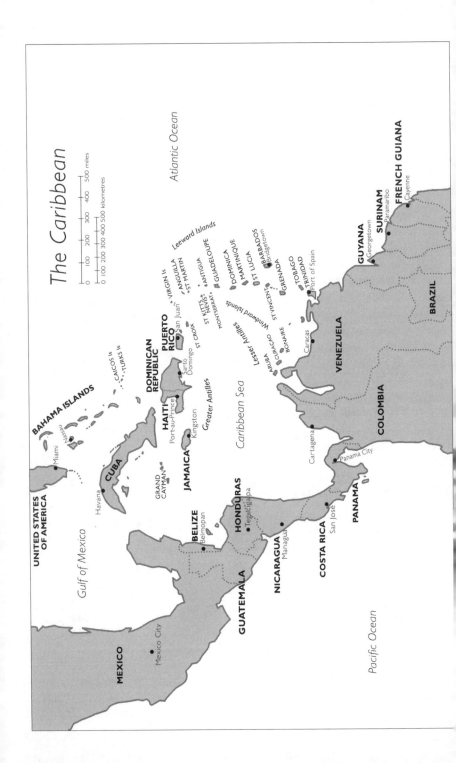

The Caribbean

Acknowledgements

My thanks to my helpful editor, Jean McNeil, who suggested this second edition; to Rod Prince, who read the manuscript; researcher Sarah Robertson; Greg Chamberlain who sent me news reports; Yves Renard for his insights; those at Tourism Concern, in particular Tricia Barnett; and, above all, to the people of the Caribbean – whether ministers or tourism officials, hotel workers or beach vendors – who so generously offered information and advice. And to my friends in Dominica, especially those living or working in the Roseau valley, who first inspired me to look more closely at the shape of the Caribbean tourism industry.

1

THE LOCK AND THE KEY:
HISTORY AND POWER

The Hilton Jalousie Plantation resort lies in a sweeping valley sloping down to the sea between the Pitons, the two great volcanic cones on the west coast of St Lucia. The site is one of the great landscapes of the Caribbean; from land, sea or air the Pitons rise up green, steep and pristine. A handful of miles away is Soufrière, the oldest town on the island, of faded charm and high unemployment. When tourists arrive at Soufrière on picturesque two-masted schooners and catamarans they are told not to throw coins into the sea for the teenage divers hanging around the jetty. They are whisked through the town to visit the nearby La Soufrière sulphur springs, known as the 'drive-in volcano'. Those once bound for the luxuries of Jalousie – 'the closest thing to paradise on earth,' claimed the original brochure – pass through swathes of cocoa, banana, citrus and avocado before turning off on to a new and better road, the approach to Jalousie. If they cared to look to their right, they would see Malgretoute ('In spite of everything'), a home for the poor and old, where figures move slowly along a wooden verandah. But this area, too, is to be transformed: the old people are to be re-housed elsewhere and in their place will be rolled out another tourist development, at Coin de L'Anse, with a hotel, apartments and a marina. As such, it will dwarf Jalousie in its scope and impact.

The building of Jalousie, which opened in October 1992, had been a battle. There were those who supported the development of a hotel between the Pitons: they included the government, Soufrière's opposition parliamentary member and some, but not all, of the local community. They believed that Jalousie's investors would bring jobs to a depressed part of St Lucia and foreign exchange to the island as a whole. At one meeting held in the town to discuss the issue, young men from Soufrière blew conch shells and shouted 'We want Jalousie!'[1]

Then there were the anti-Jalousie camps. One group, the so-called environmentalists, argued that not only were the Pitons the national symbol of St Lucia and a sacred site for the island's first inhabitants, the Arawaks, but that the ecosystem was too precious to disturb. They wanted the area to be held in common for the benefit of all St Lucians and not sold off to foreigners to turn into a ritzy tourist ghetto. There was also concern that such a resort would reduce the chances of the Pitons being declared a UNESCO world heritage site.

In a passionate article in a local newspaper, St Lucia's Nobel prize-winner for Literature Derek Walcott, wrote: 'To sell any part of the Pitons is to sell the whole idea and body of the Pitons, to sell a metaphor, to make a fast buck off a shrine...' He said that the debate was being conducted at a level which would argue that 'a casino in the Vatican' or 'a take-away concession inside Stonehenge' would provide extra income and jobs.[2] Selling the Pitons, he concluded, was like selling your mother into prostitution. The government was also faced with a proposal from a promoter who wanted to run a cable car up the Petit Piton and, so rumour had it, to flatten the summit of Gros Piton to build an 'Amerindian village' and restaurant. That bizarre idea fuelled the fury of the environmentalists who used it to attack the government.

An alternative plan for the area had been put forward in a report by the Organisation of American States (OAS). This recommended that the whole area of the Pitons, including the Jalousie estate, be turned into a locally controlled and managed national park. It was argued that this option would not only protect the environment, but that it would be the sort of tourist attraction which would generate employment through locally owned businesses such as guest houses, restaurants, and guiding services. The report estimated that the park would create 400 new jobs in the area, as well as offer opportunities for small entrepreneurs.[3]

The OAS plan, however, was criticised by yet another group, who were also against the development of Jalousie. They felt that the study was too narrow, seeking principally to justify the park on the basis of the creation of direct jobs, which was more wishful thinking than a realistic assessment. They maintained also that the methods used by the study were inappropriate: there was no consultation or local involvement. The high-handed methods of the OAS helped the government's case, as did the narrow focus of the environmentalists.

This second group had a rather wider agenda, arguing that the existence of Jalousie would conflict with a vision of integrated development in Soufrière. Yves Renard, then of the Caribbean Natural Resources Institute, saw the patrimony of the area threatened by Jalousie: he said that the community's development would not be best served by the presence of a foreign-owned all-inclusive resort, established without any participation of the host community. Throughout the Caribbean, this point of view has begun to gain authority and confidence and is an important, if still weak, new voice in the tourism debate at the beginning of the 21st century (see Chapter Nine).

Before Jalousie could be built, St Lucia's development control authority, the body with statutory responsibility over development, had to give its permission. The authority refused. Three times the government, under pressure from the owner, the British aristocrat Colin Tennant (otherwise known as Lord Glenconner, and former owner of Mustique) went to the authority and asked it to change its mind. Eventually it did the lord's bidding. The way forward was now clear for the building of Jalouise.

For the first four years of its existence, Jalousie was owned by the Swiss-based M Group Corporation, headed by Pascal Mahvi, an Iranian-born businessman. He had bought the land, once a copra estate, from Tennant (who later opened a self-consciously down-at-heel bar nearby called Bang Between the Pitons). Managed by Resort Services, an Ohio subsidiary of the M Group, the US$60 million, 320-acre resort was built with 114 cottages and suites, four restaurants, a ballroom, the Lord's Great Room furnished with Tennant's antiques, tennis courts, a helicopter pad, a hydroponic farm for growing non-traditional crops and tight, high-tech security.

When the hotel opened in 1994, on hand to deliver this service were nearly 400 workers, all St Lucians except for 14 expatriates in the most senior posts. Besides providing jobs for local people, Jalousie helped the town of Soufrière by supporting a school, a sports organisation and the queens' pageant, a kind of beauty competition. Yet the links between guests and St Lucians were controlled. In the manner of the 'all-inclusive' concept, in which guests pay for all their holiday needs in advance, non-guests could not enter the premises without buying an expensive pass.

The management maintained that the resort respected the environment: the low-storeyed buildings blended in with the landscape and, except for the Great House, were invisible from the sea, while special mooring facilities for yachts protect the coral reef from damage. The environmentalists said that this was too little, too late; the reef, they claimed, had already been damaged by silting, the after-effects of construction work, and Amerindian relics had been destroyed when the tennis court was built, probably over a burial site.

By then, however, Jalousie was featuring in international tour brochures. It had become one of hundreds of beach resorts in the Caribbean which seek to capture bookings from holidaymakers and honeymooners seeking their 'away from it all' fleeting moment of tropical luxury.

But all was not well with Jalousie. One day in May 1996, two years after it opened, Jalousie closed heavily in debt, sending its workers home. But the government – the same administration that had endorsed its opening – could not afford to lose such a flagship hotel in such a distinctive location. A rescue package was announced by the then prime minister, Vaughan Lewis, to bail out the hotel. A new company was formed, composed of the original owners, the Hilton Corporation, which was given the management contract, and the St Lucia government, which was to become – and remains – the majority shareholder. Jalousie reopened as the Hilton Jalousie Plantation in December 1997 – with Hilton having spent US$6 million on the hotel. The foreign investors were now to take a back seat, while the local government had become even more committed to the hotel than ever.

What is important about the story of Jalousie is that it is so typical. There are countless other Jalousies in the Caribbean and the story of the Jalousies, taken together, provoke an essential debate about tourism: Who benefits? And how? It asks questions about sovereignty (when beaches and valleys become foreign fields). It presents dilemmas about economic well-being and how profits are distributed. It generates arguments about how tourism can (or cannot) protect the environment, and speculates about the social and cultural relations between visitors and hosts. The decision of the St Lucian government, jostling for custom in tourism's great global shopping mall, to welcome a foreign company willing and able to build a glittering pleasure dome and so provide much-needed foreign exchange and jobs has been repeated time and time again. Indeed, in the economic and political climate of the 1980s and 1990s, Caribbean governments, with few exceptions, fell over themselves to make such an equation. As in St Lucia, governments have over-ruled the decisions of planning committees and environmental impact assessments. Finally, they have ignored alternative sorts of tourism initiatives, which might offer more long-term, if more complex, solutions based on the principles of sustainable development. The case of Jalousie was no exception.[4]

One of the challenges of tourism in the Caribbean is to forge a form of tourism compatible with local conditions. The issue is more than just whether or not to welcome a new resort but under whose terms and whether the terms can provide a long-term solution for those islands in the sun. The circumstances and conditions under which projects such as Jalousie have come into being reflect the shape and style of Caribbean tourism. In a wider sense, they also go some way towards explaining the dynamics of Caribbean societies over the last half century.

Changing Landscapes

An estimated 39 million people live on the islands of two archipelagos which straddle the Caribbean Sea from the continental landmarks of Florida in the north to Venezuela in the south. The region also comprises the 'mainland' territories of Belize in Central America and the Guianas in South America which are, historically and culturally, also part of the Caribbean. There are great disparities of size and population. Tiny Saba has 1,100 people on 11 square kilometres, while Cuba has a population of 11 million and the Dominican Republic has 8.5 million. Of the chain of small islands in the Eastern Caribbean, Trinidad is by far the largest (with a population of 1.3 million), and the rest are what are known as microstates, with populations mostly below 300,000. The distance from Belize in the west to Barbados in the east is around 2000 miles; flying time (if you could fly it non-stop in a commercial airline, which you can't) would take nearly as long as from Los Angeles to New York.

Despite its geographic and demographic diversity, the Caribbean has a common heritage, moulded by slavery, colonialism (English, French, Spanish and Dutch) and the plantation. Its people are a reflection of that historical background: the indigenous (and now almost extinct) Amerindian, European coloniser, settler and adventurer, African slave, indentured East Indian, labouring Chinese and Portuguese, small-town merchant Arab and Jew. All such peoples have fashioned the Caribbean of today, forging Creole societies in which old loyalties and traditions, dominated by Africa and Europe, compete now with the great power and hegemony of North America.

In the second half of the 20th century, the Caribbean was preoccupied with fundamental change. Many former colonies became nation states, like the already independent countries of Haiti, the Dominican Republic and Cuba, and began to etch out their own political, economic and cultural paths. Yet, like other regions of the Third World, the old economic patterns – dependency on foreign investment, foreign aid and the export of raw agricultural products – maintained their shape.

During this process the tourist industry became part of the landscape. By the turn of the 21st century, all Caribbean territories were in the tourism business. Politicians had proclaimed it 'the engine of growth' even though they often failed to give it priority when it came to policy making. Even so, tourism was much discussed: it was associated with power and prosperity; it was touted as the tool which would carry Caribbean peoples into 'development' and 'modernism' and out of their poverty on the periphery of the world.

It was not just regional politicians (of all persuasions) and the private sector who favoured this process. Invoking similar mantras and more importantly helping to make it all happen were the 'men in suits' – ranks of consultants, diplomats, international tourist industry officials, lending agencies and development banks.

International bodies such as the World Bank, which financed large hotels in the 1970s, and the United Nations endorsed tourism for the Third World; an Organisation for Economic Cooperation and Development (OECD) publication had reported in 1967 that tourism was a 'promising new resource for economic development.'[5] Later, the third Lomé Convention (1986-90), which enshrined Europe's special relationship with states in Africa, the Caribbean and the Pacific, also recognised the 'real importance of the tourism industry' and provided a broad range of financial provision. This was the first time that the Lomé Convention, which dates back to 1975, had paid attention to tourism. The fourth Lomé Convention (1990-99) took similar note of tourism, highlighting its investment potential.

Funding institutions, such as the International Monetary Fund (IMF) and the World Bank, generally support the creed that tourism makes economic sense for both tiny under-productive islands as well as for larger, more diversified if debt-laden economies, such as Jamaica or the Dominican Republic. Within the parameters of global neo-liberalism, the IMF promotes tourism through its structural adjustment programmes; the World Bank, which had closed its tourism unit in 1979, returned in the 1990s to the tourism arena, financing studies and loans for environmental or technical assistance projects with tourism components.

Such beliefs also found favour with the West Indian Commission, which recognised 'the strategic position that tourism had come to occupy in the region.'[6] The Commission was set up in the early 1990s by the Caribbean Community (Caricom), the 13-strong, English-speaking regional grouping, to seek an economic and political way forward for the region in the historic footsteps of the British West India Royal Commission of 1897 and the 1945 Moyne Commission. The Commission's 1993 report, 'Time for Action', welcomed the fact that all Caricom countries were now 'openly committed to nurturing in their economies a tourism sector geared to their particular endowments.'[7] It was not the only regional body to reinforce this position. In 1995, the first summit of the Association of Caribbean States – then a new body representing all independent countries of the Caribbean, including Cuba – said in its declaration of principles that the tourism sector 'is vital to the economies of our countries, we commit ourselves to unite efforts and actions aimed at increasing the tourist flow to the Caribbean, at improving tourism infrastructure and preserving our environment.' The declaration added that the 'full realisation of this potential depends critically on our public and private sectors being able to cooperate to address the challenges and constraints as well as to exploit the synergies' of tourism, trade and transport.

The region's declarations of support for tourism did not happen in a vacuum. Tourism was not just a regional phenomenon – by the end of the 20th century it had become the world's largest industry. United Nations figures on projected tourism arrivals had leapt from some US$664 million in 1999 to an estimated US$1.6 billion by 2020. World tourism generated around US$344 billion a year in earnings, far more than the international reserves of the economies of Japan, China and the United States put together. While in the mid-20th century, Western Europe and North America had attracted nearly all the world's tourists, by the end of the century tourists had been busy searching out what became known as 'long-haul' destinations: they were enjoying 'exotic' holidays. In 1999, for example, only 62 per cent of holidays were in the 'north' while most countries of the 'south' had increased their market share and were continuing to do so.[8]

The Caribbean's share of world tourist arrivals was 2.5 per cent in 2000, according to the World Tourism Organisation, larger than that of regions such as South and Central America and South Africa.[9] In that year, the Caribbean received 20.3 million stayover tourists and 14.5 million cruise passenger visitors. Stayover arrivals had grown by 58.4 per cent in the decade up to 2000, an average of 4.7 per cent per year. That growth was slightly faster than the growth in the worldwide movement of tourists.[10]

Armed with the statistics, it was then hardly surprising that 'Time for Action' had taken the view that tourism was a key instrument of development and modernisation. 'Out of the tourist industry radiates stimuli for a wide range of industries producing goods and services; this is the concept of tourism as an axial product. Viewed in this light, the tourism sector can play an important role in the diversification and transformation of the region,' it declared.[11] The challenge for the Caribbean, according to the report, was to retain, and possibly increase, its share of the world tourism market.

Such perspectives, however, were not new. They had been around in the 1950s, and then in the 1960s with the advent of long-haul air travel and the rise of the consumerist west. Those decades, conveniently so for the rich foreigner looking for new holiday spots, also coincided with the decline of the Caribbean's traditional plantation economies and the search for an economic replacement. For the Caribbean, one solution was migration; and there is a certain irony in the fact that tourists began to arrive in the Caribbean in greater numbers just as the poor of the Caribbean began their own more onerous journey, in the opposite direction, to find work. For those who stayed, the chosen alternative was to turn primarily agricultural economies into pastures for pleasuring the leisured.

By the beginning of the 21st century, the tourism challenge was being discussed more vigorously – some would say more frantically – than ever. Despite the recognition of the volatility of tourism, especially in fragile Third World economies and cultures, the region had become even more dependent on tourism. By then, too, the choices had narrowed: the Caribbean was saddled by debt, costs were high, prices for its goods and raw materials were in decline, and traditional protected markets had dissolved as old colonial loyalties faded in the face of free trade.

A fragmented Caribbean found itself increasingly marginalised as the world rearranged itself into a one-stop free trade shop, and free-market trading blocs such as the North American Free Trade Agreement (NAFTA) and the European Union (EU). In contrast, the Anglophone Caribbean's own regional bloc, Caricom, and the wider Association of Caribbean States made painfully slow progress towards integration. The effect, as the Caribbean Tourism Organisation (CTO) put it in 1995, was clear: 'Trading blocs such as the NAFTA and the European Community have made it increasingly difficult for traditional Caribbean manufacturing and agricultural industries to remain competitive, giving tourism an even higher priority throughout the region.'[12] In 2001, Sir Edwin Carrington, the secretary-general of Caricom, again complained that the slow pace of integration denied businesses the opportunity to flourish.

Politically, too, by the end of the Cold War, the region appeared marginalised. It no longer generated much political interest except when refugees from Haiti or Cuba threatened the Florida coast or when there was an outcry over drugs. In any case, the Caribbean was by then largely controlled by governments sympathetic to the US and had become locked into a North American neo-liberal agenda. Alternatives to tourism, such as offshore financing or data processing, offered – and continue to do so – supplementary incomes to some countries. Even so, there were problems, with such countries accused of lacking proper regulation in their financial dealings. There were also difficulties in participating in the opportunities offered by free trade. Such constraints lent themselves to a continuing emphasis on tourism. It was, after all, something that the Caribbean knew how to do and (up to a point) knew how to do well.

By the 1990s, even those countries which had previously eschewed tourism or had only developed it at the margins had begun to embrace it. The collapse in oil prices in 1973, for example, led to a new interest in tourism for both Trinidad and its sister island Tobago. Similarly, in Aruba tourism replaced an earlier dependence on oil: nearly 6,000 hotel rooms opened in the decade after the closure of the Exxon refinery in 1984. In agriculture-led economies there were similar shifts; the crisis in the banana industry, which intensified throughout the 1990s, forced Windward Island governments to put tourism at the top of the agenda. St Lucia and Grenada redoubled their efforts, while St Vincent and Dominica entered the tourist business seriously for the first time. Poor performances in sugar and bauxite exports and the debt burden pushed Jamaica towards greater tourist activity. In Cuba, an economic crisis prompted by the collapse of Soviet communism provoked extraordinarily rapid, centrally-planned tourist development. Even little-known Suriname began to include tourism in its new mixed economy strategy.

By the beginning of the 21st century, this pattern was continuing. By then, however, shifts in both the theory and practice of tourism had introduced new factors. There was growing alarm about the region's vulnerability to external events such as terrorism (see Chapter Two). Increasing competition from both new and traditional destinations like Florida and Hawaii were seen to have the edge over the Caribbean in terms of price and quality. The numbers of arrivals fluctuated. The prospect of the opening up of Cuba to the US market sometime in the future was also something that merited attention, especially for destinations close to the US mainland, such as Jamaica and the Bahamas. There was also a new awareness about the impact of unregulated tourism and concepts such as sustainable development, while words such as ecotourism, stakeholders and empowerment entered the mainstream.

Prime Minister Kenny Anthony of St Lucia, for example, told a Caribbean Hotel and Tourism Investment conference in 2002 that, while governments needed to adopt pro-market policies to stimulate investment to the region, 'societal welfare' also had to be taken into consideration. He went on to say that destinations must be 'built slowly with a cautious eye on the long-term effects of rapid growth and equally rapid resource consumption.'[13] John Bell, former chief executive officer of the Caribbean Hotel Association, made a similar point when he said that not enough had been done to provide people with a sense of participation in and understanding of tourism. There was a need for 'greater involvement of small suppliers and local communities, greater sensitivity to environmental and social considerations in tourism planning and a greater focus on the development of facilities for local use and sharing with visitors.' [14] Such comments – with their emphasis on the needs of 'ordinary people' – were new in mainstream thinking.

Alongside this was talk of a crisis in the industry: it seemed that some sort of change was necessary but no one had quite worked out what that might be or, indeed, how it might be achieved (see Chapter Nine).

Shape and Form

While tourism has made footprints in nearly every territory, they have differed in shape and size, form and style. Patterns of growth have reflected a range of factors, some dependent on natural features and geography, others on economics and politics, both within the region and globally. Furthermore, growth has taken place at different speeds. Some countries joined in early and enthusiastically, others latterly and reluctantly as their options diminished. Some, whether pioneers or late-comers, are now in the big time, and others have bit parts. Some boast marinas grand enough for Greek shipping magnates and cultivate exclusive hideaways for retired rock stars. A few have mountain wildernesses and rainforests; more have casinos, karaoke competitions and Jolly Roger pirate cruises.

Such disparate stages in tourist 'development' could be plotted on the graph of what has become known as the Butler model of tourism's life-cycle. According to RW Butler, a Canadian geographer, the first phase is the 'exploration' of a remote and unspoiled spot. Then come the stages of involvement, development and consolidation as more hotels are built and mass tourism arrives. In time, the high spenders move on and the 'product' stagnates; attempts to stop the decline with down-market tourism fail and social and environmental deterioration begins. The Butler model then suggests that the only choice is between stagnation and rejuvenation. In the worst scenario, tourists leave, discarding the people and the environment. What was once poor and unspoiled is again poor but now spoiled.[15]

Examples of these stages were identified in the Caribbean in the 1990s, although nowhere in the region has quite reached the terminal phase. There were indications that the US Virgin Islands, St Maarten, Antigua and even Barbados might fall into the Butler model abyss. But this hasn't happened. Barbados, for example, has made some serious attempts to address its problems, with mixed success. Yet the model, whether accurate or not, continues to cast its shadow over the Caribbean's tourist industry, with experts warning that tourists will depart for newer – and greener – pastures if the all-round quality of the destinations fails to deliver satisfaction.

Although new indicators and different models are always being dreamed up by academics and industry professionals, measuring the impact of tourism is a complicated – and imprecise – process. Because of this, decision-makers find it hard to assess how far along the Butler model spectrum a destination lies. In one analysis, for example, visitor spending (economic impact), average daily visitor density per 1,000 resident population (social penetration) and the number of hotel rooms per km^2 of land area (environmental impact) were all measured. What the authors called a tourism penetration index (TPI) was then drawn up of selected islands (including 21 from the Caribbean) all over the world. Of the most penetrated islands are four from the Caribbean: St Maarten (the highest ranking of all islands globally), Aruba, the Caymans, and the British Virgin Islands (although the BVI is likely ranked too high because its yachting tourism is mainly sea-based). The least penetrated, according to this model, are St Vincent, Dominica, Grenada and Montserrat.[16] A different sort of model has also been developed to assess the multiplier impact of tourism (see Chapter Two). What planners and policy-makers have to gauge is how to keep the tourists coming without endangering the environmental or social balance. The emerging crisis in the region's tourism sector has brought into focus such complex equations.

Crisis in the Making

Even before the attack on the World Trade Center in September 2001 created a global tourism decline, there was concern about how the region's tourist industry was performing. Ralph Taylor, the then president of the Caribbean Hotel Association, expressed this at the second Caricom tourism summit in the Bahamas in December 2001. At the first summit in 1992, Michael Manley, then prime minister of Jamaica, had urged the creation of an advertising campaign to market the Caribbean as a single destination. The second summit, held at another point of crisis, was more ambitious. Taylor told the assembled heads of government, tourism ministers and regional tourist chiefs: 'The simple truth is, that long before September 11, the region had been experiencing a growing crisis, as Caribbean destinations became increasingly less competitive in a fiercely competitive global tourism marketplace.' Urging the region's politicians to take action (rather than just talk), he went on to stress the importance of a tourism strategy for the region.

A regional strategy required what he called 'critical success factors'. They were: a recognition of tourism as a key strategic export industry; a review of why the region's hotels were relatively uncompetitive; the creation of a tax policy for tourism; support for a sustainable tourism fund and development and support of air services.[17] These points were not new, but put together they added up to a formidable agenda. In 2002, they emerged as an aspect of a strategic development plan put together by the CTO for Caricom (see Chapter Nine).

At the same summit, Jean Holder, the then secretary-general of the Caribbean Tourism Organisation, also made a challenging and detailed speech entitled 'Meeting the Challenge of Change', about the crisis facing the region's industry. He had said similar things many times before but this was a moment of 'urgency' when the Caribbean was more dependent on tourism than ever before. Tourism generated gross exchange earnings of US$21 billion in 2004 and employed one in seven Caribbean people. The increased dependency, he said, was a result of the marginalisation of traditional export sectors and threats to new initiatives, especially financial services. 'Nothing,' said Holder, 'can therefore be allowed to put our tourism sector at risk.' He went on:

> Global tourism is in a period of transition and Caribbean tourism has neither dealt adequately with its past nor equipped itself for the changed environment of the future. Its sustainability and competitiveness can therefore only be assured by a radical change in thinking about the industry and by the courage and political will to take the steps necessary to restructure and modernize it.[18]

Holder and Taylor are among many leading figures from the Caribbean, and especially from its private sector, to recognise that tourism is not treated with the respect it deserves. It is, perhaps, of striking significance that Caricom – the major regional institution of the English-speaking Caribbean – should have held only two tourism summits since its founding in 1973. Perhaps the history of tourism in the region can explain the lingering diffidence towards its toweringly hegemonic industry.

The Age of the Sun

Most guests still choose the Caribbean for the beach with its creamy sands and clear seas. That has, almost everywhere, been the point of seduction. Yet the beach was not where the industry first began.

At the end of the 19th century, the first tourists to the Caribbean were attracted not by its sea and sand but by its invigorating climate and balmy air (islands such as Jamaica no longer evoked associations with disease). 'The island possesses great natural beauty, and its warm, healthy climate is recommended by the medical faculty,' boasted Elder, Dempster & Co's promotional literature for its 1905 winter tours for 'health and pleasure' sailing between Bristol and Jamaica.

At that time, the tropical seascape was more likely to be admired from a veranda than from the water's edge. The particular sea-view would depend on the traveller's nationality; the English, for example, went to their colonies of Barbados or Jamaica, the French to Martinique, the Dutch to Curaçao. The Americans, for reasons of geography, went to the Bahamas and Cuba, both close to the Florida coast. At that time, too, it was exclusively the wealthy who had the time and money to travel. Early advertising blurbs for shipping lines advised 'Winter in the West Indies'; it was all too fashionable.

While wealthy east coast Americans made winter trips in their large yachts, land-based visitors stayed in pioneering hotels. The Royal Victorian Hotel in the Bahamas opened in 1861 at the cost of more than US$130,000. In the eastern Caribbean, Crane Beach, on the wild east coast of Barbados, opened in 1887, while in Jamaica, Titchfield Hotel, a look-alike Victorian stately home, opened in Port Antonio in the next decade. By 1915, Cuba had 72 hotels, over one-third of them in Havana, where everything from polo to deep-sea fishing was on hand.

The 20th century became the age of the sun: what had once been seen as a coarsening threat to white skins became the new icon. The age of sun, sea and sand tourism began in the inter-war years, although it was still only the rich who were able to enjoy it. Tanning as a symbol of affluence and mobility was part of this same process and the Caribbean benefited; its reputation was already established as a glamorous destination well before the age of mass tourism.

After the Second World War, Jamaica's north coast became associated with a glittering expatriate community, with visitors renting or building houses. Ian Fleming, the creator of James Bond, and the British playwright Noel Coward both had houses there. Not far away lived Errol Flynn on his own Navy Island. There, Flynn gave parties for film stars and popularised rafting down the Rio Grande, using the rafts which had once carried bananas down river to take his friends on all-day picnics. Cuba also gained its own reputation for macho carousing and gambling in the manner of Ernest Hemingway, one of its expatriate US residents. By the 1950s, tourism had become Cuba's second largest earner of foreign currency after sugar, and the island welcomed more than 300,000 tourists a year, most of them from the US, to savour every indulgence. By then, however, President Batista's ruthless and corrupt regime and its rotten-hearted tourism had paved the way for revolution.

When tourism overtook sugar as the region's major foreign-exchange earner, it pitched the Caribbean into a new historical phase. For the most mature tourism economies such as Jamaica and Barbados, it happened with the introduction of regular, non-stop international jet services in the 1960s. With that, a less exclusive form of tourism, alongside the luxury market, also became possible.

It was then that the scramble for tourist dollars broadened and deepened. With the potential for a mass market, the multinational organisations, such as hotel chains and tour operators, began to show serious interest in the region. This was particularly true for the nearby US and Canadian markets, which had long provided the majority of visitors to the region. Meanwhile, revolutionary Cuba had been boycotted by Washington, and Puerto Rico and the Bahamas had taken over as the choice destinations of the US. Countries, other than old hands like Jamaica and Barbados, were also beginning to be 'discovered'. The rich even bought their own islands: the Rockefellers bought part of St John's in the US Virgin Islands, and Colin Tennant, later the owner of the Jalousie estate, bought Mustique from St Vincent and the Grenadines for £45,000 (including the rights of the local population). The St Vincent government also leased away Palm Island for a 99-year lease for a rent of US$99. The British entrepreneur Richard Branson, owner of Virgin Airlines, bought Necker Island in the British Virgin Islands in 1991.

Such growth, however, had taken place against the first stirrings of concern that all was not fun in the sun. From the investors' point of view, the Caribbean seemed expensive and inefficient. At the same time, two world-wide recessions in the 1970s kept the tourists at home and the costs up. In the Caribbean itself, intellectuals questioned the co-option of the region by foreign interests, viewing it as demeaning and as recolonisation by other means. 'Tourism is Whorism' was a phrase coined at the time. The Black Power movement gained its own impetus in the Caribbean as island states struggled from colonial to independent status. The way tourism appeared to be underpinned by racism became an important issue.

William Demas, then president of the Caribbean Development Bank, lamented the tourist industry's effect on Caribbean peoples: 'We welcome foreigners, we ape foreigners, we give away our national patrimony for a pittance to foreigners and, what is worse, we vie among ourselves in doing all of these things.'[19] It was not, however, just the opinion formers who were dissatisfied with tourism. In 1966, Jamaica's director of tourism complained that the 'biggest problem we are facing isn't "selling" Jamaica to the tourist, but "selling" tourists to the Jamaicans.'[20]

Such views were not uncommon during those years. However, island administrations (with the exception of Cuba and other territories which avoided tourism) continued to promote beaches and sunshine. Their increasing dependency on tourism was highlighted by the contemptuous views of foreign hoteliers and tourism 'experts' who credited themselves with the islands' survival. For example, an American travel industry spokesman wrote in the trade magazine Travel Weekly in 1972: 'Without the large hotels, most of the islands would dry up and blow away... Hilton is probably doing more to further local island cultures than anyone else, including the islanders themselves'; or an official overseeing a multi-million-dollar aid project in the eastern Caribbean who commented, 'only tourism and drug traffic keep these islands from going down the tubes.'[21]

At that time, however, a different voice was attempting to gain a hearing. In the 1970s, Jamaica and Grenada (see Chapter Nine) both attempted to use tourism as a tool of social and economic development for their people. Neither island wished to curtail its tourist industry, but both governments believed that there were serious flaws in the way it functioned. They were convinced that they could excise the negative aspects of tourism and make it work for the people rather than exclusively for the guests.

In the event, the invasive hand of US politics and capital intervened and, for both Jamaica and Grenada, what they called 'new' tourism (see Chapter Nine) never had much of a chance to develop. Instead, mass tourism became entrenched by the 1980s. The 1990s was a period of rapid growth – the decade when all the islands scrambled to join the tourist party – helped in part by external shifts in consumer demand.

In the early 1990s, in the wake of the Gulf War, Americans turned away from holidays in Europe to resorts closer to home, such as the Caribbean. At the same time, the European market to the Caribbean was also growing, but for different reasons. Pressure on the older Mediterranean resorts, by now often described as 'ruined', but newly popular with tourists from eastern Europe, encouraged the biggest and most competitive travel companies to look elsewhere: they saw the Caribbean. Hence the growth of new mass destinations such as the Dominican Republic and Cuba. The way in which the Caribbean gobbled up these new tourists for the numbers game remains a central preoccupation.

The Numbers Game

Some territories have seen unprecedented tourist growth over the past quarter century. For example, Anguilla's stayover arrivals increased from 1,000 in 1970 to 47,000 in 2003; visitors to the Turks & Caicos increased from 2,000 to 164,000 in the same period. At the mass tourism end of the spectrum, the Dominican Republic's arrivals grew from 63,000 in 1970 to more than three million in 2003 while Cuba registered spectacular gains from barely any tourists to 1.9 million in

2003, with speculation of a long-term goal for 10 million tourists a year, according to the Centre for Studies on the Cuban Economy. [22]

According to the CTO, the most popular destination in the island Caribbean in 2003 was the Dominican Republic with 3.3 million, followed by Cuba (1.9m), Bahamas (1.4m), Jamaica (1.3m), Aruba (641,000), the US Virgin Islands (618,000), Guadeloupe (623,000) and Barbados (549,000). In 1994, the top six had been: the Dominican Republic, Bahamas, Jamaica, the US Virgin Islands, Cuba and Aruba. Together these accounted for more than half of stayover tourists and around three-quarters of the Caribbean's total receipts from tourism. Those islands with the smallest number of stayover tourists in 2003 were the tiny British territory of Montserrat (8,000), stricken by a volcano, and members of the Netherlands Antilles: St Eustasius (11,000) and Saba (10,000).[23]

To accommodate such growth, the number of hotel rooms in the region has also increased – from 131,000 in 1990 to 261,003 (which includes the Mexican resorts of Cancún and Cozumel) in 2002. The 'newer' destinations showed enormous growth, especially those in the Hispanic Caribbean, with the Dominican Republic, for example, increasing its room count from 3,800 in 1980 to 54,730 in 2002. Over this period, many others had doubled (Antigua, the British Virgin Islands, St Lucia) or tripled (Anguilla, Aruba, Belize, Cuba, St Kitts-Nevis) their room numbers. The most stagnant were the 'mature' destinations such as Bahamas, the US Virgin Islands and Barbados. However, the latter island, which lost one-fifth of its rooms between 1980 and 1995 (from 6,680 down to 5,084) has since shown signs of recovery, registering 6,742 in 2002.[24]

Tourist officials and government ministers pore over these annual reams of statistics (arrivals, countries of origin, number of rooms, occupancy rates, visitor expenditure and percentage changes) as classical diviners once peered into animal entrails for inspiration. In what has become a numbers game orchestrated by politicians and administered by officials, more, for most destinations, still means better.

Such undivided attention to arrival figures is understandable given tourism's high profile as the 20th century's 'last resort' for the region; for, over three decades, tourism has distinguished itself as the only steady growth sector. As Jean Holder has stated: 'What is unique about the Caribbean is that it is more dependent on tourism than any other region in the world. Tourism receipts are 25 per cent of our total exports. There is a great deal riding on it.'

Caribbean tourism accounted for 21 per cent of the region's gross domestic product (GDP) in 1999 and 20 per cent of its capital investment, according to the World Travel and Tourism Council (WTTC). In 1993, the Economist Intelligence Unit's report on the industry had said: 'Tourism is the only sector of regional GDP that has consistently increased its share of total income during the 1980s. In some places, tourism accounts for up to 70 per cent of national income directly and indirectly.'[25] The trend has continued. In 2000, four Caribbean states showed that visitor expenditure represented more than half of the GDP. These were Anguilla (83.06 per cent), St Lucia (63.75 per cent), Antigua and Barbuda (63.36 per cent) and US Virgin Islands (56.74 per cent). In other, somewhat more diversified, economies such as Jamaica and the Dominican Republic, tourism also made a very significant contribution to export earnings while Belize, Grenada and St Lucia, for example, earned more from tourism than from banana exports. This classic reversal of fortunes, from agriculturally dependent to tourist dependent, is now also true for the old sugar-based economies such as Barbados, the Dominican Republic, Jamaica and Trinidad and Tobago, where tourists have become far more 'valuable' than sugar.

If tourist numbers alone were the key measurement of economic success, then giant steps indeed would have been taken in the Caribbean over the last couple of decades. However, an increase in numbers is not necessarily a guarantee of increased expenditure.

One way of looking at the statistics is to work out the amount of tourist expenditure against the number of tourist arrivals. Generally, visitor expenditure increases (or decreases) as numbers increase (or decrease). For example, Jamaica's stayover arrivals increased from 976,000 in 1994 to 1.3 million in 2000; expenditure increased from US$973 million to US$1,333 million over the same period roughly in proportion to the increase in visitors. However, the Turks and Caicos Islands showed a different pattern. Arrivals doubled – from nearly 71,000 in 1994 to more than 163,000 in 2003 – while expenditure increased fourfold. St Maarten showed another pattern: its arrivals dropped – from 585,000 to 427,587 – but its expenditure increased.[26]

Variations of this kind indicate that visitor spending depends not just on heads on beds but on other factors: room occupancy rates, length of stay, the wealth, interests and social class of the tourists and the available range of attractions and shopping.

Room occupancy rate, which is calculated by expressing the number of occupied rooms as a percentage of all available rooms over a specified period, is one useful measurement of economic return. In 1987, the average year-round room occupancy rate was estimated at 65 per cent, compared with 81 per cent for Hawaii and 58 per cent for Mexico.[27] By 2002, estimated occupancy rate had dropped to 60.2 per cent with wide variations between countries – from 41 per cent in Trinidad and Tobago and 42.5 per cent in Barbados to 71.7 per cent in Aruba. (The CTO, however, suggests that the range of accommodation covered by the figures varies, and that comparisons should be used with caution.)

The all-inclusive sector shows a high occupancy rate. In 1992, according to the CTO, the all-inclusive hotels achieved an average year-round occupancy of 80.3 per cent compared with 51.7 per cent for traditional hotels. In Jamaica, the home of the all-inclusive, occupancy rates show that all-inclusives have a keen edge over traditional hotels. In 2001, all-inclusives showed an occupancy rate of 69 per cent compared with 35 per cent for non all-inclusives. The all-inclusive sector has become a vital backdrop to the overall success of many Caribbean destinations.

In some cases, rapid hotel development has created a lopsided industry where too many rooms have chased too few tourists, especially in the slow summer season. In St Maarten, an explosion of hotel building in the 1970s, when the number of rooms escalated from 400 to 3,200 in 1993, brought the room occupancy rates tumbling from 70 per cent to 45 per cent. 'We want to put a freeze on hotel rooms, otherwise things will go from bad to worse,' said Cornelius de Weever, director of the division of tourism in St Maarten, in 1994. In fact, by 1999, a drop in the numbers of rooms (3,065) had resulted in a better occupancy rate of 59.3 per cent.

Low occupancy rates (and seasonality) have a particularly painful impact in the Caribbean where high hotel construction and running costs, high food import bills and relatively high pay rolls all contribute to low profit margins. Total revenues per room in the Caribbean in 1986 were more than US$46,500, compared to the average worldwide of US$29,510. Yet the profit margin per room was estimated at only US$5,000 in the Caribbean compared with US$7,705 worldwide and US$11,500 in the Pacific.[28] The result is that room rates in the region are some of the highest in the world: the Caribbean average in 1998 was US$83.04. Even high visitor expenditure does not necessarily solve problems or bring greater economic returns if there are high internal costs and high import bills (see Chapter Two).

A Question of Control

Such figures illustrate part of the complex economic character of the Caribbean tourist industry. Yet they do not reveal another crucial dimension of the region's ever widening and deepening dependence on tourism. This is the question of control.

Historically, Caribbean economies have been driven by external forces. In many ways, tourism has not changed this, although in recent years there have been certain shifts towards local control in some states. Yet overall, the Caribbean lacks control over its one growing economic sector. This is particularly true in regard to the cruise ship industry. This is totally foreign owned: not one Caribbean cruise ship company participates in this fast-growing sector (see Chapter Seven). No other region is probably quite so vulnerable. In general, as has been pointed out by many people, both inside and outside, the Caribbean is subject to world systems not of its making. As an academic has stated:

> When a third world country uses tourism as a development strategy, it becomes enmeshed in a global system over which it has little control. The international tourism industry is a product of metropolitan capitalist enterprise. The superior entrepreneurial skills, resources and commercial power of metropolitan companies enables them to dominate many Third World tourist destinations.[29]

From the beginning, US interests and capital dominated. This was particularly true, for instance, in Jamaica. In the last decades of the 19th century, bananas from Port Antonio began to be shipped to the east coast of the US. The business was run by the United Fruit Company, owned by a Massachusetts sea captain called Lorenzo Baker. Bananas went one way and tourists, travelling the other way, spent five luxurious days on board a banana boat before arriving in delightful Port Antonio. There, Captain Baker put up his passengers at his newly-built Titchfield Hotel, where American staff served them imported American food. In contemporary economic parlance, Captain Baker had achieved 'vertical integration', controlling the two essential planks of the tourist industry – travel and accommodation.

The captain's enterprise did not go unnoticed. There were, as there would be later, two schools of thought. Some Jamaicans welcomed his business as a model for US investors to develop the island's resources. Others deplored the situation whereby foreigners came to Jamaica 'to take out of it fortunes.'[30]

The steamships of the 19th century have now become jumbo jets and those first guesthouses have turned into luxury hotels. But for the Caribbean the economic issue remains the same. Who profits from tourism and controls its component parts: land and hotels, labour and management, transport, marketing, distribution, entertainment? Is it the descendants of the United Fruit Company, the transnational companies in New York, London and Paris who run the airlines and tour operators and many of the hotels? Is it the local governments who reap the taxes and duties generated by tourism or the local elites who accrue commission fees as wholesalers and importers and who now own and manage hotels? Or do the Caribbean workers in the industry – the guesthouse owners, waiters, taxi drivers, farmers, tour guides – also benefit? Or, indeed, have those with nothing to do with the industry indirectly benefited from tourism?

Airlines, tour operators, travel agents and hoteliers are the key players in the tourist industry jigsaw. These three institutions, in particular the airlines and tour operators, are largely owned, controlled and run from outside the region. Sometimes, through vertical integration, they are corporately linked, controlling every stage of the tourist's holiday. The bigger companies continue to buy up smaller ones, thus weakening competition and choice. As this continues, so the region is faced with doing business with fewer and larger corporations.

At the same time, the Caribbean does not have any control over those industries that channel and distribute tourists to and within the region. As stated in a strategic plan drawn up by the Caricom countries in 2002, this situation is almost unique to major tourism destinations. The region's inability to develop and manage its own tourism affairs has led to 'new calls for the creation of a dedicated regionally-owned Caribbean wholesale or tour operator.'

The Airlines

It was the introduction of the long-haul jet aeroplane in the early 1960s which transformed the Caribbean, bringing it within reach, both technologically and financially, of the ordinary holidaymaker. Every day of the year, airport departure boards in Miami, New York, London, Paris, Toronto and Amsterdam flash up Caribbean destinations – Montego Bay, Nassau, Antigua, Fort-de-France.

Yet for the most part it is not Caribbean-owned airlines which shuttle to the sun. In 2000, there were 13 airlines (excluding charters) flying into the Caribbean from overseas, of which only two, BWIA and Air Jamaica, were owned or part-owned in the region. American Airlines, KLM, British Airways and Virgin Atlantic from the UK, Air France (four of the five reflecting old colonial links), and foreign-owned charter companies dominate the Caribbean skies accounting for 85 per cent of arrivals. American Airlines accounted for one quarter of all arrivals to the region, excluding Cuba. Small, under-equipped regional airlines are not only outclassed by the international carriers but, in their struggle to survive, they have lost phenomenal amounts of money. Both Air Jamaica and BWIA were privatised in the mid 1990s. Under new US ownership, BWIA began to become more competitive, while Air Jamaica was bought by Butch Stewart of Sandals Resorts. Indeed, in an interesting development Stewart was moving into vertical integration himself – flying his all-inclusive customers into his own resorts on his own Air Jamaica. 'I bought into Air Jamaica because it was part of the economy. Islands which don't have their own airline are in trouble. They will always be at the mercy of foreign carriers,' said Stewart.[31] Even so, Air Jamaica accumulated massive losses, more than US$80 million, for example, in 2002.

Despite the efforts of the ebullient Stewart, the regional situation had not much changed since 1993, when the Economist Intelligence Unit pointed out that the regional airlines were 'at the mercy of the major airline blocks of North America and Europe.' In addition, said the EIU, the collapse of PanAm, TWA and Eastern Airlines had meant that the Caribbean was dangerously dependent on American Airlines, a situation which had always caused 'great concern'.[32] This vulnerability means that the big suppliers can not only elbow out smaller airlines but, through their market power, they decide routes strategies (developing 'hubs', for example), schedules, fares and control reservation systems. The British tour operator, Kuoni, reported in 2002 that the Caribbean was still affected by 'insufficient airlift', remarking that hotels had closed in Antigua and St Lucia as a result.

British Airways has traditionally played tough in its routing strategy. In 1985, in a secret deal with the Antiguan government, it paid US$280,000 for exclusive rights to the London-Antigua route, thereby denying landing rights to BWIA, the region's only locally-owned airline flying to Europe. This arrangement ended in 1992, and by then BWIA had managed to expand into continental Europe, gaining a foothold in Zurich and Frankfurt. Yet those routes remained vulnerable, never more so than in late 1994, when BWIA's new private-sector American owners axed the European routes, much to the alarm of eastern Caribbean destinations such as St Lucia and Grenada which relied on a growing European trade.

There was another scare in 1998 when American Airlines announced plans to use Miami rather than Puerto Rico as its hub for Caribbean services. It also was reported that AA had demanded – and got – a payment of US$1.5 million per year each from Antigua, Grenada and St Lucia to support continued flights. At the same time, Air Jamaica halved its number of flights to Barbados and St Lucia, and dropped Antigua altogether (although this route was later reinstated). Another crisis surfaced early in 2001 when German and British airlines and tour operators decided to either eliminate routes or reduce frequency of flights. Britannia Airways, for example, suspended its monthly flights from Germany to the Dominican Republic: this, according to local reports, forced the closure of seven hotels.[33]

Every year, there are reports of new schedule changes. In May 2002, for example, British Airways stopped its summer flights to Montego Bay, Cuba and Cancun, Mexico, because it was not making money from these routes. Caribbean governments were told that BA needed cheaper landing slots, reduced hotel rates for cabin crew and better marketing to promote the destinations. The plight of the BA 747 stuck in wet tarmac on the runway in Antigua in 2002 (new tarmac had been laid and had not dried properly) could not have done much to increase the bargaining power of the host islands. Even so, in 2005 there were daily BA flights to Antigua.

Plans for the Caribbean region to pool resources and amalgamate their own airlines 'to make use of economies of scale instead of being burdened by them'[34] and to counter the giant international carriers have not been successful. In 1993, a modest proposal by the CTO for regional airlines to collaborate in a number of areas to save US$64 million a year was barely discussed by a Caricom heads of state meeting. Plans to merge BWIA and Air Jamaica, with British Airways as the 'strategic partner' management interest, failed in 1994, the same year that the airlines were privatised. Integration rumours returned to the agenda under privatisation. In 1998, for example, Conrad Aleong, the chief executive of BWIA, proposed that BWIA, Air Jamaica and LIAT should merge, declaring that only a creation of a single airline could provide the economic base required to 'fight the larger carriers.'[35] Similar warnings were made by Holder who urged governments to create a 'viable Caribbean air transportation system to supplement the services being provided by external carriers.' BWIA and LIAT, the state-owned airline of the eastern Caribbean, did, however, make some attempt to amalgamate in what was called a 'strategic alliance ' in 2002. While LIAT's debts mounted up although its service improved, another regional airline, Caribbean Star, was launched. Owned by Alan Stanford, an American businessman who became heavily involved in investments in Antigua in the late 1990s, Caribbean Star was competing with LIAT for customers.

The West Indian Commission's 'Time for Action' had reported, in its understated style, that the 'provision of those [air] services must not become wholly a matter of chance, depending on calculations and decisions made elsewhere in response to considerations far removed from the goals and objectives of West Indian integration.'[36] Those decisions, however, continue to be 'made elsewhere'.

The Tour Operators

If foreign airlines decide the routes, the schedules and the prices (flights have never been cheap), the tour operators and wholesalers play another crucial role. Like the airlines, the tour operators are largely foreign-owned. Based in the cities of North America and Europe, they put together the component parts that make up a holiday. They select the flights, choose the hotels, organise ground transportation and day trips. Sometimes these services are sold by travel agents broken into small sectors; more usually they come as one giant pre-packed, beribboned offering.

Tour operators deal in volume, negotiating with the airline for 'allocations', seats by the planeload, organising charter flights and booking 'block off' hotel rooms by the floor. They get good prices for large volume sales and drive a hard bargain for the best deals. Their control over the package holiday means that independent travellers to the Caribbean often find it hard to get an airline seat (the tour operators buy 'allocations' and until they release them, flights register as full).

The mass market tour operators concentrate on the larger hotels, linking them into on-line reservations systems. In such a competitive climate, smaller hotels find it difficult to work outside this network, and only in 1995 did the CTO introduce a scheme to link them into a booking system with tour operators. The internet has emerged as a new distribution mechanism. Initially, it appeared that small hotels would benefit from going on-line. It now seems that unless they can offer a 'niche product', they remain dependent on the large operators.

Tour operators are tough negotiators and put pressure on hotels to increase their discounts, especially in lean years and in the off-season. This is especially true for the smallest hotels, the majority of which tend to be locally-owned and can least afford to have their profit margins reduced. One Barbadian hotelier with years of experience in the business said, 'Tour operators beat you down. They say they can get their price at another hotel so you have to reduce your rates. Some of them are greedy. We feel the small hotels should all agree to a rate and stick to it but it doesn't happen.' Another Barbadian, Neville Bayley of Sunbay Resorts, decided to link up with the Howard Johnson chain in 1996. Bayley said that high operating costs and the inability of small hoteliers to come together had made his hotel unviable.[37]

A 1987 report for the US Department of Commerce pointed out: 'Smaller properties that want to participate (many have no choice since they cannot get their guests in any other way) have to provide rooms at extremely deep discounts.' It also said that hotels which traditionally gave discounts only during the off-season found themselves under pressure even during the peak season. The study found that some tour operators 'will not do business with a hotel that does not give them a quota of rooms at a lower than normal rate during peak periods.'[38] Small hotels seem to rarely have a future unless they develop that 'niche market' or can survive on the regional business market.

Like the airlines, the power of the tour operators lies in their ability to direct the flow of the tourist trade. At the same time, they have the power to withdraw it. 'This is an important chain,' said a manager of the once powerful Airtours. 'We are in a very powerful position. It's a strong hotelier who turns us down. My job is to make sure that the hoteliers don't go elsewhere.' Airtours, on the other hand, was free to go where it liked. The company, which had a tougher reputation than most other British tour operators, started a programme in the Dominican Republic in 1989, but then stopped for what it described as 'purely commercial' reasons. It also expanded to Cuba in 1994, but withdrew from it the next year, again for 'commercial reasons'. Both destinations were quickly back in the brochures but the power of tour operators to withdraw favours remains.

Airtours' first foray into the Caribbean was to Barbados in 1987 when it provided a Caribbean holiday (£299 for 14 nights, room only) for economy-conscious British tourists. Peter Odle, former president of the Barbados Hotel Association, had been responsible for first inviting Airtours to Barbados to help boost the summer occupancy rate. 'I cut the first deal with them. We had no summer business.' According to Odle, 'Airtours promised to increase its rates after the first season when it offered dog-cheap rates of US$22-25. Then in the second season, it played one hotel off against another and didn't give an increase. They have no loyalty to anyone.'

While tour operators are spreading their business into new islands, packaging ever more varied holidays, the financial deals take place in the metropolitan cities. As *The Other Side of Paradise* points out: 'Owing to the transnational nature of the business, payments for services actually delivered in the Caribbean go directly to the New York headquarters of Sheraton or Hertz, never even passing through agency offices in Jamaica or the Dominican Republic.'[39]

Yet, as a small Caribbean-based travel agent explains: 'Tour operators contract directly with hotels, with airlines and with ground operators. We couldn't do without them. They are the most important people in the business.' And a hotel owner in St Lucia conceded: 'Tour operators are tough. You can't make it without the tour operators because they control the airline seats. You have to court them.'

The Hotels

So if Caribbean hotels depend on foreign-owned airlines and tour operators, who owns the hotels? Local ownership has gradually been increasing. While more than three quarters of the hotels in places such as Turks and Caicos, Antigua, Cayman Islands and Bonaire are foreign-owned, there has been a strong indigenising process in countries such as Jamaica and Barbados, where there is a high rate of local ownership, in particular among the small hotels which are often all locally owned. This is also true, for very different reasons, in some smaller destinations such as Dominica and Trinidad and Tobago. The phenomenon of the last decade has been the success of the Jamaican-owned company, Sandals. In the 1980s, Caribbean governments also owned hotels, but by the end of the century few still held them.

Some of the world's largest hotel chains, such as Marriott, Hilton, Ritz-Carlton, Holiday Inn, and Hyatt, operate in the Caribbean. These companies do not own charming hillside inns; they run large, modern, formatted and computerised citadels. They are important to the region – but they always have the power to take their custom elsewhere. At the end of 2002, for example, the French group, Accor, one of the world's largest hotel chains, announced it was pulling out of Guadeloupe and Martinique. It meant the closure of 15 hotels, along with 1,500 jobs. The company, in a letter to the French president, Jacques Chirac, said that it was convinced it was impossible to make a profit in the Antilles 'no matter what aid is offered by the state.' It drew attention, among other factors, to high labour costs, strikes and the 'aggressive' behaviour of hotel staff. Such a decision exposes the impact of dependency by foreign companies on the local industry.[40]

The story of Paradise Island, off Nassau in the Bahamas, reflects the history of one hotel and its evolution: from a rich man's retreat to transnational investment. The originally named Hog Island had become a favourite picnicking spot for the Nassau smart set by the time Axel Wenner-Gren, a Swedish industrialist said to be the world's richest man, bought a slice of it in 1939. He dredged a pond to make a lake, cut canals and christened his estate Shangri-La. In 1961 he sold it for more than £3.6 million to Huntingdon Hartford, the New York railway tycoon, who began a major building expansion by investing US$10 million into Paradise Island.

Twenty years later, there were some 3,000 hotel rooms on Paradise Island. Almost 90 per cent of these were managed and/or owned by five foreign companies. These were Holiday Inn, Club Med, Sheraton and Loews and, above all, Resorts International, the former Mary Carter Paint Company, which had bought most of the island from Hartford in 1966 and came to control 42 per cent of its hotel rooms. By 1985 Resorts International owned four hotels on Paradise Island, the Paradise Island bridge, the Paradise Island airport and Paradise Airlines. At one point, it also owned more than 25 per cent of hotel rooms in the whole of the Bahamas.[41]

This was not the end of the story, however, for in 1989 Resorts International filed for bankruptcy with debts of US$913 million. Four years later, Sun International of South Africa acquired 60 per cent of the equity for US$75 million. And in December 1994, Chairman Sol Korzner, whose company also owns Sun City in the former homeland of Bophuthatswana and 31 hotels and casino resorts in southern Africa, France and the Indian Ocean, announced the opening of the renamed US$250 million Atlantis Resort with 1,150 rooms, 12 restaurants, a casino and the world's largest outdoor aquarium and lagoon. There was more to come, with the opening of the US$600 million Royal Towers in 1998. As the brochure says: 'Larger than life, as dramatically fanciful as it is magnificent in scope and concept, the US$850 million Atlantis, Paradise Islands is a glorious and wonderfully playful celebration of the lost city of Atlantis' and so on.

The theme park fantasy of Paradise Island is one aspect of hotel ownership in the Caribbean. At the other end of the spectrum is the small, locally-owned hotel. In some cases, the independent, local hotelier finds it difficult to retain a foothold. Occasionally, locals feed off mass tourism, picking up business generated by the big boys, but often the local owner has neither the contacts, the money nor the means to be part of computer tourism.

Local ownership, however, has increased and continues to do so. In Barbados, for example, Barbadians owned 83.1 per cent of all accommodation (and 100 per cent of guesthouses) by 1985, although only half of the hotels, and fewer than half of apartment-hotels. By 1997, 4,500 out of the 6,500 rooms on the island were in the small-hotel sector – and locally owned.

Under-financed local ownership brought its own problems: inadequate marketing, cash-flow difficulties, low revenues and low occupancy rates. In an attempt to revitalise the sector, which owed the Barbados Development Bank millions of dollars, the Barbados government set up the Gems of Barbados project in an attempt to breathe new life into the heavily indebted sector. The original idea, which was supported by all sides, was for 15 small hotels to be brought under the umbrella of Hotels and Resorts Ltd (HRL), a private company set up by the government. When each hotel had returned to profit, they would be handed back to their owners. A change of heart, however, meant that the properties would be signed over to HRL and the owners would be given shares minus any debts. Only three hotels agreed.

Further complications developed, with HRL buying a couple more hotels despite the fact that it had been unable to sell any shares. Various scandals, reported in the local press, emerged after 1995 when the scheme was first launched. While a snazzy brochure, Gems of Barbados, promoting four hotels was produced, by 2002 it was reported that losses from the project amounted to approximately US$17.1 million.[42]

In Jamaica, with its larger population and more diversified and sophisticated economy, a further process of local ownership has occurred. Local ownership now dominates, at around 90 per cent of the island's 23,000 or so hotel rooms. Leading the way, at an international level, are two Jamaican companies. These have broken the First World's hegemony in mass-market tourism with the successful introduction of the all-inclusive holiday. Butch Stewart of Sandals and John Issa of Super Clubs have spearheaded the development of what in the late 1980s was described as 'the most important innovation in the Caribbean hotel sector during the last decade.'[43] They have also spread their wings into the rest of the Caribbean, in particular to Cuba (Super Clubs and Sandals) and to three other islands (Sandals). Some islands have embraced the all-inclusive concept more than others: Jamaica, St Lucia, Turks and Caicos and the Dominican Republic are among the most popular all-inclusive destinations.

It is worth looking at Sandals because, like Super Clubs, it is a home-grown success and has been copied all over the region. 'All hoteliers are now calling themselves all-inclusive. When we saw that all-inclusives would grow off trees, we rolled the dice and said we're going to be at the top of the tree,' said Stewart. Success for Sandals, he claims, comes from value for money. 'We have the biggest watersports business and fitness centres, brand-new restaurants, great entertainment. You have quality choices and with all that you end up with value for money you can't get anywhere else in the world.'

Stewart, originally a businessman with a car parts distribution company, started Sandals in 1981 when he revamped an old hotel in Montego Bay as an all-inclusive couples-only resort. By 2002 the Sandals chain (the couples-only Sandals and since 1997, his Beaches properties) owned and operated 10 hotels in Jamaica, three in St Lucia, one in Bahamas, one in Turks and Caicos and one in Antigua. By then Sandals had 3,200 rooms, was providing holidays for 300,000 visitors a year, employing 9,000 people and had been named the world's leading independent resort group by the *Travel Trade Gazette* for eight years in succession.

The crucial role of Sandals in Jamaica was highlighted in April 1992 when, at a crisis point for Jamaica's exchange rate, Stewart deposited US$1 million per week into the island's commercial banks at a rate four Jamaican dollars below the prevailing rate to help prevent the Jamaican dollar's collapse. As a result, other Jamaicans moved their US dollars back into local banks and the currency stabilised. Sandals, according to its own press release, provides Jamaica with 10 per cent of its hard currency.

The enclave culture of Sandals and Super Clubs (and those other all-inclusives, such as Jalousie, which have jumped on the bandwagon of the pioneers) has introduced a new ingredient into the Caribbean tourist cocktail. Not everyone is enjoying the taste (see Chapters Two, Three and Six), but the tourist establishment has welcomed the likes of Sandals with open arms. As Allen Chastenet, a former director of tourism in St Lucia, put it as early as 1994: 'All-inclusives have brought security to tour operators and airlines. At the same time, they can also provide an umbrella for small, local developers. Sandals has a US$15 million a year advertising budget. It can help put St Lucia on the map.'

The success of Stewart and Issa did not, initially, prompt the rest of the Caribbean business community to move into the hotel business. However, Stewart thought that this would change. 'Traditionally they saw it as for those already established in the trade. They see it as a risk and have been timid, but the younger people are moving into the business,' he said. But what Stewart is particularly concerned about is quality and standards – at an international level. In 2002, he addressed the St Lucia Hotel and Tourism Association. He told them:

> The days of protectionism are over. Businesses that cannot compete internationally will fail. Tourism requires planning, investment and solid marketing like any other business. We have been voted world's best eight years in a row. We invest in training our staff to deliver top level service and we spend more than regional tourist boards to market our product. Anyone who is in tourism who is not prepared to take a world view of how the hospitality business operates will either continue to operate marginally or go out of business.

Tough and innovative, Stewart's approach remains a model home-grown success story.

Government Ownership

Caribbean governments have also moved in to, and, latterly, out of, hotel ownership. In 1987, regional governments, largely the Bahamas, Curaçao and Jamaica, owned 43 separate properties; their total of some 9,500 rooms accounted for 11.4 per cent of all hotel rooms in the region.[44] In some cases properties were taken into public ownership to save jobs (as in Jamaica and Curaçao) when private-sector interests faltered, or else to create jobs (as in the Bahamas). Yet over the years, management problems made for poorly-run hotels and low occupancy rates. Debts piled up and by the early 1990s most of the hotels had either been sold, were up for sale or, at the very least, were being managed by the private sector.

Governments were also forced to sell hotels by the privatisation agenda of the International Monetary Fund. Under IMF tutelage, Jamaica, which owned 12 hotels at one stage, began to divest through the 1980s, and by the mid-1990s all but one hotel, the Holiday Inn at Montego Bay, had been sold.

In the Bahamas, hotel ownership by the state-run Hotel Corporation was promoted by the administration of Sir Lynden Pindling, the first post-independence prime minister. Its primary aim was to generate employment for the mass of black Bahamians who had voted Pindling into power. Yet its debts became enormous, its profligacy and inefficiency renowned, and alleged corruption endemic (see Chapter Four). Between 1974 and 1993, the Hotel Corporation spent more than US$401 million buying and operating hotels, but by the end of 1994 operating losses stood at more than US$200 million.[45] The administration of Hubert Ingraham, which came into office in 1992, began to sell off its hotel properties.

The Bahamas government had owned three large hotels on Cable Beach, Nassau, two hotels on Grand Bahama, and three hotels on the Out Islands, two on Andros and one on Eleuthera. The government soon sold the Nassau hotels, but it was not until 1997 that it sold the Holiday Inn and Lucayan Beach and Casino on Grand Bahama. New owners – such as Butch Stewart of Sandals and John Issa of Superclubs – brought new energy and new investment to the industry. The sale of the hotels was one aspect of the regeneration of the Bahamas tourist industry in the 1990s and, by 2002, the government owned only two hotels.

In Barbados, government ownership of hotels had similarly begun as a way of increasing local involvement in the hotel sector. Heywoods Hotel, for instance, on the west coast was built in the early 1980s by the Democratic Labour Party government. Peter Morgan, the first president of the Caribbean Hotel Association (CHA) and the Barbados minister of tourism at the time, explains what happened: 'The idea behind Heywoods was to create five to six locally-owned and individually managed hotels on a lease-purchase arrangement. Common service facilities and conference rooms would have been used in common to reduce the costs.' Funds were earmarked from the World Bank, but then Morgan's party lost an election. The new administration eventually built the hotel, but by then it was no longer economically feasible, said Morgan. Typically, it was first leased to a

Texan management company and then early in 1994 sold to a local company, Barbados Shipping and Trading, for US$17 million, a figure, it was reported, that was largely swallowed up by overdraft payments and repayment of the World Bank loan. It reopened in November 1994 as the all-inclusive Almond Beach Village which is owned and managed by Ralph Taylor, a former president of the CHA.

As in the latter days of Heywoods, governments may have owned hotels, but they did not necessarily manage them, preferring to sub-contract management to a private, usually foreign, company. This process also occurred in the private sector. A 1987 survey of hotel ownership in Jamaica, Barbados and Trinidad and Tobago recorded that while 75 per cent of hotels were in local hands, only 31 per cent were locally managed.[46] The pressure to lock into international reservations systems with links to airlines and tour operators in Chicago or London increased the need to franchise management out to foreigners. While ownership appeared to be a necessary condition of control, by itself it was not enough.

Cuba under Castro adopted yet another pattern of hotel ownership, the joint venture, as the country began its shift away from a socialist model of entirely state-owned and operated hotels, which it had adopted after the revolution. The joint venture process began in 1982 when legislation, known as Decree 50, was introduced allowing for joint ventures in all sectors. In 1987 a state agency, Cubanacan, was formed to attract foreign capital with joint tourism ventures. Others, such as Gran Caribe and Gaviota, followed. The collapse of the Soviet Union forced Cuba to promote tourism even more vigorously, and by the early 1990s the joint venture programme had gained momentum, with companies, mainly from Spain, Mexico, Italy and France, participating in either building hotels or managing them. The Jamaican all-inclusive, Super Clubs, for example, had also signed up for a joint venture. Favourable terms, including repatriation of profits (in some cases taxes on profits are waived), often as good as in the capitalist Caribbean, were part of the deal (see Chapter Two).

By 1994, *Cuba Business* reported that the 'star' of Cuba's annual tourism convention was Gran Caribe, the state-owned hotel chain which 'had secured 48 contracts to fill around 2,500 of its rooms with some 100,000 visitors.'[47] At that time, of Cuba's 20,000 or so rooms of international standard, 1,650 were operated by joint ventures, while 27 of the major hotels were managed by 15 different management chains. This was a time of frenetic expansion, with the minister of tourism reporting that 27,000 new rooms were to be built at a cost of US$2,400 million with even more foreign partners. One particular deal, between Cubanacan and Sunrise of Bermuda, was for six new hotels to be built in six years, at a cost of more than US$100 million.

In 1999, there was no sign of a slowdown, with the announcement that 24 joint ventures had another 11,900 rooms under development. By 2000, there was a total of 33,000 rooms in nearly 200 hotels. In 10 years, the number of rooms in Cuba had more than tripled.

Such ambitious attempts to lure foreign investment (see Chapter Two) into the hotel sector is, however, characteristic not just of Cuba's crisis management, but of the whole region. As has been described, despite the increase in local ownership, the regional tourist industry continues to rely largely on foreign capital to build and fuel the big hotels that sustain the industry. In fact, in many destinations it is the large hotels – over 100 rooms – that dominate the industry. In the Dominican Republic, Guadeloupe, Jamaica, St Lucia and St Maarten, for example, 70 per cent of the hotel stock is in those of more than 100 rooms. As Allen Chastenet of St Lucia admits: 'You have to bring in people who can instil confidence into the market place. There has to be someone who can provide that guarantee to tour operators and airlines.' That analysis, partly determined by dependency, is perhaps one reason why, in the conservative political climate of the early 1990s, Jalousie opened for business while the alternative plans foundered.

That big foreign-owned hotels are a precondition for creating confidence for foreign airlines and foreign tour operators is evidence enough that the region remains partly locked into a pattern of external dependency. It is seen as an example of weakness that Barbados, for example, has only one hotel chain on the island. Yet choices – the keys to change – remain. Can and do Caribbean governments use tourism as a tool for sustainable development? The Association of Caribbean States agreed in 2001, at its third summit, to establish a 'sustainable tourism zone of the greater Caribbean' – the first, it was claimed, of its kind in the world. An action plan states the zone's commitment to creating mechanisms to certify that destinations and facilities comply with specific sustainable tourism standards. But, in the light of experience, such fine words remain in the filing cabinets of the region: the reality is sometimes very different.

NOTES

1.   *The Voice*, St Lucia, 30 May 1990
2.   *St Lucia Star*, 26 August 1988
3.   Organisation of American States, 'Proposal for the Development of the Pitons National Park', prepared for the government of St Lucia Tourism and Co-ordinated Project, Washington DC, 1989
4.   Rob Potter and Jonathan Pugh, 'Planning without plans and the neoliberal state: the case of St Lucia', *Third World Planning Review*, 23 (3), 2001
5.   United Nations, April 21 2001, Inter Press Service press release
6.   West Indian Commission, 'Time for Action: Overview of the West Indian Commission', Barbados, 1992, p. 106
7.   Ibid.
8.   Americas: Tourism Market Trends, 2001 edition, World Travel Organisation
9.   Caribbean Tourism Organisation annual statistics
10. Ibid.
11. 'Time for Action', op. cit.
12. Caribbean Tourism Organisation Press Release, Barbados, January 1995
13. Caribbean Tourism at a Crossroads, John Collins, undated, grenadianvoice.com
14. Caribbean Hotels Association, *Tourism Talk*, Issue No 4, March 2002
15. JL McElroy, 'The impact of tourism in small islands: a global comparison', paper given at the TOTAL foundation, September 2000
16. Ibid.
17. Ralph Taylor, Caricom press release, December 10 2001
18. Jean Holder, Caricom press release, December 10 2001
19. Cited in Tom Barry et al, *The Other Side of Paradise: Foreign Control in the Caribbean*, New York, 1984, p.87
20. Frank Fonda Taylor, *To Hell With Paradise: A History of the Jamaican Tourist Industry*, Pittsburg, 1993, p.169
21. Cited in Kathy McAfee, *Storm Signals: Structural Adjustments and Development Alternatives in the Caribbean*, London, 1991, p.63
22. Martha Honey, *Ecotourism and Sustainable Development*, Island Press, 1999
23. Ibid. These figures are based on statistics available in April 1995 and represent a return from 24 countries. Note that some countries, notably the Dominican Republic, include their returning nationals in their stayover arrival figures. Figures for Saba and St Eustatius provided by the Netherlands Antilles Tourist Board.
24. Ibid.
25. Economist Intelligence Unit, Tourism in the Caribbean: Special Report, London, 1993
26. Victor Curtin and Auliana Poon, Tourist Accommodation in the Caribbean, Caribbean Tourism Research and Development Centre, Barbados, 1988
27. Ibid.
28. Curtin and Poon, op. cit.
29. Britton, 1982, quoted in Paul Wilkinson and Gordon Ewing, Towards a more sustainable and competitive Caribbean tourism sector: an OAS perspective, 1999
30. Fonda Taylor, op. cit., p.54
31. Butch Stewart quoted in *The Times*, Sep 13, 1997
32. Economist Intelligence Unit, op. cit.
33. Inter Press Service, Caribbean, May 12 2001
34. *Caribbean Tourism Today*, May/June 1993
35. *Caribbean Insight*, March 1998

36.   West Indian Commission, op.cit., p.111
37.   Caribbean News Agency, May 1996
38.   US Department of Commerce, op. cit.
39.   Tom Barry et al, op. cit., p.80.
40.   *Caribbean Insight*, November 15 2002
41.   Keith G. Debbage, 'Oligopoly and the Resort Cycle in the Bahamas', *Annals of Tourism Resarch*, vol 17, 1990, p.513 et passim.
42.   *Caribbean Insight*, August 2002
43.   Curtin and Poon, op.cit
44.   Ibid.
45.   Nassau *Daily Tribune*, Bahamas, 31 October 1994
46.   Cited in Curtin and Poon, op. cit.
47.   *Cuba Business*, June 1994

2

LINKAGES AND LEAKAGES: THE PLANNING FACTOR

Keeping the flights full, the hotel lobbies buzzing, the beaches lined with occupied sunbeds and the duty-free complexes crammed with eager shoppers depends on the endeavour and initiative of the local private sector and on the support, marketing expertise and political will of governments. Like unseen and overworked stage managers who have to make sure everything is in place for the showbiz spectacular, the public sector of the Caribbean must dance attendance on its audiences for fear that reviews will be poor and that the largely foreign-owned businesses – airlines, tour operators, hotel chains, cruise lines – will next year take the show elsewhere.

The burden on Caribbean governments to organise their tourist industries largely on other people's terms was forcefully described by Herbert Hiller, a leading public relations figure in the cruise ship business who made some innovative suggestions about the region's tourism problems in the early 1970s. He wrote later:

> It takes a particular history to accept that the external manifestations of one's culture are valuable chiefly as ornamentation for hotels designed, constructed, and managed in the interests of overseas profit. In time, however, all successful Caribbean tourism administrators come to accept this about mass tourism, and few can resist giving in. Indeed, they are chosen for their ability to organise the national tourism sector in response to overseas priorities, even if these remain at odds with genuine development, with such objectives as self-resourcefulness, energy conservation, and import restrictions.[1]

Some members of the Caribbean's tourist industry would now argue with Hiller's 30-year-old analysis; others might still agree with it. Whatever the perception, ministers of tourism can never afford to take their eye off the ball of customer satisfaction.

First among the priorities, and predicating all tourist activity in the Caribbean, is the safety and comfort of the visitor. These are costly responsibilities. Host governments must possess and maintain a stable political environment, preferably sympathetic to the countries from which the tourists originate. They must also provide a suitable infrastructure for demanding tourists and shape a financial climate attractive to overseas investors. Places unable to guarantee such conditions attract few tourists.

Keeping the Peace

Tourists must be protected from political upheaval, strikes, or coups. At the first whiff of unrest, both tour operators and governments go on red alert. Jamaica, in particular, suffers from a reputation for violence. When, for example, 28 people were killed in downtown Kingston in September 2001, the general manager of the Ritz Carlton in Montego Bay, 119 miles from the capital, said, 'It is killing us. If this keeps up, I am not sure about what we are going to do.' Losses during the short period of the violence amounted to US$2 million, he claimed.[2]

Tourists must not be inconvenienced or, indeed, be disturbed at any level by local difficulties. Guided by tour operators, travel agents and governments, tourists react feverishly to bad news caused by any sort of instability, real or imagined. The result is that they stay away; there is always, after all, another beach in another place.

The Caribbean usually experiences unexpected and brief flurries of political difficulty; these create short-term loss. More damaging to the region's tourist industries, however, is long-term customer alienation. This happens either as a result of the disintegration of civil society, such as in Haiti or, as in the case of Cuba, as a result of an all-transforming revolution.

Tourism in Haiti, for example, has been virtually non-existent since the mid 1980s. First came the rumour that Aids originated in Haiti; then the fall of the Duvalier dictatorship in 1986, a long period of unrest, the election of President Jean-Bertrand Aristide in 1990, his downfall in 2004 and economic and political instability. Those events proved more unattractive to tourists than had the years of Duvaliers' violent Tonton Macoutes. In those years, American tourists continued to visit the country, albeit in sheltered enclaves, far from the ugly repression in the slums.

During the early 1990s Haiti's office of national tourism had a tourism director and six employees with nothing to do. Branch offices in Miami, New York, Montreal and Paris shut their doors, hotels closed and art and craft vendors went out of business. In fact, the whole edifice of tourism disappeared. As some sort of calm briefly settled on Haiti in the final years of the 20th century, attempts were made to reintroduce tourists to the country, emphasising its history and cultural attractions. Consultants were hired, a master plan was published in 1995, the ministry of tourism was upgraded, and wildly optimistic figures for arrivals were predicted.

In contrast, it was not civil unrest that caused US nationals to stay away from Cuba but ideological hostility and an economic blockade which prevent US citizens from travelling there, except in specific circumstances. For similar reasons, Americans also stayed away from Grenada between 1979 and 1983 when Maurice Bishop's left-wing People's Revolutionary Government (PRG) was in office. Tourist arrivals to Grenada dropped by 25 per cent overall, while the US share of the market decreased by 77 per cent between 1978 and 1982. While some argued that the decline was due more to economic factors than political ones, the pro-tourism PRG claimed that travel agencies in the US put out hostile information about the left-wing regime. Certainly, the US press followed its own government's anti-PRG line.

Visitors to Jamaica also declined during Prime Minister Michael Manley's first term of office in the 1970s. Hostile reports about Manley's semi-socialist experiments swayed US public opinion and the tourists stayed away. As Jamaica's *Daily Gleaner* put it in 1976: 'As naturally as night follows day, American investments for Jamaica dry up; the American press burn us at the stake; our tourist industry, which is almost totally sustained by the American market, begins to die on its feet, and we find that the world has suddenly become a much more difficult place to make our way in.'[3]

Natural as well as political instability also affects consumer confidence. The Caribbean suffers from hurricanes, and, less frequently, from earthquakes and volcanic eruptions. In the last 15 years, hurricanes Gilbert, Hugo, Andrew, Louis and Mitch have brought the worst destruction. Gilbert in 1988 blew its way through Jamaica just before the start of the tourist season: tourism receipts for that year dropped by nearly a third. One year later, Hurricane Hugo smashed hotels and roads in the eastern Caribbean, while Hurricane Andrew struck parts of the Bahamas in 1992. Then, in 1995, Hurricane Luis tore up eastern Caribbean islands, and in 2001 Hurricane Mitch traumatised Central America, including Belize, while in September 2004 Hurricane Ivan destroyed lives and homes, especially in Grenada.

In some cases, a whole season's income from tourism is lost in the wake of natural disasters; even when stricken areas get back on their feet, it takes time for the international press and the travel trade to note this. As John Bell, former vice president of the Caribbean Hotel Association, said after Hurricane Luis: 'You have a lot of people whose geography of the Caribbean is very, very misty. For example, they'll say, "There's a hurricane that supposedly hit Antigua, so we won't go to Barbados."' [4]

External factors with no obvious links with the Caribbean also affect the region, often disproportionately. The most dramatic recent example was the September 11 attacks on New York and Washington, which produced a sharp fall in arrivals, followed by hotel closures and staff lay-offs. Losses for the industry in some of the region's key destinations were estimated by the WTTC for the season 2001-2002 as follows: more than US$837 million by the Dominican Republic, followed by Puerto Rico at US$589 million, with Jamaica, Bahamas and Cuba facing losses of more than US$250 million. Arrivals fell in the last four months of 2001 by 18.8 per cent compared with the same period in 2000.

Roads to Development

If political and economic barometers – both externally and internally – register calm, the next task of governments is to provide a modern and reliable infrastructure. Investors require that the groundwork is prepared for them. However impoverished the living conditions of the local population, investors need 'modern', Western-style amenities to attract the tourists. Erik Cohen wrote over 20 years ago, 'a tourist infrastructure of facilities based on Western standards has to be created even in the poorest host countries. This tourist infrastructure provides the mass tourist with the "ecological bubble" of his accustomed environment.' [5]

Such 'ecological bubbles' contain airports, roads, water supply, sewerage disposal, electricity, and telephones. These facilities make the tourists' journey not just possible, but convenient and smooth. Police, immigration and customs services, currency and licensing controls must also be upgraded and expanded. All these projects are expensive. Funded partly by aid but also by expensive borrowing, they must all be paid for in the end by local people through some sort of taxation.

Leaders of the tourist industry, both foreign and regional, lobby governments to improve the infrastructure. In St Maarten, for instance, one of the key 'mass tourism' destinations, long-term government neglect boomeranged onto the hoteliers, and was one of the causes of low hotel occupancy rates. 'We think all the infrastructural needs should be upgraded to help us with the quality of the product,' said Henk Koek in the mid 1990s, then manager of the long-established Holland House Hotel, on the seafront of St Maarten's capital, Philipsburg, during a period when standards were in decline. It was a typical expression of the private sector's dependence on the public sector.

Of all the infrastructural needs, the obvious priority is an international airport which can land wide-bodied jets from North America and Europe and process jumbo-loads of arrivals. The lack of a major airport is one reason why islands such as St Vincent or Dominica have far fewer tourists than neighbouring islands such as Grenada or Antigua. Large-scale investment in the 1960s and 1970s went into building airports for tourism throughout the region. Funds mostly came from foreign governments and agencies, but the enormous sums of money needed to maintain them must be found by Caribbean governments. A manager for Martinique's international airport once estimated that the arrival of at least six jumbo jets per day was needed to pay for the high cost of running it.

Airport extensions, anticipating tourism expansion, continued throughout the early 1990s. Massive airport works in Martinique were undertaken to increase capacity to two million passengers a year in 2000, while in the Dominican Republic, the Gregorio Luperón International Airport opened in 1994 on the north coast at a cost of US$20 million. Funded by the government and foreign sources, the airport was designed to handle 1,800 passengers per hour and six planes simultaneously. Featuring a new taxiway, control tower, two-level passenger terminal, restaurants, shops and car park, it was designed to cope efficiently with the anticipated increase in passengers.[6] The airport was opened on the eve of the 1994 general election, as an orchestrated political event. Airports confer status and represent achievement and modernity.

Hundreds of thousands of Caribbean nationals do not have piped water, but tourists expect unlimited supplies: with their post-beach showers and baths, they are estimated to use six times as much water as residents. Yet many parts of the Caribbean have water supply problems, especially in the dry season, which also happens to coincide with peak tourist season. Local water companies struggle to provide supplies from inadequate storage facilities that were not built to cope with increased demand. In the Jamaican resort of Negril, for example, anecdotal evidence points to problems caused by unregulated development which means that large beachside hotels receive – and hoard – water before it becomes available to residents and smaller hotels.

The last bad drought in the eastern Caribbean was in 1994. It posed particular problems for island governments. While some hotels made up for the water shortages by trucking in supplies, this was not always enough. In Grenada, the water problem drove tourists away. The Grenada Renaissance Hotel was forced to spend thousands of dollars settling law suits brought against it by guests deprived of water.

In the same year there were also water shortages in St Lucia although a major US$65 million reservoir was being constructed to ease the problems of both tourists and locals. At one point, one of the island's major hotels had to apologise to its guests for providing no water at night or between 10.00 am and 4.30 pm. In a memorandum it said that the crisis had affected everyone in the north of the island ('those with no water reserves are without water completely'), but emphasised that 'hotels are receiving priority from the government for any possible water distribution.'

While hotels are used almost exclusively by tourists, at least some features of the tourist infrastructure are in the public domain. Tourists use airports, which also provide Caribbean nationals with direct access to the outside world. New roads are built to service tourists (the best roads often being the ones from the airport to the hotels) but they are also used by farmers, construction workers, teachers and so on. Improved water, telephone and electricity supplies, driven by the tourist agenda, can be shared by locals, at least by those living in or around the tourist belts.

However, the increase in infrastructure has often been accompanied by residential developments of villas and apartments for sale and rent. Such tourist-based initiatives have affected both the availability and the price of land, not only putting it out of the reach of local people, but also reducing the pool of land for agriculture and other uses. In Bequia, for instance, land sales to foreigners have not only displaced the best agricultural terrain, but through speculation and soaring prices, ownership has become limited to foreigners or the local elite.[7] In Barbados and other islands with a real estate boom, there has been a similar rise in land prices and local resentment. In Grenada, the government has invoked the Compulsory Purchase of Land Act at Levera estate to buy land from nationals who have refused to sell it to foreign developers. The loss of farming land for a major resort means that the local community has lost its financial independence and its social cohesion.

To pay for the high operating costs of tourist management and infrastructural development, governments levy taxes on the sector. As the Caribbean Tourism Research and Development Centre (CTRC) noted in 1988: 'Many Caribbean governments have become increasingly dependent on tourism and tourist-related economic activities as sources of direct and indirect tax revenue.'[8] Apart from direct taxation, there are airport departure and aircraft landing taxes, sales taxes on hotel room occupancy, air tickets and tourist purchases, import duties on goods and services, corporation taxes, and licensing fees, income tax on tourist employees, entertainment taxes and so on.

In many Caribbean countries, taxes on goods and services have become the major component of government revenue, while income from direct taxation has decreased.[9] This strategy has made the Caribbean even more dependent on buoyant external economic conditions and a healthy tourism 'product'.

The high level of taxation, both direct and indirect, has become an added burden on the hotel sector, pushing up already high prices in an area already known for its high rates (compared with neighbouring Florida or Mexico). Bitter complaints about an undue burden of taxation is a continual refrain heard in the private sector. Critics compare the tax burden of hoteliers with that of the cruise ships. Butch Stewart of Sandals, for example, has drawn attention to the fact that cruise ships enjoy virtual duty-free and tax-free status. 'The ship is not taxed, there is no room tax, no beverage or labour tax and the food on the table is not taxed,' he said.

Enticing Investors

To compensate for infrastructural constraints and high operational costs, governments provide a basket of generous incentives to entice the prospective investor. These usually consist of a variety of concessions including the right to import duty-free materials and start-up equipment for hotels, exemption from land tax and capital levies, tax holidays, sometimes lasting up to 35 years, and the repatriation of investment and profits. These are considerable inducements, which can act as a catalyst for both local and foreign investment.

The introduction of such legislation prompted a tourism take-off in Jamaica and Bahamas. With Jamaica's Hotels Aid Law of 1944, Montego Bay became a tourist boom town in the post-war years: between 1944 and 1956 there was an increase of almost 500 per cent in the number of rooms, while in 1958 alone about £2 million of capital expenditure was secured for hotel construction.[10] 'The foreign interests have come down like Philistines in Montego Bay,' a local MP told parliament in 1968, describing the way speculators had forced up land prices and elbowed out Jamaicans.[11]

Foreign investment in the Bahamas was encouraged in the same way in 1949 when the Bahamas Development Board was set up under the control of Stafford Sands, a lawyer, businessman and member of the House of Assembly. The Board's job was to lure tourists to the Bahamas through an expansive and expensive advertising campaign. It had a budget of US$500,000, a substantial sum at that time. It proved successful, with tourist figures increasing from around 30,000 in 1949 to 365,000 in 1961.[12] It soon also benefited from the US trade embargo of Cuba with US tourists shifting from Havana to Nassau. Over the same period investment in the Bahamas spiralled, with all sorts of speculators swarming into the islands. Perhaps the most spectacular result was the transformation of Grand Bahama by Wallace Groves, an American lumberman, from empty scrubland into the town of Freeport, a centre of commerce, industry, hotels and casinos.

None of this happened without major concessions and generous conditions handed out by Bahamian politicians. There was no income or corporation tax, capital gains tax, real estate or property tax and no customs and excise duties (except for goods for personal use). Easy terms were available under the Hotels Encouragement Act and lax regulations made offshore banking an attractive proposition. Numerous adventurers, tax refugees and crooks basked in this clement financial climate.

When, 20 years after the Bahamas' bonanza, Grenada began to seek private investors in the wake of the US invasion of 1983, the easy terms had a different impact: they drained the government's coffers. Looking back on Grenada in the 1980s, Robert Evans of Grenada's Industrial Development Corporation reflected: 'In the mid 1980s, the government believed that the private sector would solve everything and gave concessions on everything, with the United States making up the shortfall. By the time the US started to withdraw budgetary support, the government had abolished most taxes and had eroded its revenue base.' Governments which dish out concessions also have to expect that investors may abuse the hospitality and disappear on the next plane when the incentives period ends. Concessions are also not necessarily the determining factor for foreign money. Incentives for hotels were in place for years, according to Royston Hopkin, a Grenadian hotelier, but only a pro-US government and a new international airport attracted investors to build two new hotels. As a Caribbean Hotel Association draft paper pointed out in 1988: 'Most investors are looking for a stable environment rather than for special deals.' The Economist Intelligence Unit also made a similar point, concluding that 'incentives in the Caribbean would be better aimed at operating costs, which are high, than at capital investment.' [13]

Another examination into the impact of tourism incentives in the Caribbean came to similar conclusions. It concluded that 'existing incentives for encouragement of tourism investment… play a smaller role in attracting new investment than is generally ascribed to them.'[14] This is not necessarily the case in countries with an under-developed tourism 'product'; in these states, incentives remain 'pivotal' in mobilising local investment when foreign investment is hard to come by.

However, the study found that incentives do not play a major role in the decision by foreign investors to establish operations. Potential investors are more interested in political and economic stability, low training costs and high occupancy rates than in tax-free goodies. The report also noted that successful countries outside the Caribbean attracted investment partly because of the commitment and energy with which schemes are promoted rather than around any special attractions in the schemes themselves. Sandals, for example, the Caribbean's home-owned chain, has owned prime land in Barbados since the early 1990s, but no hotel has been built: the explanation is commonly held to be that costs and taxes in Barbados are too high.

Land and Planning

Strategic planning at a national level is another major public-sector task. Yet, more often than not, the scramble for tourists has seen development determined by short-term fancy rather than a co-ordinated long-term approach. Many countries, as an EIU report noted, 'still lack a clear policy and/or development plan for the sector.' Problems, specific to small-island planning in general, are intensified by the particular characteristics of tourism. Such a fragmented industry – of suppliers, consumer and providers, all with separate interests and needs – makes it difficult to arrive at a unified policy decision.

One of the results of a lack of planning has resulted in spasmodic and uncoordinated development. In the 1980s and early 1990s, before infrastructural aid dried up, governments accepted whatever was on offer: an airport from the Canadians here, a road project from the Americans there, a hotel from the British somewhere else. (Dominica's former prime minister Dame Eugenia Charles used to say she had become a very good beggar.) Alongside this infrastructural development, paid for by foreign governments, there were also private investors interested in buying up real estate for tourism development. Much of this took place on the region's coastal strips.

An obsession with tourism growth and the need to attract investment has worked alongside a lack of planning regulations, building codes or environmental restraints (see Chapter Five) to result in the uncoordinated transformation of the coastlines. When planning procedures do exist, these have often been bypassed or over-ruled by governments anxious to please foreign investors and local elites. There is also an endemic problem in small societies when self-interest and political power are one and the same – members of planning committees, for example, have interests in tourism developments while politicians, too, use their political muscle to over-rule planning decisions.

For example, the south coast of Barbados between Bridgetown and Oistins briefly became a gold coast when apartments, hotels, bars and fast-food outlets piled in to fill the gaps between the old, established hotels. But by the late 1980s, recession, overbuilding, lack of capital and a new trend in down-market tourism had created stretches of abandoned apartment blocks, broken signs, peeling paintwork, 'For Sale' signs, and deserted, locked-up villas. Only tropical vegetation disguised the junk-yard appearance of better days gone by. At the end of the century there was 20 per cent less hotel accommodation than there had been 20 years earlier.

Lack of controlled planning combined with high prices put further pressure on the Barbados tourist industry. Low hotel occupancy rates and low, if any, profits – especially in the small hotels – became a trend. As a result, there was no money for refurbishment and upgrading. The situation was worsened still further by a recession in the US in 1991. Eventually, Barbados was forced to seek 'help' from the International Monetary Fund. At one point, Barbados was cited as one tourism destination that was approaching the end of its life-cycle. Those who pointed to the inertia of thinking in Barbados at that time talked of how its government had 'adopted a laissez-faire attitude, preferring to encourage such policies as first growth, then quality control, and more recently market diversification, rather than becoming an active agent in planning for tourism development.'[15] When development plans do exist they tend to be drawn up by unaccountable overseas consultants who are paid large sums of money to make recommendations, have a limited understanding of the country's dynamics, and then leave without ensuring any effective follow-up.

At the same time as the government in Barbados exhibited such a 'laissez-faire attitude', it has not, however, been inactive in its approach to tourism. When it pleases, it acts, especially in relation to public engagement and NGO activity. An assessment of Barbados' most recent national physical development plan concluded that despite the apparent concern for sustainable development, local involvement, environmental impact procedures and so on, the government 'has ensured, by means of a series of formal and informal actions, that the development control process remains highly centralised.' It was also pointed out that the plan's policies for sustainable tourism development were vague enough to allow the minister to maintain 'ultimate power'.[16]

Political interference in planning decisions often characterises small island administrations (see Chapters One and Five). Even when environmental impact assessments (EIA) are carried out, the procedure has 'traditionally carried little weight in the decision-making process', while one EIA for a prospective resort in Grenada was written by 'someone at a desk in the US who had never been to Grenada'.[17] Governments, with re-election in mind, and with a personal interest in the development or under pressure from foreign developers, can find ways to ignore the conclusions of such assessments. Barbados, with a longer history than many Caribbean countries of carrying out EIAs, also shows such a tendency. Following the intervention of the Barbados minister of tourism, for example, luxury homes at Port St Charles were allowed to go ahead despite an EIA which concluded that the impacts on the marine environment were too great.[18]

Another constraint working against the formulation of clear, long-term policies is tourism's ambivalent status in the political hierarchy. Tourism does not always receive the attention it deserves. 'It seems that most governments and officials prefer to see the region as it was and tourism as some sort of recent and not entirely legitimate appendage,' was the trenchant comment from David Jessop, who runs the British-based Caribbean Council for Europe. And Jean Holder, the former, long-serving head of the CTO, has written: 'It is even possible to contest general elections in the Caribbean without either side dealing seriously with national tourism policy.'[19]

Holder, who has seen many ministers of tourism come and go, continued to lament the fact that most governments don't understand tourism: 'the process remains a mystery to them.' In December 2001, he told the assembled ranks of the Caribbean Community (Caricom) ministers and officials that tourism is 'an extraordinarily complex phenomenon in social and economic terms.' He added: 'It is intrusive socially, culturally and environmentally and has as much potential for irritating a host population, as for creating positive human interaction.' He went on to say that the tourist establishment in the Caribbean appear to be 'constantly baffled' that their best efforts were sometimes frustrated because of these delicate matters. In fact, he said, they deny the negatives and refuse to accept that Caribbean tourism workers could possibly be dissatisfied. Their approach, he continued, was to repeat as often possible the mantra of economic benefits but to ignore the negatives and the reasons for them.

The sometimes haphazard organisation of the tourist industry also exposes the Caribbean to charges of amateurism which, within a highly competitive and global industry, it can ill afford. As Drew Foster, chairman of Caribbean Connection, one of the UK's leading tour operators, pointed out: 'While governments understand that tourism is a major industry and as such is a major part of the economy, it doesn't get the financial backing, effort or time it warrants. It's not necessarily run by professional people.' Foster also alleges that politicians use tourism for political gain:

> Politicians are required to report percentage increases in overseas arrivals to harbour favour with their party and often put pressure on their tourist boards to deliver these increases at any cost. Excessive amounts of money with gimmicky ideas are then used to attract the required numbers. Better strategic planning would have been better employed to achieve the results often at a more sensible cost. I am afraid it's a case of numbers, numbers, and percentage increases all the time.

Yet statistical data is not always kept with appropriate attention to detail; nor is up-to-date data always available on a country-by-country basis, a point that the CTO often makes in its annual statistical reports. Such lapses make the work of statisticians and economists difficult. A major study of the economic impact of tourism on Jamaica, for example, concluded that, 'in spite of the sector's importance to the economic, social, and environmental well-being of the country, information about the economic impact of tourism has been inadequate to provide a sound basis for policy making. Moreover, tourism does not exist as a separate sector in the National Accounts.' [20]

Another problematic aspect is that the tourism portfolio is sometimes tied to other ministries – trade and industry, for example. Even when there is a minister of tourism, they are not necessarily powerful within the cabinet (nor, often, do they have any expertise in tourism). Different countries also have different ways of organising national tourist industries. Some countries run tourism from a ministry, headed by the minister and staffed by civil servants. These are often countries with more 'centralised' traditions, such as the Bahamas, or those with small, under-developed tourist industries, such as Dominica and Guyana. Others have set up tourist boards, run by a director of tourism, who reports to the minister of tourism responsible for policy. These boards, made up of a mixture of public- and private-sector interests, are usually responsible for marketing and promotion and 'product development'.

The private sector has latterly sought, and won, a more central role, especially within the Anglophone Caribbean. Yet the relationship between the public and private sector remains fraught with the private sector often accusing the public sector of an inefficient use of its budget and with an inability to go out and sell the destination (see Chapter Six). It is also scornful of the levels of competence in the public sector, with too few staff still having academic expertise in tourism. Criticism also comes from the tourism specialists. 'Most public sector tourism staff have wandered into the sector and some cope better than others,' is the somewhat disdainful verdict of a University of the West Indies paper. [21]

Barbados is one country that has suffered significantly from internal upheaval and division. One significant aspect of tourism administration in Barbados, but also in some other countries, has been the racial dimension. In Barbados, the private sector has been dominated by whites, or at any rate, the lighter-skinned. That racial underpinning has expressed itself with the key jobs in tourism, both at home and overseas, sometimes being dominated by whites. In the past, tourism ministers, too, tended to be light-skinned. In 1994 a controversy arose which some saw as exemplifying Barbados' racial divide. As the then Barbadian general secretary of the Caribbean Conference of Churches, Edward Cumberbatch explained: 'You have perceptions in the hotel industry that whites want to be handled at the top by whites.'

He said this in the middle of a disruptive dispute between the then prime minister, Erskine Sandiford, and the Barbados Tourism Authority (BTA) over the appointment of a new chief executive officer. The authority had refused to endorse Sandiford's choice, Tony Arthur, who was the acting chief executive officer, and three ministers had resigned. Later, Sandiford sacked all but two of the members of the BTA. Some people had said that Arthur had been rejected because he was 'not a good mixer' or 'too African in appearance.' [22]

Whatever the truth, considerable damage had been done to the country's tourist industry by this period of indecision and internal wrangling, which had been going on for some years. In 1993, a commentator in the *Sunday Sun* wrote: 'The political tinkering and fooling around have cost the country an incalculable fortune. The appointment of incompetents to strategically vital positions of importance cannot be afforded any longer.' [23]

The internal difficulties – revealing both ineffectual management and a lack of expertise – continued with the new government of Owen Arthur and the appointment of a series of tourism ministers. The second tourism minister, for example, re-organised the administration of the sector and increased the perks and salaries (described by local people as 'Lotto salaries') of the executives. Even so, they did not stay long. The third minister of tourism was accused of cronyism by his critics who were, among other things, also alarmed at his initiative to order an expensive participation in a trade show in Germany at a time when there were no flights from continental Europe to Barbados. Under Owen Arthur's fourth minister, who was appointed in 2001, the tourism authority was again, according to critics, staffed with top people with little or no expertise in the industry. Such instability and unpredictability do not make for efficient decision-making.

While Jamaica's tourism establishment has also not escaped criticism from the private sector, Jamaica is one Caribbean country that has made some steps to ensure the coherent development of its largest industry. Its national industry policy established twin objectives: diversifying the sector and achieving higher value-added levels. A policy framework was developed which incorporated an integrated infrastructural programme alongside tighter procedures for ensuring environmental conservation. The Tourism Product Development Company (TPDCo) was also set up to 'develop and sustain Jamaica's tourism product.' Its objectives 'to ensure its sustainability and benefits to the community' include work on anything from anti-harassment initiatives (see Chapter Four) to 'beautification', projects with schoolchildren and job training (see Chapter Three). Yet some feel that the budget does not show a commitment to that development. Jamaica's tourism budget, representing 1.1 per cent of the whole, totalled US$46.8 million. Of this, US$35.5 million went to the Jamaica tourist board, of which US$20 million was for marketing. TPDCo got $3.52 million. The contrast between the marketing money and the tourism development money is something that critics would find endorsed their belief that attention to tourism education at home is often dwarfed by proselytising abroad.

Missing Links

One overall effect of the weak organisation of the tourist industry has been that foreign capital makes further inroads at the expense of a locally-controlled sustainable development strategy. This was critically summed up by Professor Dennis Conway of Indiana University in 1989:

> Government passivity or lack of foresight has left the tourist capitalist sector virtually a free-for-all. The tourist sector has been either completely dominated by foreign capital or managed by foreign institutions in cooperation with local mercantile capital. Both of these interests, foreign and local, are committed to maintaining dependence on imported technology and imported goods and services, a major influence on the minimal level of intersectoral linkages between tourism and other economic sectors in Caribbean countries like agriculture and light industry. [24]

One of the distinctive features of the Caribbean's tourist industry is the extent to which hard-earned foreign exchange is depleted by a high import bill for goods and services. The figures are difficult to establish, but in most countries, the level of what are known as 'leakages' is very high, averaging from 50 to 70 per cent, according to a report by the Worldwatch Institute in 2001. A 70 per cent leakage means that for every dollar earned in foreign exchange 70 cents is lost in imports, taxes, profits and wages. In the Bahamas, a senior tourism official suggested in 1994 that the leakages for that country might be as high as 90 per cent. While up-to-date statistics are hard to come by, it is probably safe to estimate that the larger and more diversified economies, such as Jamaica, have been able to block the leakages more effectively. The Organisation of American States assessed Jamaica's leakage at 37 per cent in 1994, a far more respectable figure than is usual.[25]

In 1988, the CTRC admitted in a report on economic development and the tourist industry that 'food and most finished goods required by hotels to satisfy tourist demand must, at present, be brought largely from the outside, with considerable leakage of foreign exchange.' It went on: 'While a certain amount of foreign exchange leakage is inevitable in tourism, much can be done to improve the Caribbean's capability to supply a greater part of the goods and services required by tourists from internal sources.'[26] Since then, there has been some, but only some, improvement in that direction.

On the opposite side of the economic fence are 'linkages'. These are the ways in which the tourist industry utilises locally produced goods and services rather than importing them. Maximising the linkages decreases the leakages of foreign exchange. This process also lessens the dependence of tourism on outside factors while stimulating local economies and 'people development' and encouraging a greater sense of self-determination. In 1993 the West Indian Commission's Time For Action urged that 'agriculture, manufacturing and tourism be developed on a symbiotic basis.'[27]

Jean Holder, too, has pointed out that the Caribbean has 'failed miserably to maximise the possibilities for supplying the tourism sector' from local and regional goods and services.[28] Holder attributed this to policy failure by the public sector and a lack of confidence by the private sector so that ultimately buyers do not know what is available and sellers do not know what is required. The head of the Caribbean Hotel Association, John Bell, expressed similar sentiments at the Caricom tourism summit of December 2001 when he called for a greater involvement of small suppliers in the industry. This is the new 'caring' face of Caribbean tourism and one which has not until recently appeared to be central to thinking within the industry.

While the underproduction of the manufacturing sector for domestic use is one example of how the leakage problem impoverishes the

Caribbean, nowhere can this process be better seen than through the lack of interaction between agriculture and tourism. While some islands, such as the dry coral territories of Aruba and Anguilla, would find it difficult to become fertile vegetable gardens, many now unproductive islands have long histories of agricultural production, from sugar to cotton to coffee, citrus and, more recently, bananas. The land is fertile and versatile. Yet in the dining rooms of many Caribbean hotels, where millions of meals are consumed daily, the tourists do not eat the mangoes, breadfruit, citrus and bananas of every Caribbean yard. They drink orange juice from Florida, eat a banana from Colombia or stab at pineapple chunks from Hawaii. Only perhaps in countries like Jamaica, or perhaps for different reasons Dominica, can it be reasonably claimed that local products dominate tourist dining tables.

The explanation for the lack of links between farmer and chef lies buried in the history of Caribbean agriculture; the culinary tastes of tourists from Texas or Toronto, however conservative those may be, bear less of a responsibility.

Centuries of slavery and colonialism imposed an export imperative on the region; the raw materials of the land, primarily sugar, were exported in bulk to fuel Europe's industrial revolution. Away from the plantations, slaves with access to provision grounds grew their own food when their labour was not required on the estates. They grew it for their own use and sometimes to take to market; but this was marginal, subsistence agriculture and labour was always monopolised by the plantation system.

Neither emancipation nor independence changed this pattern of one-crop dependency; only the crop changed. The dominant crop is nowadays more likely to be the banana than anything else, but it is grown primarily for export, while 'provision' farming remains largely unorganised and practised very much on traditional lines. Many of these small-scale farmers are women who grow yam and dasheen and a small selection of seasonal fruit and vegetables for family use or for taking to market. As has been pointed out: 'Women farmers receive little attention from extension agents and so food production utilises traditional methods, often with low activity.'[29]

In his study of agricultural diversification in the Windward Islands, Mark Thomas found that ministries of agriculture had little marketing experience. 'Successful crops in the Windwards have always been introduced as estate crops and smallholder production has followed, once post-harvest and marketing arrangements were established by the companies and exporters associated with the estates.'[30]

Such systems have not fitted easily into satisfying the needs of luxury hotels with nouvelle cuisine menus. Agricultural practice in the Caribbean has been slow to respond to the needs of the region's growing tourist industries. As Chester Humphrey, a Grenadian trade unionist, pointed out, 'The government can't expect farmers to automatically develop the linkages with tourism because for 500 years they have been trained in a culture of export agriculture.'

The result has been that the hotels and restaurants of the Caribbean have depended heavily on imported food. Unable to rely on local supplies, the crates and containers of pineapples, concentrated fruit juice, canned tomatoes, iceberg lettuces and Californian melons pour into the islands. For the food and beverage managers of the region's hotels, it has become easier and cheaper to import than to search for local supplies of the right quality and volume.

The hotel managers of Cuba's blossoming tourist industry came to the same conclusion despite the firm control taken by the Cuban government. In the 1990s, hotels bought from a state wholesaler, paying in dollars for produce paid to the farmers in pesos. Cuban hotels have to buy local, but foreign-owned hotels can use imported items. It has been estimated that the foreign chains import 40 to 60 per cent of their food, a figure comparable to many other Caribbean countries. The reason lies in the poor quality of local food, grown with few incentives to improve standards, difficult distribution and storage conditions and no access to imported pesticides and fertilizers. The result is that 'The quality of Cuban-produced food, as measured by size, appearance, and taste, is often poor and about a quarter of it is returned by hotels as unsuitable for tourist consumption.'[31]

The likes and dislikes of tourists are a further discouragement to the local agricultural market. 'If you didn't provide what the tourist wants, you'd get so much hassle. We would have so many problems if we didn't provide beef and lamb. We had a beautiful seafood buffet, but many people wouldn't eat it,' said hotelier Peter Odle, a former president of the Barbados Hotel Association. Farmers complain that the hotels tell them that their guests only have a fish and chip palate.

So, agricultural history, the conservatism of the package tourist and the globalisation of the food network as produce is airlifted from distant fields provides a justification for hoteliers to sidestep the problems associated with local purchasing. 'To satisfy their demands the hotels and restaurants must, of necessity, buy the imported Grade A beef, "Irish" potatoes and the variety of cheeses, condiments, jams and jellies that their customers automatically expect to see on the menu.'[32] It is the excuse in any case that some hoteliers and chefs seek, especially those from Europe or North America. Chefs trained in Switzerland may not recognise Caribbean vegetables or even if they do they may have no idea how to cook with them. Despite a tightening-up of import regulations, vegetables not normally associated with the Caribbean such as broccoli, cauliflower and courgettes appear on import lists.

The emphasis on export agriculture has continued despite tourism. Once again the demands of foreign capital dictate the direction of policy. In fundamental terms the Caribbean produces what it does not eat, and eats what it does not produce. Crucially, the decades in which the tourist industry grew to maturity were also years when the banana, in particular in the Windward Islands, was riding high; spurred on by high prices, farmers cultivated every gap and hillside. However, by the late 1980s when the future of the secure preferential market in Europe was beginning to look increasingly doubtful, governments were seeking to diversify their agricultural programmes. Yet the tourist market on the doorstep was ignored. Instead, in 1988 the Organisation of Eastern Caribbean States (OECS) embarked on a US$6.2 million programme, financed by the US Agency for International Development (USAID) and called the Tropical Produce Support Project. The emphasis, once more following in the footsteps of colonial economics, was on production and marketing for export.

Despite aid money, extra-regional exports from the OECS increased very little during the early 1990s. 'Farmers were so secure with bananas that they didn't bother with other commodities. It took them a little while to change,' explained St Lucian Stephen Fontinelle. Dame Eugenia Charles, then prime minister of Dominica, had another explanation; she believed that bananas are 'man's work' and male farmers do not like dealing with non-traditional 'women's crops' such as passion fruit.

Meanwhile, questions were increasingly asked as to why some of that money, expertise and effort could not be turned towards exploiting the tourist market. An editorial in Focus on Rural Development demanded: 'Are we so stuck on developing exports for extra-regional markets, where we are at a comparative disadvantage, that we are overlooking a burgeoning market on our own doorsteps?'[33] Another reason is that governments obtain taxes and duties from imported products and that the merchant class, a significant political grouping, depends on importing for their livelihood.

Against this background of tradition, practice and ideology – none of which are determined by the needs of the Caribbean but rather by outside forces – another factor has worked against the development of effective local tourism/agricultural linkages. During the 1980s agricultural output continued to decrease as a percentage of Gross Domestic Product (GDP) in almost all Caribbean countries. Agriculture and fishing decreased from 12 per cent of GDP in Barbados in the mid 1970s to 6 per cent by the end of the century, while Jamaica recorded a decrease from 8.2 to 7 per cent.

The general decline in agriculture has, in turn, upgraded tourism; the incentives, the talk and the excitement have all been at the expense of agriculture. Benny Langaigne works for Grencoda, a development organisation based in Gouyave, on the west coast of Grenada, where tourists are rarely seen except in passing minibuses en route to the north coast attraction of Caribs' Leap. 'We are concerned about the dominant trend which is to use tourism as the motor of the economy and downplay the significance of agriculture. This results in a lack of concentration in agriculture,' he said. 'Instead, the more energetic people are drawn away from farming and into being a taxi-driver or a security guard at a hotel. The average age of the Grenadian farmer is now 55 to 60.' The shift is perhaps inevitable. As Jean Holder has said: 'People cannot be kept in agriculture as labourers by preaching to them about the virtues of agriculture in the country's needs. People are kept in agriculture by revolutionising agriculture and creating conditions that can compete with other sectoral activities.'[34] The problem is that this has not happened. Agricultural work remains for the most part badly paid, physically hard and subject to climatic and market risks.

Making Connections

Throughout the Caribbean, governments have articulated the problem of the leakages and the need to create backward linkages. Yet there has been, with few exceptions, little action to help farmers or small traders to revolutionise their methods: to learn about the necessary packaging, transport, marketing and delivery processes for the tourist industry. In any case, small farmers have little access to credit to help them expand and be more efficient.

The exceptions have been in Jamaica and Grenada (see Chapter Nine), where both experiences were initiatives by socialist-style governments of the 1970s, and, more recently in St Kitts and St Lucia. By the early 1990s, however, it was left to Grenada's non-governmental organisations to propose reforms to encourage such linkages. The report of a Grencoda workshop held in May 1993 to review and evaluate events in Grenada since 1989 stated: 'A specific area for collective enterprise and collaboration between all bodies – government, church, private sector, NGOs – was identified as the necessary and overdue marriage between tourism and agriculture.'[35]

In Grenada, most linkages between agriculture, agro-processing, fishing or manufacturing and tourism have tended to develop from individual initiative. Agro-processing, for example, which had begun to develop under the Peoples' Revolutionary Government, has been in decline. Cecile Lagrenade's business is the only one of its kind in Grenada. Based in the lush hillsides above St George's, it was started as a cottage industry in the late 1960s by her mother; it produces jams and jellies from nutmeg, guava and limes, pepper sauce and jelly and mauby and seamoss drinks. Production has steadily increased and there are plans for a range of organic products. Lagrenade buys from farmers, employs local people and uses dozens of vendors to sell her gift baskets to tourists. It seems a small but efficient business, but she said that people seemed to have lost sight of agro-processing. Similar problems exist throughout the agriculturally rich islands of the eastern Caribbean. In St Kitts, for example, Euphemia Weekes, of the non-governmental Inter-American Institute for Cooperation in Agriculture (IICA), observed: 'There are no plans for linking tourism and agriculture. It happens spontaneously. The problem is about information flow between farmers and hotels.'

Jamaica, with its larger and more diverse economy, has created opportunities for the links between farmers and hotels to flourish. 'There is now more traditional Jamaican food in hotels than ever before. You'll find yam on hotel menus as easily as you'll find Irish potatoes,' said Lionel Reid, former president of the Jamaican Hotel Association. Reid said that Jamaica's tourism industry is almost self-sufficient in food and only imports choice cuts of meat. According to Reid, the change occurred in the 1970s, when the Michael Manley government set up the Agricultural Marketing Corporation to help farmers find local markets for their crops. In a rather different political climate, Sandals Resorts now leads the way in linkages with farmers. It works with Jamaica's Rural Agricultural Development Authority to provide seeds to farmers, to arrange extension services and then buy the products from the farmers. Latest figures show that Sandals

Resorts in Jamaica purchased some J$500 million worth of produce from local farmers per year. 'The farmers like it and we like it because we get fresh vegetables twice a week instead of cooler boxes,' said one Sandals general manager.

Sandals, which introduced the system in St Lucia in 2001, claims that it will buy as much as it can from local farmers 'providing that established standards are met.' Andrew Regobert, of Micoud on the east coast of St Lucia, is one of them. A veteran farmer and agricultural adviser, he used to grow bananas but has now become one of the main vegetable suppliers to the island's Sandals resorts. He says there are many benefits from dealing with Sandals. 'For a start, they gave me the opportunity to explore the full potential of my farm.' He has also inspired other local farmers to move into vegetable production. 'Right now with sales to Sandals, it has brought some more enthusiasm back into farming.' He also believes that his farm could be a future agri-tourism destination to show tourists the links between the two sectors. [36]

Such initiatives, which offer a future to the region's ailing agricultural sector, are not yet commonplace. However, according to some researchers, there is a growing move to integrate agriculture with tourism. This is partly explained by a maturing of the region's tourist industry and the employment of larger numbers of West Indian chefs but also the result of the precarious nature of traditional exports, for which markets are now less secure in a world dominated by free trade. So farmers like Regobert in St Lucia are looking for markets closer to home.

In St Lucia, the government and the private sector began to work together in the early 1990s to improve the linkages. Its 'Adopt a Farmer' pilot programme was launched in the mid 1990s by the St Lucia Hotel Association and the ministry of agriculture to work with the largest all-inclusives on the island, Sandals and Club St Lucia. One of the goals of the original idea was that the hotels could have some control over the produce and that the farmers would have a guaranteed market. With a steady income, farmers could then gain credit from the banks. 'It made sense,' said Richard Michelin of the St Lucia Hotel and Tourism Association, who was behind the original idea. Adopt a Farmer introduced the idea of quality control. One farmer, said Michelin, used a cardboard cut-out to measure the size of the tomatoes wanted by the hotels. 'It was team work and it made sense,' said Michelin.

Another initiative of the 1990s, which showed signs of proper planning was set up in the small Leeward Island of Nevis. There, three local groups, the Nevis Growers' Association (vegetables), the Nevis Livestock Farmers' Cooperative (meat) and Daly Farm (poultry) began to trade with the Four Seasons Resort under the guidance of a task force set up by the ministry of agriculture and the Caribbean Agricultural Research and Development Institute (Cardi). The task force's role was to plan and organise vegetable production 'avoiding any gluts and scarcities,' to provide seeds and technical information for farmers, to forecast production, to regulate imports and, most importantly, to act as a negotiating agent between the farmers and the hotel. It offers the farmers a guaranteed market and in return demands high standards.

Sales started in January 1991. 'We started with providing six crops and now we provide 38 different items,' said Daniel Arthurton, who was the first coordinator of the task force. 'We supply 100 per cent of the eggs required, 35 per cent of fruit and vegetables, 15 to 20 per cent of fish. We are fine-tuning constantly. Four Seasons now come and ask us to try and grow different varieties. It's a tacit understanding that they will take our produce if quality standards are maintained.'

According to Arthurton, the project changed not only incomes, but also attitudes. 'Some farmers decided to go into commercial large-scale production with drip irrigation and production extended all-year-round and not just the rainy season.' The manager of Four Seasons said that the hotel now also buys most of its lettuces from a hydroponic farm. 'We would prefer to buy more locally produced and grown ingredients,' he said. 'We continue to rely heavily on the importation of fresh items.'

Apart from agriculture, mechanisms for stimulating tourism's linkages with the wider economy are also missing. Within the manufacturing sector, for example, the constraints for developing this linkage were described in a 1991 report from Caricom's Export Development Project. It described how regional manufacturers had limited marketing and sales expertise and little experience of competing within an international market; they also had a reputation for sub-standard products and unreliability. Small-scale businesses and high prices also compounded their problems along with hoteliers reluctant to change their long-time business practices of buying from Florida suppliers. The study revealed a high correlation between hotel ownership and local purchasing, with local hoteliers more likely to buy local. In the smaller countries with largely foreign-owned hotels, manufacturers, inhibited by a lack of raw materials, and marketing and capital restrictions, have great difficulties in competing for hotel contracts.

Cuba's larger industrial base would suggest better opportunities for fostering linkages. Yet, until recently, the enclave nature of Cuba's tourist industry with its dual-currency economy limited that potential. When tourism in communist Cuba first began to develop in the late 1970s most of the hard currency it earned remained in circulation within the sector, minimising the trickle-down effect. The recent development of a private sector, with tourists staying in private homes and eating in small private restaurants, has given many more Cubans access to the dollar economy – although at a price, as the government takes a heavy tax on these 'private' enterprises. There are also outlets for Cuba's manufacturing industries to supply the tourism sector with such items as furniture, mattresses, linen and building materials. But quality, as in agricultural production for hotels, has remained a problem; Fidel Castro himself once noted that the standard of work in Cuba's elevator factory was not good enough for luxury hotels. [37]

The Ripple Effect

The essential fact about the economic benefits of tourism is that the wider the range of goods and services an economy can supply, particularly those that relate directly or indirectly to tourism, the greater the proportion of tourist expenditure remaining within the country as income. Conversely, those countries that are more heavily dependent on imported goods and services will enjoy less income per tourist dollar spent. There are, however, different methods of working out the relationship between cost and benefit. One method is called the ripple or 'multiplier' effect, which is the degree to which tourism expenditure filters through an economy and contributes to income and employment.

In the Caribbean different experts have come up with different results. One report by H. Zinder, undertaken for USAID and produced in 1969, put the tourism income multiplier for the eastern Caribbean at 2.3. This meant that for every US$1 spent by a tourist some US$2.3 would be added on average to the national income. The Zinder report fell under heavy criticism for using a flawed methodology that essentially double-counted the impacts of tourism. Later studies undertaken throughout the 1980s and 1990s by John

Fletcher, an economist and head of the International Centre for Tourism and Hospitality Research at Bournemouth University, produced very different results. Looking at selected countries, including those in the Caribbean, Fletcher estimated the tourism income multiplier for Jamaica at 1.23, the Dominican Republic at 1.20, Antigua at 0.88, the Bahamas at 0.79, the Cayman Islands at 0.65 and the British Virgin Islands at 0.58. Only two South Pacific states recorded lower multipliers.[38]

In more recent years, Fletcher has taken his research on tourism impacts in a different direction, believing that much of the information provided to tourism ministries is inaccessible, often out-of-date and therefore unhelpful. Fletcher, a pioneer of the use of input/output models to measure the impacts of tourism, has created interactive computer models for a number of countries including two in the Caribbean – St Lucia and Bonaire. His latest models are installed on computers in the ministries and are able to simulate the effects of changes, real or hypothesised arising from tourism. The impacts included in these models are no longer confined to the economic effects but also include environmental and social indicators. 'The models are comprehensive planning tools that can be used to forecast future impacts,' said Professor Fletcher. 'The ability to understand how tourism interacts with impacts on the other sectors of the economy is vital for sustainable tourism development.'

Meanwhile, small islands, with small populations and few natural resources, generally score lowest on the multiplier scale. In contrast, the Jamaican tourist industry's high score on Fletcher's multiplier reckoning reflects such factors as a relatively large population with a relatively well developed industrial base. Combine these factors with high levels of local ownership of hotels, a steady growth rate in tourist arrivals, and you get a relatively low leakage rate.

Small islands, with small populations and few natural resources, generally score lowest on the multiplier scale. In contrast, the Jamaican tourist industry's high score on Fletcher's multiplier reckoning reflects such factors as a relatively large population and land mass, high local ownership of hotels, a steady growth rate in tourist arrivals, and, importantly, a relatively low leakage rate.

Yet despite its mature, large and what many see as an energetic tourist industry, Jamaica remains vulnerable. Firstly, it remains heavily dependent on the economic and political climate in the US in terms of tourist arrivals and fluctuations in the exchange rate. It also has much poverty, a severe balance-of-payments deficit and a huge foreign debt. These difficulties contribute to volatile and sometimes violent social conditions, which create problems for its image as a relaxed holiday playground (see Chapter Four).

The Jamaican government's task has been to balance the needs of its people – its poor crowded into city slums or scattered on rural hillsides – with the requirements of a rapacious tourist industry. The answer, for Jamaica, as elsewhere in the region, has been to turn to tourism as a generator of jobs, whether at the airport, in the hotel bar, duty-free shops, construction sites or on the beach. That has offered one way of easing those burdens.

NOTES

1. Herbert L. Hiller, 'Tourism: Development or Dependence?' in Richard Millett and Will, W. Marvin (eds), *The Restless Caribbean*, New York, 1979, p.53
2. *Caribbean Insight*, September 2001
3. Cited in Frank Fonda Taylor, *To Hell With Paradise: A History of the Jamaican Tourist Industry*, Pittsburg, 1993, p.184
4. *Caribbean Week*, September 16-29, 1995
5. Erik Cohn, 'The Impact of Tourism on the Physical Environment', *Annals of Tourism Research*, vol 5, 1978, p.215
6. *Santo Domingo News*, Santo Domingo, 20 May 1994
7. Neil Price, *Behind the Planter's Back: Lower-Class Responses to Marginality in Bequia Island, St Vincent*, London, 1988, p.206
8. Caribbean Tourism Research and Development Centre (CTRC), Caribbean Tourism – Economic Development, Tourism Management, Barbados, June 1988
9. Ransford W. Palmer, 'Tourism and Taxes: the Case of Barbados' in Dennis Gayle and Goodrich, Jonathan (eds), *Tourism, Marketing and Management in the Caribbean*, London, 1993, p.58
10. Fonda Taylor, op. cit., p.163
11. Ibid., p.176
12. Philip Cash, Gordon, Shirley and Saunders, Gail, *Sources of Bahamanian History*, London, 1991, p.292
13. Economist Intelligence Unit (EIU), *Tourism in the Caribbean*, London, 1993
14. 'The Impact of Tourism Investment Incentives in the Caribbean Region', Organisation of American States and Caribbean Tourism Organisation, 1990
15. Paul Wilkinson, *Tourism Policy and Planning in the eastern Caribbean: Anguilla, Barbados, Dominica and St Lucia*, York University Press, 1993
16. Robert Potter and Jonathan Pugh, 'Physical Development Planning in Barbados', *Singapore Journal of Tropical Geography*, 21 (2) 2000
17. Ibid.
18. Ibid.
19. Jean Holder, 'The Caribbean: Far Greater Dependence on Tourism Likely', *The Courier*, no 122, Brussels, 1990
20. Cited in OAS, op. cit.
21. Kenneth Hall et al, Caribbean Tourism and the Role of UWI, *Social and Economic Studies*, Vol 51, No 1, March 2002

22. *Caribbean Contact*, Barbados, March/April 1994

23. Cited in Graham Dann and Potter, Robert, 'Tourism in Barbados: Rejuvenation or Decline?' in D. Lockhart and Drakakis-Smith, D (eds) *Island Tourism: Problems and Perspectives*, London, 1995

24. Dennis Conway, 'Tourism and Caribbean Development: Opinion Aside, What is Needed is Measurement ansd Appropriate Government Management' in Gayle and Goodrich, op. cit., p.174

25. OAS, op. cit.

26. CTRC, op. cit.

27. West Indian Commission, 'Time for Action: Overview of the Report of the West Indian Commission', Barbados, 1992, p.99

28. Jean Holder, 'The Caribbean Tourism Organisation's Role in Caribbean Tourism Development Towards the Year 2000' in Gayle and Goodrich, op. cit., p.217

29. Janet Momsen, 'Caribbean Tourism and Agriculture: New Linkages in the Global Era', in *Globalisation and Neoliberalism*, edited by Thomas Klak, p.119, 1998

30. Mark Thomas, 'Agricultural Diversification: the Experience of the Windward Islands', Institute of Development Studies, University of Sussex, 1989

31. Momsen, op. cit.

32. Caribbean Farmers Development Company, Focus on Rural Development, St Lucia, no. 3 1992

33. Ibid.

34. Jean Holder, 'The Caribbean', op. cit., p.78

35. Grenada Community Development Agency, communiqué, 1993

36. onecaribbean.com, 4 May 2002

37. Derek R. Hall, 'Tourism Development in Cuba' in David Harrison (ed), *Tourism and the Less Developed Countries*, London, 1992, p.117

38. John Fletcher, 'Input-Output Analysis and Tourism Impact Studies', *Annals of Tourism Research*, vol 16, 1989, p.515-29

3

FROM BANANA FARMER TO BANANA DAIQUIRI: EMPLOYMENT

For every new hotel room in the Caribbean, roughly one more new job is created. In a region beset by chronically high unemployment, any job, even though low-paid, seasonal, unskilled and with few prospects, might seem welcome. For as Jean Holder, former secretary-general of the CTO, has said, employment in tourism is 'the difference between social order and social chaos.'[1] Tourism provides not just direct employment in hotels, casinos, restaurants, shops and transport, but also indirect employment in the services and industries it has spawned. It also fuels a peripheral informal sector – the economic belt where the poor strive to earn an income from selling or providing services to tourists on a casual basis.

Whether tourism is an efficient generator of jobs is a matter of debate, but what is significant is that the Caribbean relies on a strategy that equates jobs with tourism. On the tiny island of Aruba, for instance, the pursuit of tourism brought unemployment down from 40 per cent in 1985 to virtually zero a decade later. The assumption that tourism will provide reflects the region's dependency on tourism; at the same time it highlights the lack of alternative forms of employment, especially in the smaller islands.

This view finds telling expression in the formal opening of a new hotel. The gala occasion where government bigwigs, local celebrities, airline executives, hotel owners, public relations officers and tourist board officials rub shoulders for cocktails and long speeches is not only used as a demonstration of faith by the – usually foreign – investors in the stability and well-being of the country. It also provides an opportunity for local politicians to celebrate the biggest job creation scheme since, most likely, the opening of the last hotel.

When the Rex Grenadian Hotel opened in appropriate style, the then prime minister Nicholas Brathwaite was there to savour the moment; his speech revealed the extent to which Grenada has come to rely on tourism. Pointing out that some 150 people were to be employed at the 212-room hotel – the island's largest – he indicated that 'workers must regard themselves as stake-holders with everything to lose if the venture fails.' The Rex, part of the Rex Resorts group and marketed and managed by Marketing and Reservations International, had instantly become one of the island's biggest employers. The local newspaper *Grenada Today* pointed out that more than 75 per cent of the hotel's staff had been previously unemployed and had no experience of hotel work.[2]

In one generation, the coming of tourism has changed the pattern of employment and the structure of communities for ever. Peasant economies have been moulded into service sectors where cane-cutters become bellhops and fishermen are turned into 'watersport officers'. Where statistics exist, the slide away from agriculture into the service sector in the last 40 years (and in some islands in the last 15 years) looks dramatic. Rural communities, first dislocated by migration, now find that the young move to the tourism-dominated coastal areas looking for casual work in the way that in other parts of the world they drift to the cities. Traditional life-patterns are altered as women become wage-earners, often for the first time, in the hotel sector where the demand for domestic work is high. Economic interests become more stratified with the higher-class locals identifying with the tourist interests and better able to exploit the opportunities offered by foreign capital and personnel than the unskilled majority.

Throughout the Caribbean, an estimated one in seven jobs is to be found in the tourist industry; a higher percentage than in any other region of the world according to the World Travel and Tourism Council (WTTC). The CTO admits that accurate figures for the numbers of jobs generated by tourism are hard to come by (it blames its member nations for not providing adequate statistics), but estimates that some 300,000 people were employed in the accommodation sector in 1999. This, of course, does not take into account direct employment in other aspects of the tourist industry, which brings the total to 900,000, according to the CTO; furthermore, it does not include the many 'faceless', who work unofficially in the industry. The WTTC offers a much higher overall figure: the Caribbean's tourist industry – direct and indirect employment – accounted for 2.4 million jobs in 2004, with this figure rising to 3.2 million by 2014.

In general, it is the countries with the most 'mature' tourist industry, the biggest hotels and the least diversified economies that are most dependent on tourism employment. The mass tourism of the Bahamas, for instance, supports 45,000 jobs, representing 35 per cent of formally employed labour. In more diversified economies, such as the Dominican Republic or Jamaica, the percentage of those employed in tourism compared with the rest of the economy is lower, despite the importance of tourism to the economy as a whole. In contrast, work generated by tourism in countries such as Trinidad and Guyana has made, to date, little impact on employment statistics. Figures from the WTTC showed that, in 2004, tourism provided (directly and indirectly) 11.8 per cent of jobs in Cuba, 31.8 per cent in Jamaica and 58.3 per cent in Barbados.

In the hotel sector, Caribbean nationals are largely concentrated in unskilled jobs. Until very recently, they tended not to be in the top jobs at all. However, they are now moving into senior positions in greater numbers. There are Caribbean general managers – nearly all of Sandals' general managers are, for example, from the region – who are at the very top of the industry. Middle management posts too are often held by Caribbean nationals, while white-collar jobs in the front-office and sports sections of hotels are sought after by the school-leaving children of the local lower-middle class.

One of the few studies to analyse the make-up of a tourism work force was done in 1994 and again in 2001 in Negril, Jamaica. The research by Dunn & Dunn, commissioned by the Jamaica Tourist Board, showed that in 2001 men just outnumbered women in the tourism workforce, but that women were a growing percentage. Most workers were between 25 and 35 years old. In 1994, just over a quarter of the group had had a high school education; in 2001 this had increased to 46 per cent. Women still received lower wages than men in 2001 but the wage gap had closed: males earned an average of US$67 a week and women US$62.[3]

The majority of the workers in the Dunn & Dunn studies had been on training courses, particularly in tourism awareness. The longer the workers had been employed in tourism, the more training they had received. They were generally proud to work in tourism and thought it created lots of jobs. However, the study revealed a high turnover among new employees. Asked to state what other work they would like to do if they had a choice, most of the workers chose jobs with a higher social, skill-level and income status than the jobs they currently held. 'Overall, the findings indicate that employment in the tourism industry is a stepping stone to other careers.'

The message was that management would have to respond to an educated workforce that would depart for fresh pastures unless conditions and pay were seen to be adequate. 'Training workers who will then use the industry as a stepping stone to other jobs outside the sector will not be cost-effective,' warned Dunn & Dunn.

What then are these jobs that such workers (in Jamaica, at least) briefly experience and then abandon? Most, but not all, hotel work is relatively low grade: the security officers at the gate, bellboys in the foyer, 'room attendants' servicing the bedrooms, gardeners sprucing up the foliage, cooks, barmen, waitresses in the restaurants and bars, watersports 'officers' and deckchair attendants. Many of these workers remain 'unskilled', and especially in smaller establishments are not offered proper training. Sometimes it appears that tourism is used as a desperate measure to soak up the unemployment rates of the unskilled. Or even as Derek Walcott put it:

> ...These were the traitors
> who in elected office, saw the land as views
> for hotels and elevated into waiters
> the sons of others, while their own learnt something else.[4]

For a region steeped in poverty, there is no shortage of recruits for such jobs. Supply in most cases, in fact, far outstrips demand, although in some islands such as Antigua, St Maarten, Aruba and the US Virgin Islands, a labour shortage has required migration (particularly by women) from other islands, such as Dominica and St Kitts, to fill the jobs at the bottom of the pile. In Aruba, labour was even brought in from the Philippines. For tourism still offers, as Gordon Lewis wrote 30 years ago, opportunities 'at once more comfortable, more exciting and more socially prestigious than work in the agricultural sector.'[5] In larger hotels with high occupancy rates, a (rare) all-year-round clientele and trade union representation, employees may be reasonably well paid; a 'room attendant' with good tips, for example, can make more in the peak season than a shop assistant or a clerical worker.

A long-standing trade union movement within the hotel sector has helped to improve wages and conditions, especially in the more mainstream resorts. Indeed, one reason given for the reluctance of investors to buy into the Caribbean is what they consider to be high labour rates. According to the Economist Intelligence Unit, total payroll and related costs were 13 per cent of room revenue in the Caribbean in 1990, compared with 6.1 per cent in Africa and 9.2 per cent in Latin America. Only Europe and North America had higher costs.[6] The regional comparisons have not changed significantly in the last decade.

However, for most hotel employees, especially in the smaller establishments, both the perception and the reality of the industry is of seasonal work, low wages, poor conditions and scant security. Yet for both men and women, any sort of paid employment offers a certain status, an opportunity for a guaranteed income, however small, which is not subject to the sun, rain or to a fickle market. For women, hotel work is regarded as suitable employment since it takes place in 'respectable surroundings' and is an extension of traditional domestic skills. Indeed, women switch to hotel work from domestic service as 'helpers' because of higher pay, regular hours and better conditions despite the disruptions to family life caused by shift work.

Men see employment in the tourist trade as preferable to traditional work in fishing or agriculture for similar reasons. A young man from Bequia explained: 'Man, when I working in de hotel in de harbour last year, even though I getting paid really bad wage I at least know dat each week I gonna get dollar for pay for food and thing. An when I finish work I know I ain't hafi think about going fishing or nutting.'[7]

Indeed, one of the few surveys into worker attitudes in Caribbean hotels found a high 'worker satisfaction' rating. Of 654 hotel employees interviewed in 1990 at 12 of the larger hotels (including six all-inclusives) in Jamaica's main resort areas of Montego Bay, Ocho Rios and Negril, almost every worker felt 'very positive' about being part of the tourist industry. 'The hotel workers in these larger hotels have a strong tourism self-image and feel a sense of pride in being part of a vital industry,' commented the survey carried out by the Jamaican pollster, the late Carl Stone.[8]

Most of the interviewees also enjoyed their work: they liked working with people, dealing with foreigners, learning about foreign countries, learning useful skills, getting basic training and experience. The job satisfaction was far higher than that for the Jamaican labour force as a whole: 87 per cent compared with 61 per cent (in the 1982 national work attitudes survey). Of those who did not like their work, most complained of unfair accusations of stealing guests' property, management harassment and poor relations with other workers.[9]

In contrast to the high rate of job satisfaction, there was general dissatisfaction in relation to other criteria. Except for employees at the all-inclusive Sandals Resorts, workers complained of 'relatively low wages and meagre benefits' and did not believe that 'they were getting a fair share of the benefits.' At Sandals, which prides itself on paying its 9,000 staff higher wages than its rivals – a strategy aimed at creating confidence and worker satisfaction – only 35 per cent felt that they did not receive fair shares, but 73 per cent of the other hotel workers said wages and benefits were low. The resentment of these workers was fuelled by the belief that the hotels were making hefty profits. Grassroots opinion supported the view of workers: asked whether they thought hotel workers got full benefits from tourism, between 70 and 78 per cent of respondents outside the industry said they thought wages and benefits were very low.[10] It is the small resorts with the smallest hotels, often locally-owned and staffed, which for the most part pay the least, provide negligible training and offer the least job security. The bottom end of the market is also less efficient in creating jobs.

A later survey in Jamaica, conducted again by the Carl Stone pollsters in 2002 reinforced the earlier findings, although it should be noted that it was carried out for Sandals, with its 6,000 workers in Jamaica. It showed that all-inclusive hotel workers in Jamaica had a job satisfaction rating of 94 per cent compared with 92 per cent of non all-inclusive workers. Similarly, more all-inclusive workers (54 per cent) said that they got a fair share of the benefits of the tourist industry compared with 21 per cent of non all-inclusive employees.

While the debate on the benefits or otherwise of all-inclusives continues (see below), the job-generating capacity of the all-inclusives appears to outstrip those of other hotels. In 1994, the Caribbean Tourism Organisation found that 'guest ratio at all-inclusives tends to be higher than in conventional hotels of the same standard.' This is because all-inclusives staff more services for longer periods. For example, it found that the 151-room all-inclusive Almond Beach Club in Barbados provided year-round employment for 230 staff compared with a maximum of 137 staff when the property had been operating as a conventional hotel. In St Lucia, the average number of employees per room at all-inclusives was 1.58 compared with an estimated 1.16 for conventional hotels. As the survey pointed out, some of these jobs or services had previously been provided by independent operators outside the resort. While a job is a job, there are clearly economic – as well as social and political – implications in the capacity of the all-inclusives to sweep up a wide band of jobs.

In Cuba, the tourist industry has a different dynamic – and a different worker profile. For a start, it has attracted many middle-class, professional people: visitors to Cuba often comment that their waiter is a former professor of philosophy or that the chambermaid has a post-graduate degree in electronic engineering. The reason? Wages are better in the tourist industry than elsewhere. Even though employees in tourism are paid in pesos, they gain crucial dollar tips and gifts. According to one report, tipping was encouraged by the government to generate foreign exchange and to motivate the workforce (Cuba has a lacklustre reputation for service).[11] In the early 1990s, hotel workers had to turn over their dollar tips to be exchanged for pesos; not surprisingly, compliance was low. Such petty restrictions meant that tourists left gifts in kind, such as soap or shampoo (although these, too, were supposed to be registered with the management), for the workers. For Cubans, work in the tourist industry – with its access to the dollar economy of the joint ventures and, of course, to the tourists themselves – offers opportunities not available to other Cubans. The social impact (see Chapter Four) of tourism in Cuba has its roots in such inequalities.

Tourism has also exposed racial divisions within Cuban society. When tourism was a minority interest of the Cuban government in the early 1980s, many black Cubans worked in tourism. Now, in the tourist boom, blacks are not seen to have the same opportunities as whites in the tourist industry. Evidence is hard to find but occasional papers and interviews expose the prejudice of white Cubans and foreign managers involved in the joint ventures. 'It is so rare to find black women in tourism that when there is one people comment that she must be going to bed with an important boss,' commented one Cuban female manager of a tourism corporation. From the same source came another comment, this time from a white Cuban guide: 'I do agree that there is an aesthetic criteria in the selection of tourism personnel that favours whites. In my company out of 60 workers there are three blacks.' Researchers have found it difficult to discuss racism among foreign investors and managers since they are the key figures in the Cuban government's tourism development strategy.[12]

Trade Unions

One reason why the bigger hotels in the more developed English-speaking Caribbean countries offer better pay and conditions is that a well-organised trade union movement has operated in the hotel sector for some 40 years and has, on occasions, used its muscle.

Where trade unions have established a foothold in the hotel sector, they have often managed to negotiate collective agreements on behalf of a large percentage of the sector. In Barbados, for example, some 40 per cent of the 8,000 employees in the hotel and hotel-based restaurants are unionised; indeed, all employees are covered by any agreement. In Antigua, for example, where the first agreement was made with 13 hotels in 1962, the Antigua Workers' Union (AWU) represents most of the island's hotel workers. It negotiates three-year agreements which set wage rates (for three grades of hotel) and conditions. Agreements include clauses on equal pay, maternity leave, redundancy payments, holiday and sick pay although there is yet to be a clause about pensions. In Grenada, where unions have been involved in the hotel sector since the birth of the union movement on the island in the 1950s, workers have negotiated similar clauses including pensions and profit-sharing. Similar union agreements exist in other islands. One big omission, however, is the Sandals chain, which remains non-unionised, except in Antigua.

One important issue that aggravates relations between management and union is that of job security – or rather the lack of it. Throughout the region, workers are laid off when hotels, in particular the larger ones, change hands, which often means changing 'chains'. When this happens, there is no guarantee that staff will be kept on: new employers find it more convenient to 'train up' new employees rather than take over staff not trained in the 'culture' of the new management. In Antigua, in the wake of September 11, many workers were laid off by hotel closures in 2001 and no redundancy was paid. The employers, according to the Antigua Workers Union, say they cannot pay.

Workers are more regularly laid off in the summer months, the traditional low season. This period may last as long as seven months, and most workers will have no unemployment benefit. In some cases, seasonal contracts and an overall cut back in staff have been introduced, according to union leaders. 'In the past, there was a core of permanent staff who were added to in the season, but now a lot of properties are not adding to the core,' said Le Vere Richards, a former assistant general-secretary of the Barbados Workers' Union. Another method that hotels in Barbados adopt to reduce the wages bill during tough times is to use non-union labour by contracting out hotel services such as gardening and cleaning.

When recession hits the industry, hotel employees are the first to suffer. As competition intensifies, demand shrinks and costs rise, the labour force is reduced. In 1991, hotel workers in the Bahamas lost their jobs when US tourists, affected by a slump at home and the effects of the Gulf War, began to cancel their holidays. By May of that year, some 1,500 workers had lost their jobs with many more on short time. Workers marched through Nassau in protest at the job losses, and Leonard Archer, secretary-general of the Trade Union Congress, said that the unions would 'close the whole damn country down' if any more workers were sacked.[13] In the event, job losses slowed down for a time. More recently, the events of September 11 2001 caused a regional cut-back of hotel and ancillary staff. The World Travel and Tourism Council had predicted a loss of 365,000 jobs in the Caribbean. In the Dominican Republic, the *Daily News* reported that nearly 10,000 employees, about 20 per cent of the total, had been laid off in the wake of the attacks.

But lay-offs can occur without the help of terrorists. According to the Caribbean News Agency, even before September 11 at least 50 per cent of the workforce had been laid off in Antigua at the end of the 2000-2001 tourist season. Some 600 workers were asked to go on shorter weeks and surviving managers agreed to a 20 per cent salary cut. Responsibility lay with the usual suspects: charter airlines were no longer flying to Antigua, marketing had been inadequate and more competitive destinations such as Cuba and Mexico had pinched Antigua's customers. Such is the transient nature of employment in the hotel and restaurant business.

Official industrial disputes in such a precarious industry are rare; more typical are occasional – and brief – wildcat strikes. During disputes governments appeal for a settlement and warn of the dire consequences of disrupting the tourist industry. The last major strike in Barbados, for example, where labour relations are usually 'relatively peaceful and harmonious,' was in December 1993. It was the start of a new tourist season; a two-year wage freeze imposed by the IMF's structural adjustment programme had run its course but no agreement had been reached with the hotel workers on a gains-sharing scheme. So when the Barbados Workers' Union called out its 6,000 hotel workers on a three-day strike, the then minister of tourism, Evelyn Greaves, appealed to both sides to reach an agreement, which they duly did. A peaceful industrial relations climate in Barbados has more recently been attributed to the 'national social partnership,' a pact agreed to by employers, trade unions and government to work towards the national interest.[14]

The Informal Sector

Beyond the hotels, restaurants and casinos, an unknown amount of 'indirect' employment is generated by the tourist industry, especially in agriculture and handicrafts, transport, construction (in the boom hotel building years) and some manufacturing. The extent of this employment depends on how effective the linkages are between the different sectors of the tourist economy (see Chapter Two).

Taxi drivers are a major feature of Caribbean tourism. It sometimes seems that every middle-aged man with a car and a driving licence turns to taxiing, waiting at hotel entrances, airports, cruise ship terminals and town squares, often for hours between jobs. Those with minibuses may get a job with the cruise ships, ferrying groups on island tours. Scaramouche, the singing taxi driver in Grenada, is one such guide. A veteran calypsonian, who talks nostalgically about the days when calypsonians learnt their trade in Port of Spain's Nelson Street, he sings to his clients, improvising flattering calypsos about their personal charms. In general, the familiar complaint of taxi drivers is of slow times and of too many drivers chasing too few tourists.

Other paths for small-time entrepreneurs are to gain a foothold in the accommodation sector. Many of the small hotels and guesthouses (often converted family homes) in the Caribbean, like those along the south coast of Barbados, dotted around the St George's basin in Grenada and at Negril in Jamaica, are owned by women. In the same way as women have gained hotel jobs as an extension of domestic work, running a guesthouse has historically eased the way for lower middle-class women to become financially independent.

Yet most of the employment generated in this area is limited to family members helping out in a largely informal way. While this sector offers some opportunities for the small business class, the high costs and lack of access to credit means that their profit margins are slight and their financial base shaky. As one St Lucian small hotel owner complained in the mid 1990s: 'The government has no policy on tourism for locals – their attitude is that they prefer outsiders because they bring in money.'

In the hinterland of the formal tourist industry, hundreds of thousands of Caribbean men, women and children earn a living in the markets, on the street or the beach. Every day, all over the Caribbean, vendors cluster in the public spaces anxious to sell to tourists as they leave the controlled 'private zones' of their well-protected hotels. Like the Antiguan women who walk two miles up the sun-baked hill to the tourist look-out of Shirley Heights with a supply of T-shirts on their heads or the Haitian vendors in St Maarten with their paintings in cramped side-streets. Or the Grenadians who cruise the beaches for the chance to sell jewellery, straw hats, T-shirts, imported Taiwanese tat or finely crafted sculpture. Or the small boys in St Kitts with a plastic bucket of peanuts ('Nice lady, buy something from me'). Or the women who braid hair in Jamaica or cook chicken on coal pots in Tobago. Or the boys who shine shoes in Dominican Republic or the young men everywhere who offer their services as guides or as suppliers of casual sex.

So what is known about the vendors? Not very much – mainly because no one has asked them. One survey does, however, tell us something of their demographic profile and their perceptions of their role in the tourist industry. It is worth taking a look at this study, which features in Dunn & Dunn's book *People and Tourism*, and examines craft vendors in Negril, Jamaica, both those who have a fixed place of sale and the itinerant ones.

The study found that the majority of vendors in designated locations were women and that selling craft offered an opportunity for women with domestic duties to control their own businesses, however modest. Eighty per cent of these vendors were between 25 and 49 years of age (young people no longer find such work attractive) and most had only a basic education (very few had been to high school). Most had dependants, either adults or children to support, and lived outside Negril in low-income communities travelling to and from Negril each day, at considerable cost and difficulty. The vendors were reluctant to answer questions about their economic returns but it appeared that for many their business was not cost effective.

The itinerant vendors showed a different sort of profile: most were young men who came from outside Negril. They sold crafts, music tapes, watches, clothes, jewellery. Unencumbered by overheads and unregulated, their products were cheaper than those of the established vendors (a point which caused resentment). While the first group had had some training in tourism awareness issues such as visitor harassment, the itinerant group appeared less aware of the problems around harassment and failed to realise that their behaviour often caused irritation (see Chapter Four).[15]

All such vendors are survival strategists. However their income is earned, it makes a significant financial contribution to families and communities. Yet the vendors are more marginalised than formal-sector employees and they often find themselves threatened by the tourist authorities, who wish to 'tidy them away' or eliminate them altogether. Their fate is nothing new: historical accounts describe Kingston's streets as teeming with beggars, unofficial tour guides and vendors selling liquorice seeds and postcards in the early years of the 20th century. In response, extra police were sent out to patrol the streets, and magistrates fined and imprisoned the 'harassing' masses.[16]

The modern tourist industry has introduced less punitive, if sometimes equally restrictive methods to curb the vendors. As tourism has become more organised, the fortunes of the vendors have changed. While in theory more tourists mean more customers, freelance hustlers sometimes find that as the tourist trade expands and as the big hotel chains and large-scale businesses move in, their opportunities are reduced. Responding to the perceived holiday needs of the tourists, official policy towards the 'informal sector' is often to tighten up its operations.

Sosúa, on the north coast of the Dominican Republic, for example, became a tourist area during the 1980s, in particular after the 1983 opening of the international airport at nearby Puerto Plata. The numbers of street and beach vendors increased as the town experienced a tourist boom, but when the formal sector of large hotels, villa conglomerates and smart restaurants arrived in town, the vendors found that the places they were used to working in were no longer available. Signs saying 'vendors prohibited' began to spring up. Some of the vendors even believed that eventually they would be forced out of business.[17]

On the other hand, unofficial vendors and guides often discover that as their numbers increase, the tourist establishment can no longer afford to ignore them. The vendor who walks the beach or the guide who hangs around the beauty spot becomes a 'problem' as numbers increase and officials worry that they are harassing tourists. One by one, the islands of the Caribbean have responded in the same way by organising them, demanding that they purchase a licence and take a 'course' in tourism awareness and eventually restricting them to corners of the beach or to special booths or plazas in urban areas. In effect they are dusted down, spruced up and educated into the acceptable face of guest-host relations.

In some instances, this process contributes to resentment of tourism in local populations (see Chapter Four). The issue of the beach as a function of the tourist industry rather than as an intrinsic part of local life has caused particular controversy. In the 1980s, Jack Dear, the then chairman of the Barbados Tourist Board, was instrumental in restricting beach vendors to booths for the first time. Mighty Gabby's popular calypso of the time, entitled 'Jack', expressed the popular sentiment of distaste for the new regulations. One verse went:

I used to sell coral and lime
But Jack insists that is a crime.
Now when I see the Police face
I run in haste with my briefcase.

The vendors who tend to like the system least are the beach boys who cruise the beaches with an eye to selling whatever is available. 'I work this beach and can make a lot of money doing this,' said Pine Boy on Rockley Beach, a popular south coast stretch in Barbados, while keeping a lookout for patrolling police and wardens. 'I can get you anything and sell you anything you want – mainly smokes, sometimes aloe, sex.' He and his friends occupied the less picturesque end of the beach, hanging out by an abandoned guesthouse around the back of a beach bar where they filled discarded bottles with the juice of aloes which they sold to sun-bathers as an 'after-sun gel'.

But not all vendors dislike the changes, even though they have to pay rent for a beach booth. Some, especially the older women, who no longer want to walk the beach, prefer to have a permanent stall. Heather, a middle-aged woman, braided hair at Rockley Beach. She charged US$40 for a full braid (with your own choice of coloured beads) which takes two hours. She was quite happy with her patch alongside the other vendors selling clothes. 'People come from all over and ask for me,' she said proudly, producing a book of photographs of her crowning glories fading behind cellophane. She had been on a course, she said, where 'they told us how to behave to tourists and how to dress nice.' On Barbados' posher west coast, the elderly women selling strips of chiffon beach-wear along the beach from the exclusive Sandy Lane Hotel complained that the tourists are 'haughty and puffed up', but they were glad to have a permanent pitch and not have to walk the beach any more. It gave them a little status.

In Grenada, vendors walked the three-mile stretch of Grande Anse Beach until the end of the 1990s. Ras Ian (to rhyme with lion), a wiry veteran beach vendor with a licence to sell coral jewellery, used to walk Grande Anse beach with a board hung with coral and seedpod earrings; he made a better living on the beach than he could in agriculture. He claimed that he was harassed by the hotels for trying to sell to the guests so he would not mind selling from a booth. However, he envisaged difficulties in working with other vendors in a confined space. 'It might make people jealous and create nastiness. On the beach you are free up to move.'

The vendors' market was duly built between the beach and the road and it became illegal for vendors to try to sell on the beach. As a tourist official commented – not unreasonably: 'People don't want to be disturbed while sun-bathing on the beach when they probably won't have their purses with them.' Ras Ian's walking days were over.

A somewhat similar process was also underway in Dominica, where the fledgling tourist industry was beginning to experience similar conflicts of interest. There, a growth in tourist arrivals, mainly from the cruise ships, stimulated a steady stream of visitors to Trafalgar Falls, the twin waterfalls at the head of the Roseau Valley. With this increase in tourist traffic, the young and unemployed men from the village of Trafalgar began to offer their services as guides, escorting people from the car park area to clamber up to the hot springs pool at the base of the larger waterfall.

Congregating around the car park where the minibuses and taxis dropped off the tourists, they became more obtrusive as they competed for guiding jobs. Other locals who had invested money and skills to be professional guides were discomfited by the 'pirate' guides, some of whom it was claimed were aggressive, offered drugs to tourists and abused the women visitors. The Trafalgar guides, who denied that they behaved badly, recognised the opportunities to make money from the tourists but had neither the skills nor resources to do it within a more formal framework. As a result their presence tended to create problems for everyone.

In response, a plan to regularise their position – to train some of them, and to give them official status – was introduced; at the same time, access to the Falls was restricted to tourists with tickets. What had happened was all too familiar: the inability of the tourist industry to retain an 'informal' relationship between host and guest as numbers increased. The shift is from an informal personal engagement to a formal economic contract.

Throughout the Caribbean, the need to contain the vendors and the guides who are the unofficial face of tourism illustrates a fundamental unease about encounters between host and guest. Implicit in the thinking of the establishment is that the casual, untrained vendor poses a threat to the tourists' well-being and the region's reputation and thus to its economic survival.

'Smile Please'

It is not just the freelance vendor whose behaviour creates unease within the industry, but the whole range of encounters experienced by the guest, from the first exchange at the immigration desk. The holiday brochures make sure tourists are primed, putting a euphemistic gloss on sometimes indifferent service, for instance, by describing a 'laid-back attitude to service' which reflects 'the slow pace of life', and tourists are urged to enjoy it as part of the atmosphere. Yet at a more profound level, the issue is not just about different approaches to service, but also about the unequal and racist historical relationship between blacks and whites and the lack of a positive service tradition. 'Ensuring quality service in a fragmented industry of multiple and diverse suppliers poses special training and management problems, particularly in former plantation islands without a positive service tradition,' was the observation from two academics.[18]

The parameters of this issue have to some extent been ignored by tourism administrators. Instead, the problem of the encounter has been approached pragmatically, as an educational exercise in which the burden and learning process has been placed on the Caribbean national rather than on the tourist. As a poster in Dominica in the early 1980s put it: 'SMILE. You are a walking tourist attraction.'

The failure of the Caribbean population to be 'nice' to all tourists at all times, with its implications for the tourist industry, is the reason for the concern. Criticism of poor 'attitude' is common in newspapers and the radio, including phone-ins, and is identified by Caribbean nationals as much as by expatriates, although the tone of the upbraiding is different.

Caribbean Week (now defunct) once carried an article entitled 'Smile Please', by its columnist Garry Steckles, an expatriate Englishman. He described how a tourist leaving Golden Rock airport in St Kitts gave a hefty tip to two young porters who had carried her bags for a couple of minutes. 'In return, she didn't get as much as smile or a nod, much less a thankyou,' wrote the indignant Steckles. He continued: 'And as the two youngsters wandered off counting their money, I was left pondering, not for the first time, how long we in the Caribbean are going to be able to keep attracting visitors while so many people working in the tourist industry seem to have a totally indifferent attitude toward the people who are providing them with a living.'

Steckles went on to argue that until the Caribbean learnt to provide pleasant, efficient and courteous service, the future of its tourist industry would be in doubt.[19]

Another article in the same newspaper was written by Peter Morgan, Barbados' first minister of tourism. Morgan wrote:

> In small communities, which most of our Caribbean islands are, everyone is involved in tourism, whether they believe it or not or like it or not because it is the total impression of his or her vacation which decides a person whether or not they plan to return. The price might be right, the climate perfect, the rum just what the doctor should have ordered but, above all, if a person doesn't feel welcome then he is not coming back.[20]

The view of the outside 'expert' was expressed in a consultant's report on Dominica's service sector submitted to the ministry of finance and development in 1991. A summary of the major findings concluded: 'Poor worker attitudes manifest themselves in a variety of ways – lack of concern about punctuality, absenteeism, low productivity, an acceptance of under-employment, low career expectations and a failure to accept responsibility for problem solving.'[21] These attitudes, surmised the report's authors, would have a particularly detrimental impact on productivity and profitability in the services sector. Dominica would not have been the only country to have such an evaluation made of its workforce.

With the Caribbean in open competition with the rest of the world, the region is sensitive to criticism as delivered by, for example, the summary verdict of the Economist Intelligence Unit: 'Given that the Caribbean is expensive, second-rate service simply will not do.'[22] The remedy is, according to the mandarins of the Caribbean's tourist industry, professionalism and excellence. 'The day of the enthusiastic amateur is over,' wrote John Bell, executive vice president of the Caribbean Hotel Association (CHA),[23] while management consultants call for 'high service performance' and 'customer-friendly personnel'. Sandals' Butch Stewart has been in the forefront of insisting that the Caribbean must compete – and win – on the international stage.

Some experts have identified cultural conflicts as the problem. Peter Goffe, for example, a Jamaican-born academic, defined in consultant-speak what he calls a 'service performance gap' caused by 'mismatched cultural values' which occur when foreign multinational managers trained in an 'efficiency' culture are in charge of a local staff who do not share such goals.[24] Indeed, the prescriptions for change require the adoption of a new culture, of new business practices.

A New Slavery?

The legacy of slavery underpins much of contemporary Caribbean culture and the expression of it pervades many aspects of tourism. It is a thread which, significantly, Jean Holder of the CTO identified, when he wrote: 'there appears to be a deep-seated resentment of the industry at every level of society – a resentment which probably stems from the historic socio-cultural associations of race, colonialism and slavery.' He added that the Caribbean is 'forced to choose between an industry it "deep down" does not really want, and the economic fruits of that industry which it needs and which, it seems more and more, only tourism will provide.' Holder concluded that significant numbers of employees 'are not proud of what they do, and harbour resentments rooted in the inability to distinguish between service and servitude.'[25]

Many of the 'problems' associated with the tourist industry stem from slavery and colonialism, this folk memory lingering in the shadow of every encounter: that black people have served white people for hundreds of years and that before they did it for a wage, they did it under servitude. As Maurice Bishop, the former prime minister of Grenada, said in a speech to regional policy-makers on tourism in 1979:

> It is important for us to face the fact that in the early days and to some extent even today, most of the tourists who come to our country happen to be white, and this clear association of whiteness and privilege is a major problem for Caribbean people just emerging out of racist colonial history where we have been so carefully taught the superiority of things white and inferiority of things black.[26]

Indeed, tourism in its early days rekindled memories of slavery. For a start, the best jobs in Jamaican hotels were reserved for white Americans, while black Jamaicans were left with the most menial tasks. The predominantly American tourists brought their own racist attitudes and behaviour on holiday with them, and Jamaicans often found themselves unwelcome on the beach or in hotels, treated as dehumanised curiosities and exotic objects in the tourist literature. In Cuba, the resort area of Varadero, which was developed from 1880 by the textile magnate Dupont, banned native Cubans. Thus, tourism began to marginalise Caribbean peoples in their own countries.

Service in turn-of-the-century Jamaica had also left much to be desired. One visitor commented that the hotel staff behaved 'as if it were gall and wormwood to their haughty souls to have to wait upon the white person.'[27] Those early travellers referred to the generous hospitality of the white planter class, but in contrast, the black Jamaican showed little but discourtesy, being 'unpleasantly familiar and cheeky'. From the outset, there were the echoes of slavery in the dynamics of the tourist industry; indeed, the languid behaviour of black hotel employees evoked the passive resistance practised in slavery.

Indeed, it should be no surprise that whenever there are conflicts between locals and often foreign management (less often, between locals and tourists), this underlying discourse is articulated. In a letter to an Antiguan newspaper, a member of staff at a restaurant complained about poor working conditions: 'How are we to work right through the day from 7 am until 3.30 pm with only one meal on empty stomach; ARE WE SLAVES?'[28] In Bequia, staff expressed their grievances about their subservient role at work by asking: 'Dey think we is still slaves?'[29] A nurse training for her new job at a Grenadian hotel described how the staff have to eat their lunch under a tree, 'like we were back in massa's time.'

This connection between slavery and tourism was made by the Trinidadian-born writer V.S. Naipaul, who argued in the 1960s that the Caribbean had this time chosen its path to a 'new slavery'. In *The Middle Passage,* he wrote: 'Every poor country accepts tourism as an unavoidable degradation. None has gone as far as some of these West Indian islands, which, in the name of tourism, are selling themselves into a new slavery.'[30]

Before Naipaul, the Martiniquan polemicist Frantz Fanon wrote in *The Wretched of the Earth* that tourism recreated the labour relations of slavery and the colonial situation. More directly than Naipaul, Fanon blamed the local bourgeoisie as the enablers of this 'new slavery': 'the national middle class will have nothing better to do than to take on the role of manager for Western enterprise, and it will in practice set up its country as the brothel of Europe.'[31]

Jamaica Kincaid's satirical essay on Antigua, *A Small Place,* wrote that the hotel school taught Antiguans how to be good servants. 'In Antigua, people cannot see a relationship between their obsession with slavery and emancipation and their celebration of the Hotel Training School (graduation ceremonies are broadcast on radio and television).'[32]

In the 1990s the argument was picked up and developed by Hilary Beckles, professor of history at Cave Hill, the Barbados campus of the

University of the West Indies (UWI). In his analysis of the relationship in Barbados between the white business elite, the state and the people, he called tourism the 'new plantocracy'. 'The new financial tourism base means that the state has become the overseer,' says Beckles. 'The feeling is that black people are more marginalised now, that there is a return to colonialism. Because whites own all the land, commerce, and have all the major duty-free outlets and now the sea ports – the same group is in control. In tourism, blacks have no status in terms of decision-making.' In neighbouring Antigua, opposition politician and journalist Tim Hector observes a similar pattern. 'In the beginning a tiny, foreign elite in ownership and management, controlled sugar. In the end a tiny, foreign elite, in ownership and management, controls tourism. Slavery or wage-slavery has been our lot.'[33]

The same points were still being made at the turn of the 21st century. Willi Momm, director of the Caribbean's International Labour Organisation office, for example, said in 2002: 'It is surprising that so few people with responsibility in the tourism industry, be they investors or local policy makers, seem to notice or to care that the tourism industry in this region is, to a large degree, resented by the people. Many investors appear content to buy up the best chunks of land and beach and to close them off from the local population, ignoring its protest.' He went on to say that there was 'a minimum of creativity and ingenuity to reverse this state of affairs.' Reflecting on his own interest in the tourist industry, he said 'the best guarantors that the industry will flourish and expand in the years to come, are decent conditions for workers in the tourism industry and decent opportunities for workers outside the industry to benefit from tourism.'[34]

Training and what is now called 'human resource development' is a vital, albeit late, arrival on the tourist industry scene in the Caribbean. It is, as is now recognised, essential to the region's economic survival and the competitiveness of its tourism.

Training

Training has been the industry's poor relation. Training is the key to a well-equipped and finely tuned army of employees. But until recently it has been a low priority, with money more likely to be budgeted for the upgrading of buildings than of people's skills. The EIU found a 'lack of investment in training facilities, shortage of experienced trainers and an uncoordinated approach to training in the region.'[35] There were not enough systematic and effective training schemes to go round at all levels, whether for graduate managers or chambermaids. According to the CHA's John Bell, writing in 1993, training at all levels needed to be 'dramatically upgraded' and 'significantly enhanced and expanded' if the Caribbean is to be successful 'in the 21st-century crucible of increasing international competition.'[36]

What training then does the region provide for its tourism workers? In tertiary education, a hotel management degree and a post-graduate diploma have been offered by the University of the West Indies since 1977. Started on the Mona campus, Jamaica, it was transferred the following year to the College of the Bahamas in Nassau. Some 630 students, the majority of them women, have graduated from its Centre for Hotel and Tourism Management with a notable increase in numbers over the years: 330 students graduated between 1996 and 2002 compared with 300 graduates in the 17 years up to 1995. Since 2001, the College of the Bahamas has also handled a distance teaching programme for 85 middle managers.

Graduates have gone on to do well in the industry as training directors, directors of human resources, general managers, marketing managers of tourist boards, one minister of tourism and so on. Prejudice against women in the tourist industry has lifted in the last decade, according to Ainsley O'Reilly of the College of the Bahamas in Nassau. While there remains some stigma to attracting the brightest and the best into tourism, O'Reilly believes that tourism is now considered part of the fabric of the region's economies. Graduates come from all over the Caribbean but more than half are from Jamaica, followed by Trinidad and Tobago (17 per cent) and Barbados (14 per cent).

Caroline Gibbs is a young Barbadian and a tourism graduate from UWI. Before going to university, she worked in a hotel for two years. But the UWI course gave her a different perspective: for a start, she was able to see for herself how the bigger and more mature Bahamian tourist industry worked. Despite her enthusiasm, she feels that there is still a negative attitude towards tourism graduates:

> We have difficulties getting a job in contrast with people who have worked their way up – they are the ones who get the jobs. You don't get respect if you have a degree in tourism. People don't see education in tourism as respectable or as hardworking, for example, as a degree in engineering. But I see the industry as being so dynamic

– all qualities and management skills are so important. I want to have my own company – I dream to own my own little place – to be unique, to contribute to the industry.

Despite the growth of the degree course in the Bahamas, the gaps in UWI's provision for tourism and hospitality students had, by the late 1990s, become something of an embarrassment. 'UWI has been sensitive to the criticisms levelled against it... and as such, has made major efforts to design and implement relevant programmes, and to deliver courses that meet the need for more flexible and accessible modes of training for the industry.'[37] To this end, a range of degree and diploma courses has been instituted at various locations throughout the region. Further brainstorming concluded that a Caribbean School of Tourism and Hospitality Management at UWI should be the main umbrella organisation for advanced academic and vocational training resting on partnerships between academia and the public and private sectors throughout the region. A great leap forward in tourism education is envisaged. A proposal for an Institute of Tourism Research, operated by UWI, was agreed at Caricom's tourism summit in December 2001.

The current initiatives reveal past limitations. Apart from university provision, the development of tourism education as a whole has been seen to be piecemeal and ad hoc, with the different hospitality schools offering a patchwork of courses of different quality and at different levels. Many have been and remain under-funded and under-staffed with education and tourism ministries sometimes not engaged in the necessary 'joined-up writing' of government. Caricom's 2001 tourism summit also agreed that a tourism development fund should be established to strengthen the hospitality institutions and tourism awareness programmes at national level.

The region's first hotel schools were set up in the 1960s in Jamaica and Barbados to teach basic hotel skills. At that time, its students had to sit external exams set by the American Hotel and Motel Association. The one in Jamaica spawned the Trinidad and Tobago Hotel School and the Bahamas Hotel Training College. Now there are some 24 hospitality schools and programmes throughout the region offering a variety of courses of different scope and quality. As Ainsley O'Reilly of UWI has written: 'Most of these schools have not been developed properly, have poor facilities and are generally under-funded.'[38]

'Training is a relatively new concept within the region. There is a gap of formally trained people,' admitted Antiguan Shirlene Nibbs, former director of training and curriculum development of the

Antigua-based Caribbean Hospitality Training Institute (CHTI) and now Antigua's director of tourism. The CHTI, which is the training arm of the Caribbean Hotel Association, was set up in 1980. Its role – to professionalise and regulate training on a regional basis – is crucial.

According to Nibbs, the private sector had been more active in providing training than the public sector, where 'human resource development is secondary to providing tourism infrastructure.' Yet even within the private sector, she said: 'Training is very spotty – some hotels understand the training role and have a training manager. Even then when you examine what they have to offer and ask, is the training beneficial, are there proper systems in place, generally speaking the answer is no.' In both sectors training programmes are often badly coordinated and duplication occurs. In the public sector, she pinpointed groups such as immigration and custom officers, national tourism office staff and even government ministers as in need of training.

Nibbs had 45 trainers working with her in a 'travelling university' to provide short-term, custom-built courses on food and drink, front-of-house, accounting, management skills and customer-related work. One aspect of these courses reveals the complicated cultural imperatives of working life in the Caribbean: trainers do not give courses on their home ground. According to Nibbs, this system was adopted because students are more receptive to outsiders than to their own people. Being unreceptive to instructions from superiors and the inability to make decisions and to 'manage' are two major problems throughout the Caribbean. Nibbs explained:

> Firstly, there is a lack of skills and knowledge and on top of that is the syndrome common to small communities of finding difficulty with decision-taking. For example, two maids from the same village work at the same hotel. When one is promoted over the other, problems arise. We try to equip the supervisors to manage and to explain that it is critical that they disconnect their personal life from their professional one.

A St Lucian hotel manager agreed that workers found responsibility difficult; because of community and family ties they found it hard to reprimand other workers. 'This is a culturally embedded attitude. I've found it difficult myself when I've known someone on a personal level. You have to learn that you have to make decisions and that those decisions are fair.'

The way that the now giant resort group Sandals deals with training does not reveal such cultural subtleties. What directors of the Sandals Training and Development Institute, formed in 1995, emphasise is the 'Sandals employee value triad: train, empower and reward. The mantra is that happy employees equal happy customers. 'We hire the smile and train the skills; we hire for attitude and train for competence.' It is easy to mock such corporate language but between 1994 and 1999 Sandals spent US$22.4 million training its employees into the values of the 'House that Butch Built'. Sandals claims that turnover is very low, that Sandals employees 'feel good about themselves' and that the rewards are not only in professional opportunities – with 120 hours of training a year – but, as we have seen, in conditions of employment. Sandals also sends employees to do degrees in the US and assists children of employees in their education. 'They feel good because they're with the best,' maintained Carl Hendriks, general manager of Negril Beach Resort and Spa.[39]

The Expatriates

While there is no significant disagreement between Caribbean nationals and expatriate experts about the need to improve standards in the tourist industry and to increase the numbers of skilled and trained locals, some Caribbean nationals do not believe that the industry is creating structures to secure their employment at senior levels. Despite the high investment in local skills at Sandals, in many hotels throughout the region it is not unusual to find that the general manager, the food and beverage manager, the accountant and executive chef are white expatriates from Europe or North America.

In Antigua, Keithlyn Smith of the Antigua Workers' Union said that the government closed its eyes to the work permit situation. The Labour Code states that a local must understudy an expat, but this is ignored. However, he believed that although few Caribbean nationals were right at the top, they were moving up in the supervisory levels. Sandals, he said, was a significant employer of Caribbean peoples.

In the French départements of Martinique and Guadeloupe, the racial imbalances remain. In Guadeloupe, for example, the senior management is entirely metropolitan French and white. 'Guadeloupeans are rarely found in management,' said one black hospitality manager. 'This causes resentment and makes them more nationalistic than ever. And they don't want to be nice to the tourists. We have to tell them how to behave and see the person as a person.'

Training Caribbean nationals to occupy the top jobs is part of the educational process. CTO's Jean Holder argued that there were no gains from employing 'untrained, unqualified and inefficient personnel simply because they are nationals, or to satisfy a political objective.'[40] Those within the tourism establishment are irritated by what they see as the over-sensitivity of nationals. 'Tourism is an international industry; it's an advantage to have an infusion of new blood,' retorted Allen Chastenet, former director of tourism for St Lucia. Others call those who complain about the job situation 'obsessed and xenophobic'.

However, the work permit situation has negative effects. Firstly, it creates tensions between the expatriate and local staff. 'Expats come with ideas that we are swinging in a few mango trees,' said a trade union leader. 'They push their weight around; they are very young, it may be their first job and they are under pressure from absentee bosses who are looking to make profits. That creates tension and insecurity.' The presence of expats at management level also re-emphasises the 'mismatched cultural values'.

The division of labour between expatriates and local labour is shown at its extreme on Richard Branson's Necker Island. In an article in the *Guardian* newspaper, the writer comments:

> A dozen or so staff live on the island, all young, fair-haired and bronzed... [they] tend to the guests, teach tennis and sailing and drive the speedboat on sunset cruises. They seem disconcertingly like the Midwich Cuckoos come of age, but they are more than happy to treat you, me and 'Richard' as their equals. The cleaning and general maintenance is performed by a further staff of 20 who are brought in for the day from Tortola, but not in the speedboat.[41]

The casual enforcement of the work permit legislation suggests to local workers that there is a glass ceiling in the hotel industry. While the CHTI is busily trying to convince students that 'if you have the skills and the ability, you can reach any level,' there is a deep-rooted sense that this is not the reality. As a result, admitted Nibbs, the industry does not attract the best candidates: 'People don't have role models, so the brightest don't go into tourism.' Her own family had experienced the doubtful reaction of neighbours: '"How can you allow your daughter to go into that business?" they said.'

The ambitions of the Caribbean middle classes have been directed into becoming economists or lawyers, not hotel general managers. This is another legacy of colonialism and the result is a small pool of local management material. 'The kids are just not coming into the business,' said one St Lucian hotelier. 'Sometimes I see no end in sight. It's shameful to have to advertise and get an expat.'

UWI and the CHTI is working to counter these attitudes, to promote the idea that tourism is for high-flyers rather than the unskilled, to insist that tourism does not end with carrying bags or serving banana daiquiris. The Caribbean nationals at the sharp end of the industry who try to make it work are anxious to set up a new set of images about tourism. They want to portray a modern, efficient, go-ahead environment offering a variety of jobs and an iconography that makes tourism everyone's business. At the same time, they are fighting to overturn negative images of tourism, the mindset replay of colonial relationships where smiling waiters and limbo dancers attend to the needs of white foreigners, not in great houses but in marble-lobbied hotels.

Where role models of successful locals exist, this has helped to dissolve the problems surrounding the host community's workers. This view was held by Peter Odle of the Barbados Hotel Association: 'The confidence is slowly coming. It shows in the way guys approach me. Our education is beginning to work. The idea of service and not servitude is filtering through. Tourism used to be for the lower classes, but now it's everyone at every level and that has made a tremendous difference.' This is reinforced by Le Vere Richards of the Barbados Workers' Union who believes that the 'attitude' problem was decreasing with the increase in black tourists, local people using the hotels and more Caribbean nationals in senior positions in the industry. 'The workers in the industry don't go along with the colonial concept of service any more. A lot of our workers travel and they see that in other countries the waiters are white.' In Jamaica this change in perception was achieved in the late 1970s by promoting holidays for Jamaicans within Jamaica. As a result, hotel waiters, for example, began to understand that not all tourists are white and that the needs of a Jamaican holidaymaker were no different from that of a foreigner's.

Tourism Awareness

While foreign management technique experts and commentators have probed the 'attitude' problem, and training schemes are belatedly working with the hotel sector, tourist boards throughout the region now run 'tourism awareness' programmes for the population at large.

The Caribbean's generic message, 'Be Nice to Tourists', is not just directed at hotel employees, but at customs and immigration officers (the 'welcoming committee'), taxi-drivers (the 'service ambassadors') and at market women, beach vendors, farmers and schoolchildren. The whole population, charged with a responsibility towards the tourist, is encouraged to feel part of the tourist industry. A television advertisement put out by the Barbados Government Information Service in the mid 1990s, entitled 'Tourism and You', featured two men playing dominoes on a beach. 'We need all the tourists we can get,' said the first character. 'We all got a part to play,' he continued. 'But I never come in contact with tourists,' said the second man. 'You'll get your chance,' says the first man. 'If they come and talk with you in the street... Make them feel at home.'

The 'tourism awareness' programmes are basically aimed at educating local populations into understanding the nature of the tourist industry. At best, they open up a debate about the nature of tourism, discuss how tourism can be used for sustainable development and explain what opportunities exist for careers within tourism, not just as waiters and bellboys but as architects or interpreters. At worst, they crudely promote the idea that tourists' needs are paramount.

With a varying degree of success, intensity and sophistication, the word is being taken into every corner of every island, into schools, villages and rum shops by television, newspapers, car stickers and posters. What is publicly acknowledged, however, is always the positive side of tourism. In Dominica, where serious attention to tourism development is a recent phenomenon, children from a primary school in Roseau came up with this calypso:

We will always give our best
At a reasonable price
Give good service
To Mr Tourist

A somewhat different approach is applied in the Bahamas where the Bahamahost programme has been used to train workers for nearly 30 years. 'We didn't say you have to be nice to the guests,' explained Beverly Saunders, a former co-ordinator of the Bahamahost programme ('Bahamahost serves with dignity and pride'). 'We went back to basics. We said let's look at ourselves as individuals and instil our own value system, to have a positive attitude about the industry and to show that it does offer viable career choices.' There was also a need, added Saunders, to teach Bahamians about their country, a subject ignored by the colonial educational system.

The Bahamahost programme was started in 1978, only a few years after independence, and by 2002 it had more than 20,000 graduates, including teachers, bankers, as well as those directly connected with tourism. Students attend a series of lectures in subjects such as the history of the Bahamas, effective communication, culture and folklore and basic first aid, and take an exam at the end. Participants are told: 'Our aim is to increase the awareness of the importance of tourism to our economy and to set the stage for attaining the highest level of customer service satisfaction in the world.' As one hotel manager said: 'We're trying to get a positive feeling about the industry throughout the community. They shouldn't just be turning on a smile when they come to work.'

Saunders and her team won the contract to train the senior expatriate team of Sun International when they were about to take over Paradise Island in 1994. 'Expatriates have skills,' she says, 'but they need to understand the Bahamian psyche.' The Bahamahost programme should be mandatory for expatriate management, recommended the Bahamas Tourism Task Force of 1993 in a check-list of initiatives drawn up by the ministry of tourism. In 2002 it had become mandatory for taxi drivers and tour buses.

Jamaica, too, takes training seriously. The mandate of the island's Tourism Product Development Co (TPDCo) includes training. It describes it thus: 'The quality of Jamaica's tourism product is highly dependent on having a workforce that is skilled and capable of delivering an excellent service.' Training in Jamaica is both about specialised skills and tourism awareness. Team Jamaica, a training initiative of the Jamaica Tourist Board, puts on a mandatory training programme and by July 2001 more than 12,000 workers throughout the island had participated in it while another project takes tourism workers for 'fam trips' to show them how tourism works island-wide.

In the eastern Caribbean, St Lucia has the most extensive tourism awareness programme. The slogan 'Let's be the Best' is found on bumper stickers, posters and T-shirts and is highlighted on television and radio slots where profiles of local success stories in the tourist business are publicised. Yet the public awareness programme only began in 1992; before that there was nothing. 'People didn't understand their role in tourism; they didn't know how to get into it. They thought it was just about hotel work,' said a St Lucian tourism officer. To counter this, a tourism awareness programme was launched along with a parallel programme for primary schools, based on *Hello, Tourist!*, a textbook for primary school children.

Hello, Tourist!, probably the first of its kind in the Caribbean, was first used in St Croix in 1977. Other countries have since used it: St Lucia in 1992, Antigua in 1996 and St Maarten in 1998, where it was described as bringing the importance of tourism into 'hearts and minds'. *Hello, Tourist!* explains that tourists are not necessarily all rich ('Mr and Mrs Brown saved $3,000 over a 10-year period so they could celebrate their silver wedding anniversary in St Lucia'), or indeed, particularly nice ('They may be insensitive or rude; they may drink too much and be unruly'). It points out that tourists, who come in all colours, ages and sizes, want to holiday somewhere clean and friendly and that they are interested in things that St Lucians might take for granted. It emphasises the ways that tourism benefits St Lucia and how St Lucia needs tourism. Using the image of a money tree which nourishes the island with jobs, it says: 'We must nurture the roots, fertilise them with the pride we feel about our island by keeping it clean, by not acting rude, by making sure we don't pollute our beautiful water, by smiling and being friendly.' It concludes with a long list of jobs which are connected, either directly or indirectly, with tourism.[42]

A new initiative to standardise tourism in education was launched by the Caribbean Tourism Organisation in 1997 when it was mandated to establish the Caribbean Tourism Human Resource Council. By 2002, it had produced teachers' manuals at primary and secondary school level and workbooks for primary school level. These free resources standardise the teaching materials – in the past they had been either island-produced, imported from other islands or non-existent. While tourism still has to be squeezed on to the curriculum as part of geography or social studies, the CTO resources deliver regional material and a regional message. It's an attempt, according to a CTO spokesperson, to present tourism as a 'career choice', to show its ever-widening parameters and, above all, to send out a positive message about the industry.

New professionals like Shirlene Nibbs and Beverly Saunders and the new institutions are helping to make workers feel positive about tourism. A poem entitled 'Tourism' by Augustus Saltibus, of the kitchen department in Club St Lucia, catalogued the island's problems with the banana industry and appeals for support for the tourist industry. This is the last verse:

De Tourism Ministry appealing
To all ah we
Bar man, Chef Compton, T John
Make this a priority, Lucians in majority
Who really love their Country
And of course their family
Support the Tourist Industry.

Public Opinion

Much of the debate at an intellectual level has been about the disputed economic benefits of tourism (see Chapter One and Two). What Caribbean citizens outside the industry feel about the costs and benefits is even more difficult to assess. Commonly held assumptions are that it is foreigners and local entrepreneurs who benefit. Such views have not changed much in a century. This comment comes from a Jamaican newspaper in 1904: 'All de storekeepers dem in Kingston and de big tabern-keper, dem is de county and see we working in de ground, dem is not going' to do anything fa we, but take picta and laugh at we. Chu! me bredder, only de buckra [whites] dem will profit.'[43]

One of the few objective polls that has asked the views of ordinary people was conducted by Carl Stone in three Jamaican tourist resorts, Montego Bay, Ocho Rios and Negril, in 1990. Polling 662 citizens, who included vendors, small business people, workers in small hotels, taxi-drivers and residents not involved in the tourist industry, Stone asked them: 'Do you feel that people like yourself benefit from tourism in this town?' The small business people and taxi-operators were most satisfied: 75 per cent answered 'yes', with 25 per cent saying 'Yes, but benefits could be better.' Hotel workers also overwhelmingly (98 per cent) saw tourism as beneficial, although 68 per cent of them said the benefits could be better. Vendors and higglers were less satisfied: 32 per cent of them had a negative view and saw tourism as only benefiting the big hotels and the business elite. Two-thirds of the residents unconnected to the industry saw it as largely beneficial. As Stone concluded: 'Grass roots criticisms of the industry tend therefore to centre most on who gets what benefits from the industry, while accepting the industry as being something positive and beneficial.' What the survey discovered, moreover, was that the benefits were seen mainly as economic, while the negative aspects of tourism were associated with its social impact (see Chapter Four). As Stone observed, 'policy makers in the area of tourism and hotel development often ignore the views of both small business interests in the industry and the average citizens in the resort areas whose lives have been greatly affected (positively and negatively)' by tourism.[44]

A further study in Jamaica, undertaken by Dunn & Dunn in 2001, was based on focus group discussions. More than half the respondents were either involved themselves or had family members involved in tourism. Asking the respondents 'who benefits?', only a quarter thought that the community benefited a lot or reasonably well from tourism. There was a clear perception that the 'big man' (owners of all-inclusives, travel and airline operators, in-bond merchants) benefited the most while the 'small man' (taxi drivers, vendors, farmers, hotel workers and small guest house owners) benefited the least. This was most forcefully felt by the young and dispossessed who lived on the edge of a tourist area but did not perceive benefits to themselves or their community. 'Tourism leave out the vendors, craft people, ghetto youths and poor people in general,' said one of this group.[45]

In the same study, one respondent at a community meeting in Rio Bueno, a fishing community on the north coast of Jamaica, was a Rasta artist, the owner of a craft stall. He said it was people like himself who were the ones who truly represented his country to the tourists, not the big hotels or the beaches – they could be found all over the world. People, he argued, came to Jamaica for the hospitality of the Jamaican people and its unique products such as music and culture. The people who most needed to change their attitude, he said, were the tourism planners who were 'sucking up' to those he called the 'money gods in the big hotels'. Tourism workers like himself, he said, who were vital to the success of the industry, got little help from the tourism authorities.

In Bequia, attitudes were also divided between those who appear to benefit from tourism and those who do not, according to Neil Price in *Behind the Planter's Back*, published in 1988. While there was a general sense that it brought employment, those with enough resources to open their own small businesses also saw that foreign capital is a necessary condition of growth. However, the community was aware that foreign investors do not reinvest their capital in Bequia and that the government had largely abandoned its control. Among the lower classes, feelings were similar to those of turn-of-the-century Jamaica: 'Dem rich honkies done take all dey money back home for make more... And dey de only people de bank prepare for give loans to... Dey ain't for give nutting back to de island or de people of Bequia. It just de same as robbery.'[46] For them, tourism means a shortage of affordable land and housing, inflation and a decline in wage labour opportunities.

What has highlighted the gap between those who gain and those who lose from tourism is the growth in the number of all-inclusives. This is particularly the case in Jamaica and St Lucia where all-inclusives have become a crucial ingredient of the tourist product.

The All-Inclusive Controversy

The rise of the all-inclusive resort throughout much of the Caribbean in the late 1980s reawakened many of the hostile sentiments of the 1970s about tourism. While the all-inclusive has been around for a generation in the form of Club Med, whose self-supporting little empire in the sun seemed tucked away and a law unto itself, the increased number and the distinctive vigorous marketing of the all-inclusives, led by the Sandals group, triggered new waves of resentment. Yet the all-inclusive sector, led by Sandals, has become the most successful and well-run sector of the industry. High occupancy, lots of promotion – in the international marketplace – and the source of steady jobs for thousands of nationals are features of the all-inclusive.

The first of the new wave of all-inclusives – indeed the first in the world – opened in 1978 as Couples, owned by John Issa's SuperClubs, in Ocho Rios, Jamaica. Since then, all-inclusives have sprung up in most of the established tourism destinations in the region. They spread fast: in the five years from 1988 to 1993, for example, the number of rooms almost doubled – from 7,629 to 14,283, a faster increase than the overall tourist accommodation stock over that period.

While for the tourism establishment, all-inclusives are an expression of the industry's confidence and are pivotal in contributing to economic growth, the perception at grassroots level is the opposite. Public opinion, expressed by those in indirect employment such as taxi-drivers and vendors as well as people working in local restaurants and small hotels, is bitter about the glittering ghettos which have opened in their midst. They appear to further corral the tourists, offering everything bigger and better than anywhere else and for free because the tourists have already paid back home and have 'left their wallets behind.'

Nowhere has the presence of all-inclusives caused as much of a stir as in St Lucia, a small island, which had only developed its tourist base at the end of the 1980s, but by the early 1990s had accumulated the highest percentage of all-inclusives in the region. By 1994, eight out of St Lucia's 12 major hotels were all-inclusive. According to the Tourist Board, the invasion of the all-inclusives had 'just happened' – the process accelerated by the arrival of the Sandals chain, taking over from two conventional hotels. Hilary Modeste, then head of the St Lucia Hotel Association, claimed that the arrival of Sandals had done a lot for St Lucia, as it maintained a high occupancy rate and therefore a high level of staffing. Yet the St Lucia Hotel and Tourism Association reported that its members in the restaurant and small hotel sector had suffered a 75 per cent fall in business to 'barely a survival level' since the growth of the all-inclusives.[47] It was not just the informal sector and the poor who had seemed to have lost out in the scramble for dollars, but also the local elite who normally reaped the benefits from tourism. Together with the vendors and the taxi-drivers, the entrepreneurial class also felt threatened. In St Lucia, the economic fall-out from the all-inclusives fuelled a social response (see Chapter Four). As a result, a leading St Lucian concluded: 'I used to welcome tourists, give them a lift if they looked lost, extend my hand of friendship. Nowadays when I see them with their plastic wrist-tag, I pass them by.'

The debate in St Lucia prompted the setting up of a task force in 1993 to investigate the role of the all-inclusives. It concluded that it would not be practical to control the growth of that sector – the market had to be the determinant factor. However, recommendations were made to curb, for example, the types of ancillary services inside the resorts. The debate came to prominence again in 2002, when Sandals Resorts, which already ran two resorts on the island, acquired a third: the former Hyatt Regency Hotel, which had opened and closed in the space of two years, reopened in late 2002 as Sandals Grande. Prime Minister Kenny Anthony, who some years earlier had said that no more all-inclusives would be welcome on the island, again said that he could not dictate to property owners as to whom they sold their hotels. However, he did say that non all-inclusives would be granted greater concessions and incentives than the all-inclusive sector.

All-inclusives remained good news, agreed Berthia Parle of the St Lucia Hotel and Tourism Association, although she understood the concern of the small tourism business sector. Once a policy for incentives was in place, she said, no one needed to fear the might of the all-inclusives. At the same time, there was some worry that diversity was desirable and that having a chunk of the hotel sector in the same hands was a potentially high-risk situation. The president of the association in 2002, Rodinald Soomer, said that if the government adopted a moratorium on all-inclusives, the association would support it.

The ambivalence around all-inclusives was revealed in a poll taken in Jamaica, the home of the all-inclusive. The popular view was that they were 'big money spinners for the big hoteliers, but stumbling blocks in the path of the small interests in tourism.' Only a small minority believed that they had made a very positive contribution to the development of the area, while 11 per cent believed that their impact was all negative. The positive respondents said that all-inclusives created new employment and that they earned dollars for hotels and country; the negative respondents said that all-inclusives took business away from local entrepreneurs, with their customers spending nothing in Jamaica and remaining isolated from the people.[48]

The truth, according to a 1994 OAS analysis of Jamaica's tourist industry, lay somewhere in between. The OAS obtained financial statements from 11 out of Jamaica's 19 all-inclusive hotels in its detailed survey. It drew some interesting conclusions about the role of the all-inclusives compared to other types of accommodation. Firstly, it found that 'all-inclusive hotels generate the largest amount of revenue but their impact on the economy is smaller per dollar of revenue than other accommodation subsectors.' Secondly, it concluded that all-inclusives imported more and employed fewer people per dollar of revenue than other hotels. This information confirms the concern of those who argue that all-inclusives have a smaller trickle-down effect. However, in terms of direct impact, all-inclusives made the largest contribution to GDP, with the biggest non all-inclusives second.[49]

Carl Stone's survey also looked at the all-inclusives' finances, but from different angles and in a smaller sample. It analysed the foreign exchange contribution made by six all-inclusives (four Sandals and two of the Issa group) and six conventional hotels (among them Trelawny Beach and Holiday Inn) during the 1989-1990 financial year. According to Stone, all-inclusive hotels in the sample lodged 81 per cent more US dollars per room than the other hotels. Sandals averaged US$51,100, the Issa hotels US$45,800, and the other hotels US$27,000.

However, one non all-inclusive, Half Moon, came out top, just pipping Sandals Negril for highest contribution per room.[50]

While received opinion is that all-inclusive tourists spend little money in Jamaica, Stone's poll found that, in fact, they spend more on shopping than guests in other hotels. However, they spend more in hotel shops and less with small shop-keepers and vendors (whose goods Stone suggested sometimes lack variety and quality). The survey did not inquire about expenditure on taxis, tours or restaurants, all areas that all-inclusive guests traditionally eschew.

Stone was enthusiastic about all-inclusives. He said that they represented 'the strongest component of the Jamaican tourist industry.' Far from being an obstacle in the path of progress of small business and vendors, 'these hotels have assisted the expansion of the tourist market in various important ways.' Stone believed that public education was needed to 'dispel and remove the many myths surrounding the all-inclusive hotels and to turn widespread ambivalence about all-inclusive hotels and their value into a more positive and supportive body of public opinion.'

If the verdict on the economic impact of all-inclusives in particular and tourism in general appears more or less favourable, there is even more ambivalence about the industry's social impact on the region as a whole.

NOTES

1.   Jean Holder, 'The Caribbean: Far Greater Dependence on Tourism Likely', *The Courier*, Brussels, no. 122, 1990

2.   *Grenada Today*, Grenada, 11 March 1994

3.   Hopeton S. Dunn and Leith L. Dunn, *People and Tourism*, Arawak Publications, Kingston, 2002

4.   Derek Walcott, *Omeros*, Faber, London, 1990, p.289

5.   Gordon K. Lewis, *The Growth of the Modern West Indies*, New York, 1968, p.140

6.   Economist Intelligence Unit (EIU), *Tourism in the Caribbean*, London, 1993

7.   Neil Price, *Behind the Planter's Back: Lower-Class Responses to Marginality in Bequia Island, St Vincent*, London, 1988, p.175

8.   Carl Stone, 'A Socio-Economic Study of the Tourism Industry in Jamaica', *Caribbean Affairs*, Trinidad, vol 4, no 1, 1991, p.12

9.   Ibid.

10.   Ibid.

11.   Gillian Gunn, 'The Sociological Impact of Rising, Foreign Investment', Georgetown University, Cuba Briefing Paper Series No 1, 1993

12.   Alejandro de la Fuente, 'Recreating Racism', The Caribbean Project, Centre for Latin American Studies, Georgetown University, No 18, July 1998

13.   *Caribbean Insight*, London, June 1991

14. Tayo Fashoyin, 'Fostering Economic Development Through Social Partnership in Barbados', International Labour Organisation, 2001

15. Dunn & Dunn, op. cit.

16. Frank Fonda Taylor, *To Hell with Paradise: A History of the Jamaican Tourist Industry*, Pittsburg, 1993, p.119

17. Brian M. Kermath and Thomas, Robert N., 'Spatial Dynamics of Resorts: Sosúa, Dominican Republic, *Annals of Tourism Research*, vol 19, 1992, pp.173-190

18. JL McElroy and K de Albuquerque, 'Problems for Managing Sustainable Touirsm in Small Island States', in *Island Tourism and Sustainable Development: Caribbean, Pacific and Mediterranean Experiences*, edited by Y. Apostolopoulos and D.J Gayle, Praeger, 2002

19. *Caribbean Week*, Barbados, 14 May 1994

20. *Caribbean Week*, 4 April 1992

21. Dorothy Riddle and Jay, John, 'Dominica's Service Sector: Overview and Assessment', Dominica Ministry of Finance and Development, 1991

22. EIU, op. cit.

23. John Bell, 'Caribbean Tourism in the Year 2000' in Dennis Gayle and Goodrich, Jonathan (eds), *Tourism Marketing and Management in the Caribbean*, London, 1993, p.229

24. Peter Goffe, 'Managing for Excellence in Caribbean Hotels', in Gayle and Goodrich, op. cit., p.150

25. Holder, op. cit.

26. Maurice Bishop, 'Opening Address, Regional Conference on the Socio-Cultural and Environmental Impact of Tourism on Caribbean Societies', Grenada, 1979, mimeo

27. Fonda Taylor, op. cit., p.90

28 *Outlet*, Antigua and Barbuda, 9 July 1993

29. Price, op. cit., p.224

30. V.S. Naipaul, *The Middle Passage*, London, 1962, p.210

31. Frantz Fanon, *The Wretched of the Earth*, London, 1967, p.123

32. Jamaica Kincaid, *A Small Place*, London, 1988, p.55

33. *Outlet*, 14 October 1994

34. Willi Momm, director, ILO Caribbean office. Speech to the 24th annual Caribbean tourism conference, 2002

35. EIU, op. cit.

36. Bell, op. cit., p.229

37. Kenneth Hall et al, 'Caribbean Tourism and the Role of UWI in Tourism and Hospitality Education', in Social and Economic Studies, Vol 51, no 1, March 2002

38. Ainsley O'Reilly, 'Past, present and future of tourism and hospitality education in the Commonwealth Caribbean', paper 2000

39. B. Henry and Burchell, 'A world class workforce', Sandals Training and Development Unit, 2000

40. Jean Holder, 'The Caribbean Tourism Organisation's Role in Caribbean Tourism Development Towards the Year 2000' in Gayle and Goodrich, op. cit., p.215

41. Ben Mallalieu, *The Guardian*, 6 Jan 2001

42. Hello, Tourist!, Project St Croix, US Virgin Islands, 1977

43. Fonda Taylor, op. cit., p.110

44. Stone, op. cit.

45. Dunn & Dunn, op. cit.

46. Price, op. cit., p.214

47. *Caribbean Insight*, September 1993

48. Stone, op. cit.

49. OAS, op. cit.

50. Stone, op. cit.

4

'LIKE AN ALIEN IN WE OWN LAND': THE SOCIAL IMPACT

In the Caribbean, calpyso is a vehicle for social change and political protest. 'Alien', sung by Saint Lucia's the Mighty Pep and written by Rohan Seon, a teacher at Derek Walcott's old school St Mary's College, was an enormously popular hit, playing continuously on local radio and heard in buses, rum shops, offices and homes throughout St Lucia during the carnival period. Like any good calypso, 'Alien' touched a chord with St Lucians by articulating strong feelings against the dominance of all-inclusive resorts on the island. According to the calypso, all-inclusives are 'buying up every strip of beach, every treasured spot they reach.' The chorus line, 'Like an alien, in we own land', was particularly cheered by St Lucians because all-inclusives, unlike other types of hotels, restrict the entry of non-residents to expensive day passes, thus effectively barring the majority of islanders from the premises.

This is part of the calypso:

All-inclusive tax elusives
And truth is
They're sucking up we juices
Buying up every strip of beach
Every treasured spot they reach.

Some put on Sandals
Exclusive vandals
It's a scandal
The way they operate
Building brick walls and barricades
Like a state within a state.

For Lucians to enter
For lunch or dinner
We need reservations, passport and visa

And if you sell near the hotel
I wish you well
They will yell and kick you out to hell.

Chorus:
Like an alien
In we own land
I feel like a stranger
And I sensing danger
We can't sell out whole country
To please the foreign lobby
What's the point of progress
Is it really success?
If we gain ten billion
But lose the land we live on.

The popularity of 'Alien' had also been fuelled by a dispute between Ronald 'Boo' Hinkson, a well-respected St Lucian musician, and the all-inclusive resort, Sandals La Toque. Hinkson had gone to Sandals one evening to drop off two friends when a security guard demanded to search his car, saying that the procedure was company policy. Hinkson refused to give his permission, was held against his will, and as a result sued the company for wrongful imprisonment.

Echoing the words of 'Alien', Hinkson expressed his outrage at what had happened at Sandals in an open letter to the minister of tourism, Romanus Lansiquot: 'No matter how many jobs, airline flights or US dollars Sandals brings into this country, they cannot buy the authority to trample on the rights and human dignity of the St Lucian people.'

A similar episode from another island touched the same nerve. A former prime minister of Antigua, Lester Bird (a man of impressive height and girth), was apparently once barred from the all-inclusive Club Antigua when a zealous security guard, not recognising him, refused him entry because he had no pass. The weekly newspaper *Outlet* (usually no friend of Lester Bird) commented:

Antiguans and Barbudans who literally give millions of dollars to these very all-inclusive hotels in customs duties and taxes, do not, cannot, will not, and must not be asked to accept by those to whom we give, that we are not allowed in these halls, except accompanied by a trailing Security Guard. There was a time, in the long and far off times, when people of this country had to have a pass to be out of doors after the ringing of a Church bell at night. We overcame that. We did not overcome that in those long and far off times to have it reimposed in another form in these present times.[1]

The calpyso and the treatment of Hinkson and Prime Minister Bird raise particular issues about Caribbean tourism and its social impact on the region. For a start, they reflect the region's distaste for a tourism which denies Caribbean peoples access to parts of their own country. Echoing a widely expressed view, one St Lucian who has lived in Europe for many years would never go back because 'I can't walk along the beach in my own country.'

In theory, there is no such thing as a private beach in the Caribbean, since all land up to the high-water mark is public in law. (The conformation of many Caribbean beaches, however, means that there is often only a narrow strip between sea and high-water mark.) Yet in practice, access to the beach has been, and in some cases remains, restricted. While popular sentiment endorses claims such as 'the beach is the birthright of the people', more and more hotels are on the best and most accessible beaches yet access to the beach is barred by hotel security. Even when access is not forbidden, some locals, especially older ones, often feel uncomfortable or unwelcome sharing the sea and sand with tourists.

As a result, on many islands there are beaches such as Friar's Bay in Antigua which have become refuges for local people, where they go for a barbecue or a family outing away from the hotel strips. In the 1970s, the Jamaican authorities fought a rearguard action to protect local access by putting up signs saying, 'Reserved as a Public Bathing Beach'. However, such beaches were not usually the best spots as those were 'reserved' for the tourists. By that time, a contributor to the *Gleaner* wrote, 'The day could come when the ordinary Jamaican doesn't know what a good beach looks like.'[2]

Either by design or effect, the restrictions on locals sharing beaches with tourists are part of a strategy to 'safeguard' tourism for the visitors. Within the hotel grounds, the tourists' environment can be controlled, but the beach remains, in law at least, a public space. Yet with the arrival of tourists, this area also becomes part of the holiday-makers' sphere of influence. As a result, not only do casual vendors tend to be restricted (see Chapter Three), but local behaviour begins to be scrutinised and contained.

One of the major strategies used by tourism officials has been to employ wardens and/or police (and in a few cases the military) to patrol the beaches. In Barbados, the issue first became hot in the early 1980s when Jack Dear, the chairman of the Barbados Tourist Board, was responsible for introducing wardens to the beaches. 'There was a problem of beach harassment, mainly sexual, in which women were called lesbians if they rejected the beach boys,' said Dear. 'The situation got worse and worse and became a major issue for the industry. My solution was to get them off the beach. Some people who cursed me then went on themselves to impose control.' The introduction of wardens (who 'want the women, too', according to the beach bums) and, later, the police to Bajan beaches did not make Dear popular. His critics promptly interpreted the new policy as a means of keeping black Barbadians off the beach. Again, a calypso sums up local sentiment of the time. This one, pointedly called 'Jack', begins:

I grow up bathing in sea water
But nowadays that is bare horror
If I only venture down by the shore
Police is only telling me I can't bathe any more

And the chorus includes the lines: 'I want Jack to know that the beach belong to me/That can't happen here over my dead body/Tell Jack that I say that the beach belong to me.'

Two decades later, the issue was still not dead. In 2000, articles in the Barbados' *Daily Nation* drew attention to a newly-built wall at Mullins which threatened to block access to the beach. Peter Morgan, a former minister of tourism, wrote in his column: 'It cannot be acceptable that local people should have to pass down narrow lanes, not well marked, to arrive at the beach only to be confronted by security guards who make them feel like interlopers.' Commenting on the continuing purchase of chunks of the west coast by non-nationals, he said: 'If something is not done soon, residents of St James and St Peters will soon need to catch a bus down to Brandons [just north of Bridgetown] to get a dip in their own sea.'

The problem clearly has not gone away; wherever large resorts are built, they take beach access from someone, usually local residents. In 2000 in Canouan, one of the islands of the Grenadines, an Italian-owned company, Canouan Resorts Development, leased two thirds of the land for its planned Carenage Bay Beach and Golf Resort. A local man, Terry Bynoe, president of the Canouan Progressive Movement, argued his rights – and those of other local residents – for access to Godahl beach, traditionally one of the most popular beaches in the north of the island. A stone-throwing incident involving Canaouan residents and Israeli security guards was reported in September 2000, in the same month as a high court judge granted an injunction to the developers barring Bynoe from the property. Later that year, four people, including Bynoe, were charged with a variety of offences during a demonstration against the Carenage Bay project, with residents accusing police of using 'brute force' against those involved in demonstrations.[3] The issue of public access still clearly creates an emotional response for the people of the Caribbean.

In Cuba it is not just the question of access to beaches that has caused dismay among local people. In the 1990s the re-emerging tourist industry practised a virtual economic and social apartheid, barring Cubans from restaurants, bars, nightclubs, hotels and 'dollar' shops, unless accompanied and paid for by foreigners. 'It's disgusting. We are second-class citizens in our own country. And for what? The US dollar, the symbol of our old imperialist enemy,' one Cuban cabaret dancer told a journalist.[4]

While locals may feel corralled and controlled, tourists sometimes behave as if they own the place. Many, for example, like photographing the local 'scene' although most guides ask them not to take pictures of people without first asking permission. In less touristy islands such as Dominica, tourists cannot resist taking 'picturesque' images of market vendors, women washing clothes in the river, or of the indigenous Caribs. Local people are not always greatly thrilled by this intrusion.

It is difficult to calculate the effect of strangers, with and without cameras, invading the domestic and working lives of Caribbean peoples. Many locals, especially in non-tourist driven areas, continue to live and work as they always have done. What is clear, however, is that tourists are not always treated with the flattering cheeriness demanded by both tourist boards and visitors. The British novelist Martin Amis wrote in an essay on St Lucia: 'The street-wanderers of Micoud regard us with ambiguous levity. We stop for a can of orange juice and are unsmilingly overcharged. Although you wouldn't call them hostile, they are no more friendly than I would feel, if a stranger drove down my street in a car the size of my house.'[5]

Bad Influence?

Caribbean intellectuals express concern about how the ethics of materialism transfer to the resident population. Tourists parade their wealth before people whose experience of First World lifestyles are perhaps second-hand and received through media images. Tourism, it is argued, promotes hedonism and superficial experiences; it does not build self-confidence and discipline. Such thinking is also part of a broader analysis which blames tourism for undermining national identities (see Chapter Eight) and for the spread of a general malaise within Caribbean societies.

Central to this idea is the so-called 'demonstration effect' in which tourism is said to create a demand for western lifestyles and attitudes. In pre-war Jamaica one observer noted that Jamaicans 'assume the bovine loud aggressiveness of the tourist manner.'[6] In this context, the supposedly malign influence of tourism ranges from the corruption of local youth, changes in consumption (burgers and supermarkets rather than bammies and coalpots) to the mimicry of western styles of entertainment and architecture. While this demonstration effect is in part a consequence of tourism, other factors exist alongside tourism: the emergence of a Caribbean middle class, travel, contact with relatives abroad and, more importantly, widespread access to North American media.[7]

But tourists get the blame, especially when there is stress and economic hardship. 'The poor now see that there is no one out there seeking out their interests, therefore they become mercenary too,' said Bob Evans, a former technical manager of Grenada airport. A Rastafarian called Ras Herb noticed a similar effect among his own community. He described another Rasta, who lives around the tourist area of Grande Anse beach, as follows: 'Living among the tourist and other people in that area, has made him hook on worldly materials and fantasy. To "I", he is an exaggerator, an inciter and one who will always make a talk for food.'

Joseph Antoine, a Grenadian community worker, also watched the way tourism changed communities. He believed that tourism has serious social implications:

> When people move to tourist areas, there is a break-up of community and family. People then start turning away from traditional foods – they begin to think that bottled drink is better. Then people want to

sound like tourists, too. Tourism 'demotivates'; only a small percentage benefit. Unless tourism is tied to aspirations of political development; anything else leaves people deficient.

Tim Hector, the former editor of *Outlet*, blamed the nature of tourism in Antigua for similar negative effects. In one issue in 1994, he wrote:

> And where sugar was succeeded by Princess Tourism, the fragility of the industry, and the industry itself has introduced new social relations. Where sugar brought people together, working together on large estates, tourism brings people together at hotels, without it seems, the same social bonding. Everyone is on his own. Imitating the life-style of the holidayers whom he or she serves. More and more tourism alienates. Especially when tourism is in foreign hands.[8]

A more extreme description of how tourism corrupts came from Gerardo Mosquera, a Cuban art critic, who has watched Cuba realign itself with foreign investors while holding on to a centralised economy. This contradictory situation creates such ironies as doctors working as hotel waiters: a paradox beyond the imagining of the rest of the Caribbean. Yet, that is the extent to which the Cuban population can enjoy the fruits of tourism, according to Mosquera. 'The Cuban people have had to confront neoliberal policies without even having the option of legally participating in the informal economy. This curious mixture of "socialist" fundamentalism and "neoliberalism"' has created corruption, widespread theft, marginality, the black market, mass exodus, and jineterismo [prostitution] as survival strategies,' he wrote.[9]

Imitating the tourist culture is, in part, a legacy of colonialism. Aspiring to imitate others, labelling others as better, led to V.S. Naipaul's concept of the 'mimic men', his contemptuous put-down of the region's psyche. One way in which such insecurity expresses itself is in the observance of public prudery and respectability.

Outward propriety reflects both the Caribbean's conservative (and religious) mores and recognition of a history of poverty. While elegant French tourists on St Martin go barefoot as an expression of tropical hedonism, for the Caribbean, bare feet are an image of poverty; going barefoot has connotations of struggle and slavery, not of carefree indulgence. Conversely, to be well-dressed is a mark of social status and economic well-being.

This contrast in economic and cultural values between host and guest is expressed at a public level in dress, exemplified by the manicured nails and high heels of the bank clerk changing the travellers' cheques of tourists dressed in sarongs and sandals. In an attempt to assert its own values and to 'protect' its people from tourist values, most Caribbean countries issue a 'dress code'; this implores visitors to observe local customs while reassuring them that locals are not out to spoil their fun.

The St Kitts tourist magazine, for example, has a section entitled 'Proper Attire' which advises: 'By all means go native while you are here, but please understand that to us "native" means no short shorts, bikinis or bare chests in public places. In the pursuit of fashion, please remember to dress conservatively. Beach attire is just that and is not considered appropriate for around town, in shops and stores, or in restaurants.' Barbados takes a more jokey approach with drawings of a woman tourist in a bikini pushing a supermarket trolley, with a caption: 'When you're in town or just shopping around don't be confused. You may be a peach but leave swimwear for the beach.' Beneath a drawing of a fat male tourist in a shop, is the caption, 'We know your business and we know that you're cool but please leave exposed tummies for around the pool.'

The 'rules' also extend to the beach, where nudity is unacceptable (there are exceptions in Guadeloupe, Martinique, St Martin and in Negril, Jamaica) and going topless is frowned upon. In Barbados, wardens and police enforce the dress code on the beach by clapping their hands loudly in disapproval whenever they see a naked breast.

Sex Tourism

Distaste for beach nudity may, in part, be an expression of religious propriety, but it also underpins the region's attempt to discourage what are seen as unwelcome foreign sexual mores. A report by the Caribbean Tourism Research and Development Centre in 1980 concluded that: 'There is a general feeling that tourism corrupts the moral values of the youth and that a lot of tourists have sexual relations with the local population. Respondents are also of the opinion that tourist sexual values are loose compared to those of local people.'[10] Yet, sex tourism flourishes in the region and is subliminally promoted through the sort of advertising which associates the Caribbean with 'letting your hair down' and hedonism. The tourist industry condones, if not colludes, in this image.

There is a contradiction, however, when it comes to gay and lesbian tourists. They have sometimes found themselves unwelcome, their sexuality pilloried by local church groups who use the Bible to justify homophobic attitudes. In 1998, the Cayman Islands, a British Overseas Territory, banned a visit by a cruise ship chartered by gay organisations. The charter company then declared its intention to visit the Bahamas. The outcry in the Bahamas was sufficient to merit an intervention by Prime Minister Hubert Ingraham. In a powerful speech on national television, Ingraham was highly critical of the anti-gay lobby. He described the media coverage as 'a sea of bitter, poorly reasoned diatribe' and 'un-Christian'. While saying that the constitution guaranteed freedom of speech, he also said: 'Quite simply, it is not the role of the government to investigate and pass judgement on the sexual behaviour of consenting adults so long as their activity is conducted in private.' It was a brave and radical speech for any Caribbean politician to make, for the Caribbean's adherence to a fundamental, wrathful Christianity remains widespread, and homophobia is commonplace. Ingraham was also being pragmatic for in his speech he emphasised the importance of tourism – 'our economic lifeblood'; the Bahamas could ill-afford to exclude any visitor, whatever their sexuality.

While public morality remains conservative, especially among the old generation, it would be fanciful to think that Caribbean heterosexual conventions, let alone the behaviour of the majority of Caribbean men, owe much to traditional 'family values'.

Tourists whose expectations of the Caribbean are of one long bacchanal are rewarded by dollar-seeking locals, who cannot afford to be bothered too much by stereotyping. This goes as much for the bored singers who mouth 'No Woman No Cry' at American cruise tourists eating pizzas on St Maarten's casino-packed beachfront as for the 'professional' hustlers of Montego Bay cruising the beaches for single white women. The tourist industry supplies whatever is required and by whom: by the women who have fun learning to 'wine' in hotel dance lessons ('learn to reggae with Errol') or by the groups of middle-aged Europeans pawing their teenage 'acquisitions' in the bars and hotel foyers of the Dominican Republic.

While much sex tourism in the Caribbean, especially that between local men and women tourists, exists within an informal framework, more formal prostitution has become a matter for concern, especially in the Dominican Republic and Cuba. There is also evidence of traffic in prostitutes, notably from the Dominican Republic, to other islands and to Europe, and some participation of organised crime in prostitution networks. The situation is such that a decade ago the Caribbean Conference of Churches (CCC) set up a regional arm of the Ecumenical Coalition for Third World Tourism. The then general secretary of the CCC, Edward Cumberbatch, said that he was determined that the Caribbean should not go the way of Asia, in particular in the proliferation of child prostitution and crime.

At a deeper level, local dislike of sexual relations between locals and tourists has less to do with sexual puritanism than with the perception that poor locals, whether men or women, are being racially and economically exploited by tourists. Their availability is made more seductive by received images: the 'exotic', easy 'native' woman with a hibiscus behind her ear; or the beachboy whose sexual prowess has been defined by white culture. It is also resented that the only encounters that most tourists have with local people are either as waiters or beachboys. There are no representations of 'ordinary' people in the tourists' experience. As one Barbadian advertising executive said: 'Tourists only meet beach boys, therefore the idea of a Barbadian man is restricted to that image.'

Such perceptions are encased in a familiar cultural currency. In a short story published in the Barbadian magazine *Bim* in 1969, a character says: 'I was a Barbadian, a man of the tropics, wild, untamed, supple, POTENT – what every northern woman wishes for. It was a generally accepted idea among us men on the island that the only thing that women from Canada, England and the States came down to the West Indies for was to sleep with the Natives.'[11]

In the English-speaking Caribbean, unofficial anecdote dates it all from the planeloads of French-Canadian women who visited the Caribbean on charters in the early 1960s. Nowadays, the beach boys are jokingly called 'The Foreign Service' and the practice of male prostitution is known as 'Rent a Rasta'. Public opinion still maintains that French-Canadian women remain the most available for sex, although the British and Germans are also on the beachboys' agenda (with Americans, according to received opinion, the least approachable).

Like many other aspects of the tourist industry, the beachboy phenomenon is based upon the dependency of the host. Young men and sometimes women, usually poorly educated and unemployed, offer their sexual services in return for money or temporary support to affluent, often middle-class, white tourists, whose age and marital status are pretty well irrelevant. While it might not be called prostitution, the contract has a barely disguised financial basis, with the tourists providing meals, drinks, transport, money and clothes in exchange for sex.

The beach is usually the territory for the initial encounter. Male sex workers, for example, hang out at the scruffier ends of the tourist strips; if they have something to sell so much the better. In Barbados the beach bums sell aloe, good for sunburn, which they use as a way to introduce themselves. 'I work this beach,' boasts one Barbadian hustler, proud of his ability to get anything any tourist wants to buy. 'I can make a lot of money doing this. Lots of the tourists buy sex – they have to give the boys for their time. I can get anything you want – drugs, except heroin; even boys, for US$500.' If they have nothing to sell except themselves, they adopt approaches such as a request for a cigarette or a pick-up line such as 'you lookin' lonely'.

The trend is growing, according to one researcher, Joan Phillips from the University of London, who told the Democratic Labour Party in Barbados in 2002 that teenage boys were leaving school 'to go on the beach to get the big money.' She observed that sex tourism was 'the new commodity on sale for the tourist dollar and the newly liberated in search of the post-colonial Mandingo.'[12]

Across the Caribbean Sea, in Jamaica, a satirical book called *How to Be Jamaican* describes the 'North Coast Hustler' and his way of life. 'He is easily recognizable. Almost inevitably, he wears locks, has a trim figure (quite often with a few knife scars), carries an ornately carved stick and is a walking collection of gifts from happy clients: chains, rings, Gap and Banana Republic jeans and T-shirts, and Nike, Adidas or Reebok sneakers, as well as Sony Walkman or ghetto blaster...' The description continues:

> The hustler, enigmatic behind mirrored glasses, sits and 'grooves' waiting for two teachers from Iowa eager to see the 'real Jamaica' to pass by whereupon our hero will grin and say 'Greetings to the daughters'. Such an ethnic introduction works wonders and the women are soon asking the locksman about Bob Marley who was, of course, his 'personal idren' [brother]... He casually tosses his locks and the goosepimples begin for the Iowans. Soon they are off, listening to learned discourses on Rastafari, an invitation to a fish and bammy feed. They drink it all in, enthralled. Excitement... Can the Big Bamboo be far behind?[13]

This account is a recognisable parody of reality. It illustrates the calculated nature of the hustler's role, it understands that the tourists do not recognise this (at first they are just responding to 'native friendliness') and ultimately it evokes the frisson associated with a holiday romance and a dreadlocked boyfriend.

What the account does not point out is that these encounters reverse more conventional gender roles and also confuse race and class roles. Within Caribbean societies, a lower-class male is never invited by a middle-class woman for a drink in a hotel, but women tourists do not recognise (nor care about) such sanctions. From the beachboy's point of view, as one study in Barbados put it: 'The mere presence of the beachboy on tourist premises thus represents a personal triumph in having overstepped such racial boundaries.'[14]

From the woman's point of view, a black boyfriend, however temporary, offers more than a 'holiday romance'. It gives her power over a man in a way she does not have in New York or Manchester. Her economic power means that she can choose to treat him sympathetically or contemptuously. As one Antiguan tour representative put it: 'She takes him home from the disco by taxi but she'll only give him the money for the bus the next morning.'

For the beachboy, however, each 'client' represents more than a means of survival and a triumph over the racial/class system of his island. It also represents temporary access to the First World. In one of the more closely observed accounts of sexual tourism in the Caribbean, Neil Price described the patterns of this transaction in Bequia, where relationships with white women offer the possibility of escape from the restrictions and frustrations of island life. As one young man, who had been in serial relationships with young Italian women visitors, says: 'If a girl done love you, she gonna do everything she can for get you to be near her. For dese Italian girls wid rich family, it possible dat dey gonna get enough money for give I a ticket to Europe... Man I just waiting...'[15] The fact that the ticket to Milan was a day dream did not deter the young men of Bequia.

The impact of their behaviour on their own community, however, was disruptive. Firstly, relationships between women tourists and locals were resented by local women and provoked tensions between partners. Secondly, Price noted that disputes broke out between the youths over women, while relationships between young men and the older generation became tense. One man who had been seen sleeping on the beach with a tourist had caused his father embarrassment: 'De way he done carry on is just worthless. He ain't got not respeck, and he making so I done lose my own respect in de village...'

In the Spanish-speaking countries of the Caribbean it is often young mulatto women who serve the tourists, although male prostitution also flourishes. This is particularly true in the Dominican Republic, with its reputation in the world of sex tourism for 'dusky beauties'. Women sex workers, usually impoverished young women with children who turn to prostitution from economic need, sometimes find what are known as 'amigos', men who will send them money long after their holiday is over, and express interest in a more long-term relationship. Such women provide 'fun' for ageing Europeans while stylish boys, sometimes known as sanky-pankies, ply the beach for sex with either men or women. The Dominican Republic has now joined Thailand and the Philippines on the list of countries known for its exploitative sex industries.

Cuba, too, has become distinguished by its reputation for sex tourism. Before the Revolution, Cuba was known as the 'brothel of the Caribbean', its tourist industry controlled by American mobsters; after 1959 both tourism and prostitution virtually disappeared. The eradication of prostitution was one of Castro's proudest boasts. Now, with more tourists and more hardship, sex tourism is back. As one 21-year-old prostitute and sometime pimp says: 'I don't know if this is good or bad for the country. But I know I don't have clothes. I don't have money. For me, this is the only way.'[16] A 14-year-old boy writing in the Spanish newspaper El País said that it seemed that most of the tourists in Cuba went there for sex. He ended his letter, 'I believe that one of the principles of the revolution was to eliminate prostitution.'[17]

Yet in every hotel lobby in Varadero and Havana, there are young women holding stilted conversations with middle-aged European men, while, wherever there are tourists, teenage girls, known as jineteras, in lurex and hotpants, hang around discos to be picked up for a meal or a dollar or two. 'The only thing that's a bargain here is the sex,' says an octogenarian German. Sex tourism has also exposed the limitations of Cuba's claims to be a non-racist society with Afro-Cuban women being disproportionately seen to engage in the sex industry and thus to be a conspicuous target for police clamp-downs.

Cuba's response to sex tourism remains largely punitive for prostitution is officially seen not as a reflection of economic desperation, but of moral laxness. An article entitled 'Flowers of Fifth Avenue', a reference to the young women who hang around a street in Havana's Miramar district, endorsed the official line. 'More than 60 per cent of them are working or studying and none of them are prostituting themselves to eat daily or have a roof over their heads.' Or, as the Cuban Women's Federation said in 1998: 'We find these women have poor moral and social development and that they prefer material things to normal values of love and family.'[18] The moralising against jineterismo continues to define the official response to both formal and informal sex between Cubans and visitors. At Cuba's 15th annual tourism convention, held in the beach resort of Varadero, Tourism Minister Osmany Cienfuegos could not ignore the prostitution problem. He blamed foreign tour operators for projecting a distorted image of Cuba for their own propaganda: 'Our women are not a commodity,' he said. President Castro also warned: 'We don't want the image of a country of gambling, drugs and prostitution: we want the image of a country with a high cultural level, a healthy country both morally and physically, an organised country that looks after the environment.'[19] Jineterismo continues to be interpreted negatively by the Cuban establishment, for example, 'a consumption virus, which is alien to the spiritual values of the revolution.'[20]

Meanwhile Aids has arrived in the Caribbean. In Haiti, Aids became the ultimate deterrent to the sex industry. The dramatic decrease of US visitors to Haiti in the winter of 1981 to 1982 from 70,000 to 10,000 was seen as the direct result of the US medical establishment's pronouncement that Haitians were one of the four Aids high-risk categories. When lurid press reports in the US press suggested that Aids originated in Haiti, its considerable sexual attractions dissolved overnight. As the Cuban historian Juan Antonio Blanco told *Time* magazine in 1993 in another context: 'Tourism is a sort of chemotherapy. You have cancer and it's the only possible cure, but it might kill you before the cancer does.'[21]

Most worrying for those campaigning against sex tourism are the growing numbers of children in the Dominican Republic who are involved. Mark Connolly, an international consultant on children's rights, went to Sosúa and Boca Chica, two beach resorts in the Dominican Republic, to investigate the sexual exploitation of children. He had been told that in the northern resort of Sosúa, where the T-shirts are printed with 'Jump 'em, Pump 'em and Dump 'em', 'most of the households probably have at least one kid who has sold his/her body for dollars.'[22]

By talking to both Dominican adolescents and European tourists in Sosúa and Boca Chica, Connolly concluded that the sexual exploitation of both girls and boys was condoned 'and most likely promoted' by the government, tourist services, travel agencies, and hotels. For example, in Boca Chica, most hotels and other rented accommodation allow guests to take visitors into their rooms. One real estate company, which rented out condominiums mainly to single European men where 'almost everyone had young kids' in their rooms, said that children could also be 'delivered' to the condo as part of the rental deal. Hotels in Boca Chica and Salinas, for example, have been closed down but occasional reports in the country's newspapers point to continuing exploitation of children. An ILO survey of child prostitution in Jamaica identified children, both boys and girls from the poorest of families or from the streets, between the ages of 10 and 18 engaged in sex with tourists (among other customers).

So whatever the sexual fantasy, it can come true in the Caribbean. The controlling issue is money, which gives the power to make it happen. So, depending on your gender and your particular fantasy, the Caribbean is populated by 'little brown fucking machines', 'cool' black women who love to party, 'primitive-smelling' black studs who only think of 'pussy and money' or 'respectful Latin gentlemen who love women.'[23] Sex, Aids, materialism and envy, changing values and tensions within the community are some of the reasons that go towards a negative picture of the social impact of tourism on the region.

The Drugs Connection

For many Caribbean islands drugs, just as much as sex tourism, have threatened local communities. Among the thousands of T-shirts on sale in every cruise port is one of a puny, camera-laden male tourist and a Rastaman holding a large spliff; beneath the picture is printed 'Different Island, Same Shit'. Tourists attract drug-sellers (most will be offered drugs, mostly ganja, but everything is available) although the exact links between drugs and tourism are more complex and difficult to disentangle.

The most obvious connection between tourists and drugs consists of locals supplying tourists with their holiday highs. It is a largely peripheral and small-scale business. However, at a more general level the Caribbean's tourist trade provides an infrastructure in which the drug trade can flourish. The daily network of planes and cruise ships makes trafficking easy with large numbers of tourists, crews and officials constantly on the move. Hotels and good telecommunications make life convenient for the traffickers and their agents in their own secretive sub-cultures.

Since Havana's heyday in the 1950s, those behind the drug trade and other illegal activity have seen the Caribbean as a useful transit point and as a launch-pad into the US. By the end of the 1990s, US officials estimated that 40 per cent of all drugs reaching the US mainland passed through the Caribbean; this was four times the percentage of a decade earlier.[24] The routes for the huge drug traffic from Latin America, in particular cocaine from Colombia, have been through the small, scattered, ill-policed and underpatrolled islands of the Antilles. The deserted islets, coves and cays of the Grenadines, the Bahamian Out Islands, the Virgin Islands and many other spots are ideal for drug drops, by sea or air. The Florida coast (40 miles away from the Bahamas at its nearest point) can be reached 'before a milk shake melts' in a fast motorboat known as a 'go fast' or 'cigarette boat'.

The US Department of State Bureau of International Narcotics Matters (INM) publishes an annual country-by-country summary of the Caribbean's drug activity. Its assessment often mentions the way that tourism facilitates drug trafficking with sophisticated and organised drug rings from South America making use of the traditional advantages the area has to offer, augmented by an ample network of airline and cruise ship connections and large and mobile volumes of tourists. The drug 'corridors' through Jamaica and the Bahamas are regularly mentioned, with Cuba – and its large tourist industry – becoming a new channel for drugs destined for Europe.

Behind the movement of drugs are the drug cartels. Tourism coexists with organised crime in a kind of symbiotic relationship and the US State Department reports also emphasise this link between tourism, money-laundering and off-shore banking. For example: 'Money laundering fostered by the off-shore banking and casino and resort industries on Aruba, Curaçao and St Maarten flourishes on these islands. Aruba and Curaçao have also witnessed an increase in such drug-related crime as shootings, robberies and murders between rival drug gangs vying for territory.'[25] What is good for casinos is good for organised crime.

By the 1990s, it was thought that other countries, which had been formerly riddled by money-laundering corruption, had to a large extent cleaned up their act. But not before enormous sums of money had been laundered and island states corrupted, with politicians charged and convicted on drugs charges and open economies susceptible to drug-related money-laundering activities.

British lawyer Barry Rider, a former head of the Commonwealth Secretariat's commercial crime unit, said in the mid 1990s that the institutions of some Caribbean countries had been so effectively penetrated by the vast amounts of money generated by organised crime that they could be described as criminal states. Aruba, for instance, fitted that description, with drug cartels moving there in the 1990s attracted by its rapidly developing tourist industry. In February 1993 slot-machines shipped from the US Virgin Islands to Aruba were found to contain millions of dollars in secret compartments. 'There is concern that drug money is "integrated" into the Aruban economy through real estate purchases,' the INM observed.[26]

Organised crime is efficient, said Dr Rider. 'It tends to be conservative and protects those it has corrupted.' It operates best where it can work unhindered, undetected and in conditions of political stability. This, he concluded, was one reason why Jamaica had not been infiltrated by organised crime (it has its own 'Yardies' in any case): its politics are too volatile. Organised crime does not like, and will not allow, petty crime or political violence to get in the way of its activities. Even so, Jamaica's reputation has been damaged by the publicity given to the extensive use of Jamaican 'mules' as drug carriers on flights to the UK, and accounts of holiday-makers from the UK also participating in drug smuggling.

In some cases, a busy tourist industry can offer a suitable cover for criminal activities; it can also provide opportunities for investment. When the drug cartels looked for avenues to invest their billions, they found plenty of opportunities in the tourist industry where they could use their laundered money in legitimate operations.

Perhaps one of the most telling examples of how tourism can provide an ideal cover for corruption is the Bahamas, close to Miami and Atlantic City, where casinos and real estate development flourish. This happened both before independence, when the so-called Bay Street Boys, the white merchant elite, ruled, and also afterwards during the premiership of the multi-millionaire Sir Lynden Pindling.

When in 1967 Pindling (who later was himself the subject of a corruption investigation) set up a commission of inquiry into the running of the casinos and to investigate whether any politician had received any financial reward from their operation, the main accusation concerned Sir Stafford Sands. The report stated:

> The fee of £200,000 which Sir Stafford Sands was paid so promptly for his work in obtaining the Certificate of Exemption for the Amusements Company, was, even by Bahamian standards, out of all proportion to the legal services which he rendered... The enormity of the fee demanded and the speed and manner with which payment was effected... leave us in no doubt that he was selling his services

primarily as an influential Member of the Executive Council and not as a lawyer.[27]

One of the central contentions of the commission was the recurring and numerous conflicts of interest in which consultancies were granted in exchange for an exemption certificate to run a casino. Indeed, running through many deals made for all sorts of tourist activities in the Bahamas, and indeed in other countries, is a common factor: local politicians and foreign developers fostering close relationships. Politicians have often shown themselves to be badly advised, weak and easily corrupted by sophisticated criminals.

By the 1980s, Lynden Pindling himself was under investigation. The charges, relating to allegations made in the *Wall Street Journal*, were that Pindling and other top officials had been paid by Robert Vesco, the fugitive financier, and Colombian cocaine boss Carlos Lehder to allow drug smuggling into the US through the Bahamas. A royal commission confirmed the claims but could not prove the charges against Pindling, who survived the scandal. Two cabinet ministers, however, resigned. One was Kendal Nottage, minister for youth, sports and community affairs who became a front for Salvatore Caruana, a member of the American mafia. Caruana 'loaned' Nottage US$400,000 to buy the Islander Hotel in Freeport; the loan was only to be paid back if the hotel was sold. Meanwhile, Nottage and his wife set up front companies for Caruana.[28]

Such activities were typical of the evidence that emerged from the commission's 500-page report which recorded a hugely complex catalogue of shady business deals, in which millions of unaccountable dollars changed hands. What is relevant here is that most of the deals involved real estate or airlines, hotels or villas, casinos or catering firms, each one an intrinsic part of the tourist industry.

The international network of organised crime is such that it was not surprising that Sol Korzner of Sun City resort, southern Africa, allegedly involved in money-laundering activities, moved into the Bahamas in 1994. In a legitimate operation he bought Paradise Island Resort in Nassau (see Chapter Two).

Casino Economies

Gambling, as well as drugs and sex, is part of the package of alien and undesirable imports which is seen to undermine the moral well-being of the Caribbean people. While this view is largely church-based, a broader coalition has expressed unease about the economic and social consequences of casinos (gambling on horses and the lottery is considered a separate issue and more acceptable).

As early as 1979, a regional conference on the socio-cultural and environmental impact of tourism on Caribbean societies was held in Grenada, during the days of the People's Revolutionary Government. It concluded that gambling was not 'productive', that professional gamblers only spent money in the casino and that there was a 'high correlation between gambling and organised crime.' The 'gut feeling' of the conference was that 'gambling is not considered necessary or desirable' nor a useful extra 'attraction' for the tourist industry. It recommended that 'great caution' should be exercised by governments in deciding their policy on gambling.[29]

At that time, only a handful of Caribbean countries allowed gambling. Yet by 2002, this had changed and there were casinos in 16 Caribbean territories, including Aruba, Bonaire, Curaçao, St Maarten, Antigua, the Bahamas, Haiti, Guadeloupe, Martinique and the Dominican Republic. Of those, the Bahamas, Aruba and St Maarten in particular have built their tourist industry largely on the back of their casinos.

At an economic level, casinos provide employment and government income. In Puerto Rico, for example, its 17 casinos employ thousands of people and gross US$2 billion annually. Whether they boost tourist arrivals is another question, although the casino culture appears to be on a global roll. Cruise ships, too, have added casinos to their unending list of attractions (see Chapter Seven) while, on land, hotels continue to promote their casinos as a desirable night-time attraction.

So the pressure to introduce casinos has gathered pace although the 'no to casinos' lobby remains in place. The classic approach is for a developer to agree to build a hotel only if a casino licence is included in the deal. The St Lucia government, for example, turned down a casino-hotel complex on Pigeon Point causeway only after churches and other island organisations campaigned against it in the early 1990s.

In Barbados, attempts to introduce casinos have been rebuffed for many years. 'We don't have casinos in Barbados,' said the permanent secretary in the ministry of tourism in February 1994, 'but tomorrow is another day.' Indeed, less than one year later, the new Barbados Labour Party government of Prime Minister Owen Arthur announced a commission of inquiry into casino gambling but later accepted its recommendations against the introduction of casinos – a policy that remains in place.

In Jamaica, Butch Stewart of Sandals resorts commented that the traditional anti-casino view has become outdated. What was important, said Stewart, was to ensure that the casino management was impeccably regulated. In Jamaica, hotels have installed gaming rooms with computer-simulated versions of casino games, while yet-to-be-built resorts are planned with casinos. In Dominica, the idea that casino gambling might boost flagging tourism arrivals prompted the minister of tourism not to dismiss the prospect entirely while a tourism official said that the government would have no choice if it was part of a hotel investment package.

Even Cuba, as it expanded its mass tourist base, relaxed its anti-gambling laws when in 1994 a cruise ship, the Santiago de Cuba, operated the first casino in Cuba since 1959. The ship, jointly owned by Italian investors Havana Cruises and the government enterprise Havanatur, began its day trips with gaming tables and one-armed bandits open once outside territorial waters. There, Cubans with dollars gambled alongside foreigners. Once the gambling capital of the Caribbean, if not the world, Cuba was being lured back into the world of blackjack by tourist demand and joint-venture enticements. Even so, in 2003, while inaugurating a new resort, Castro said, 'You won't see any casinos here.'[31]

Street Crime

Drug dealing, political repression and institutionalised corruption have less impact on arrivals than the one-off shooting of a tourist or serial muggings. Tourism attracts crime, while at the same time crime repels tourists. It also creates conditions which attract crime in the street as well as in boardrooms, in particular when First World wealth meets Third World poverty, and especially where there is mass tourism. Crime directed against tourists, largely robbery and mugging and often drug-related, is a feature of tourism in the Caribbean, as it is in many other countries.

Yet, the overall level of crime against tourists in the Caribbean has remained small. Barbados, for example, recorded only 245 crimes against tourists in 1998 when arrivals numbered more than half a million. An earlier analysis of reported crime in Barbados, between 1989 and 1993, found that residents were much more likely to be victims of violent crime than tourists. However, according to this police report, 'guests are disproportionately victimised by property crime and robbery. The tourist as victim is likely to be caused by perceptions of wealth, the relaxed, holiday mode of the tourist and so on.' Even so, a parallel survey of crime against tourists, commissioned by the Barbados Hotel Association, reported that 92 per cent of tourists rated Barbados as safe. And even in violence-flecked Jamaica, only 1,500 tourists (or 0.02 per cent of the total arrivals) reported being victims of crime.

A country-by-country assessment on safe travel is proffered by the UK's Foreign and Commonwealth Office (FCO) in London. It provides a guide to tourists (and an insurance for the FCO). In 2002 Haiti was the only Caribbean country featured in its list of pariah states which should not be visited 'unless on essential business' while advice for other countries in the Caribbean contained the sort of information that one might expect. For Barbados, for example, the FCO declared that: 'Most visits to Barbados are trouble free. However, armed and violent crime does occur on the island and has recently increased. Visitors should take normal common sense precautions.' It does not, in fact, suggest any alarming local conditions, and its advice could apply to just about anywhere.

High crime levels within communities and, in particular, against tourists strike horror into the hearts of tourism officials, especially when the reports are given high-profile coverage in the international press. Throughout the region, increasing crime rates are met with conferences and workshops, with demands for government to take a stand against criminals and with calls for the execution of convicted murderers. The tourist industry knows that flurries of cancellations, especially from the ultra-sensitive US market, come swiftly in the wake of gruesome crime reports.

Jamaica, in particular, with more than 1,000 murders a year, continues to suffer from high rates of drug-related organised crime, political violence and gang shoot-outs by hardmen from the yards of Kingston. From time to time such activity spills over into the tourist areas, especially the resorts of Ocho Rios, Montego Bay and Negril. A survey of residents in those three Jamaican resort towns revealed that sex, drugs and crime were the issues thought to contribute most to the negative effects of tourism.

When, for example, two middle-aged Americans were robbed and shot while rafting on Jamaica's Rio Grande river, one of the island's most popular and imaginative tourist attractions, the response from the local tourist leaders was characteristic. Hotelier Butch Stewart of Sandals said that crime, if left unchecked, would destroy the tourist industry, and the Jamaican Hotel and Tourist Association demanded 'swift and decisive punishment' for those convicted of such 'heinous acts'.[32] In a flurry of activity, the government announced that armed military patrols would patrol resorts. Some hoteliers did not welcome these moves, arguing that soldiers and guns sent out 'the wrong message' to holiday-makers, while others said that crime had dropped and that the gun-toting officers had not worried the tourists. (Stewart's own long-term solution to the problem has been to make his hotels all-inclusive resorts so that his guests have no need to move beyond the well-patrolled perimeter fences of his properties.)

Concerned that Jamaica's reputation has been tarnished by its high murder rate, Tourism Minister Carlyle Dunkley announced another initiative to tackle security: this time a joint police and military task force was put to work to round up drug dealers and illegal vendors. Such attempts to contain violence against tourists lie at the more extreme end of the crime and tourism spectrum.

Most Caribbean islands do not experience anything like the violence of Jamaica, although many are reporting higher crime rates than before. Even so, the first regional conference on crime and tourism in the Caribbean was not held until 1993. The conference concentrated on the practical difficulties involved in protecting tourists given the limited resources of police and judicial systems. The problems ranged from inadequate policing and police training, poor hotel security and the fact that even when a crime against a tourist is reported to the police, it rarely comes to court because of a backlog of cases. Grenada, for example, introduced night sittings of magistrates' courts to try and deal with this and changed the law to give beach security officials powers of arrest.

One of the most pressing concerns at a sub-criminal level involves the harassment of visitors by beggars, unofficial vendors, drug sellers and self-styled tour guides. The first survey to gather and analyse data on harassment took place in Barbados between 1991-94. Of the nearly 7,800 visitors surveyed, 59 per cent said they had experienced some sort of harassment. It mainly took place on the beach, followed by the streets and while shopping in the capital, Bridgetown. Both men and women experienced harassment, with men being pursued by drug sellers and women by vendors, and women subjected to sexual harassment. Younger visitors were more likely to be harassed than older tourists while first-time visitors reported more harassment than repeat visitors, who had become more adept at dealing with harassers. The main problem, experienced by 80 per cent of visitors, was harassment by unofficial vendors, followed by drug peddlers (27 per cent), verbal abuse (14 per cent), sexual harassment (8 per cent) and physical abuse (2 per cent).[33]

In response, the tourist authorities suggested a number of measures to combat the problem: police patrols on beaches and main tourist areas who would both protect visitors from harassment and also pursue unlicensed vendors while some hoteliers provided booths for vendors to work from. A new law was also introduced; however, this targets vagrants rather than vendors. The problem with all these initiatives is that the 'harassers' themselves do not percieve that they are behaving badly; they cannot see that they are a nuisance and they emphasise their need to make a living.

To move towards the criminalisation of harassment is not a simple procedure. In 1994, the CTO commissioned a study to determine whether legislation was required so that harassment could be legally codified. It also recognised that in taking that approach, it created the potential for 'developing laws for the protection of tourism.'[34] However, there is some thinking that harassment is not a matter for the police but a social issue which requires an educational approach and turns on the fundamental problem of attitude and benefit.[35]

This is sometimes ignored by tourist boards and hoteliers, in their demands for greater punishment and tightened-up security. Yet the contrast between the conspicuous consumption of hotel life and the economic stress and poverty beyond the security gate presents fundamental questions about the impact of the tourist business. As Jean Holder put it: 'As Caribbean countries become more dependent on tourism, as other economic sectors fail (putting more and more people out of work), as wealth and poverty are brought into greater proximity, the levels of crime due to need or greed, and harassment of visitors by hard-selling vendors, can be expected to increase.'[36]

An even more forthright view was provided by Orville Durant, former commissioner of the Royal Barbados Police Force. At a conference on crime and tourism, Durant pointed out that the Caribbean was a 'post-colonial society' in which no recognition had been given to the problems and needs of such a society. The emphasis of the tourist industry was, he said, 'only in terms of increasing the numbers of visitors without any regard to the negative impact of that increase on the society, particularly where legitimate alternatives are limited and balanced economic development is non-existent.'[37]

In one academic analysis of crime in the Caribbean, the authors concluded that public education, of both tourists and locals, is an instrument for improving visitor safety. Such initiatives, however, 'can only be effective in crowded, fast-paced mass destinations when combined with a strong comprehensive policy that reflects community control over the size and direction of tourism and that emphasizes widespread local participation in industry benefits.'[38]

Similar conclusions were drawn by Dunn & Dunn in their look at public perceptions about Jamaica's tourist industry where a majority of visitors (55.8 per cent in 1997) said they had been harassed. In response, the government introduced an anti-harassment programme and increasing penalties for street harassment. Dunn & Dunn, however, looked at alternative solutions. Their findings centre on the importance of education (some of the hustlers did not perceive that their behaviour had a negative effect on tourists) and planning (embracing the offenders by engaging them in mainstream tourism as guides). They also urged the importance of public awareness programmes (see Chapter Three) to educate people in the link between harassment and a decline in repeat visitors and the fact that harassment drives tourists into all-inclusives. Anti-poverty and employment programmes were wider initiatives which would have to underpin any attempts to reduce harassment.[39]

So perhaps it always comes back to that calypso, 'Alien', with its chorus of frustration and loss:

What's the point of progress
Is it really success?
If we gain ten billion
But lose the land we live on.

It is a succinct enough popular interpretation of the warnings of the policeman (Durant) and the bureaucrat (Holder) to suggest that the social impact of tourism can damage the well-being of both visitors and hosts.

Most governments and development institutions have long ignored the social impacts of tourism. 'Few destinations have made it an active point to incorporate social indicators in order to monitor the impact of tourism on a given locale,' wrote Kim Thurlow, who has examined social capital in relation to tourism development in Dominica.[40] Nowhere, she said, does Dominica examine the social impact of more tourists except to say that communities should be involved in the process of tourism development. The emphasis is all on economic indicators. This position is certainly not unique. And while measuring social capital – the value of social networks – is complicated, understanding how tourism affects social organisations and relationships between individuals is a key to understanding the way tourism affects small vulnerable communities, such as those in the Caribbean.

There is a faint hint that the tourism establishment has begun to acknowledge the social impact of tourism. The CTO's strategic plan includes the following words: 'Tourism will have been placed squarely within a national policy framework of social and economic development that encourages and strengthens linkages with other sectors, and speaks to the issues of poverty alleviation, sustainability and conservation of the national patrimony by reorienting policies, attitudes and perceptions related to tourism.' This statement acknowledges that tourism must be linked to the people and must be endorsed by them; at the same time, tourism policy must address the basic needs of the poor. The responsibility for the social parameters of tourism has now been acknowledged, if only tangentially.

While, within the private sector, an interest in environmental accountability is evolving (see Chapter Five), this has, so far, not been matched by the idea of corporate social responsibility. The social issues around tourism, as this chapter has pointed out, are particularly complex and sensitive and require far greater discussion and analysis.

NOTES

1.   *Outlet*, Antigua and Barbuda, 14 October 1994
2.   Frank Fonda Taylor, *To Hell With Paradise: A History of the Jamaican Tourist Industry*, Pittsburg, 1993, p.171
3.   *Caribbean Insight*, 10 November 2000
4.   *The Independent*, London, 5 August 1991
5.   Martin Amis, 'St Lucia' in *Visiting Mrs Nabokov and Other Excursions*, London, 1994, p.72
6.   Fonda Taylor, op. cit., p.153
7.   See Robert Potter, 'Urbanisation in the Caribbean and Trends of Global Convergence-Divergence', *Geographical Journal*, vol 159, 1993, p.1-21
8.   *Outlet*, 11 March 1994
9.   Gerardo Mosquera, 'Hustling the Tourist in Cuba', Poliester, London, vol 3, no 10. (Jinetear, literally meaning riding or jockeying, is the slang term used in Cuba for providing services, particularly sexual, to tourists.)
10. Cited in Peggy Antrobus, 'Gender Issues in Caribbean Tourism.' Paper given at conference on Tourism and Socio-Cultural Change in the Caribbean, Trinidad, 1990
11. Paul Layne, 'Sunny Barbados', *Bim*, vol 13, Barbados, 1969, p.48
12. *Daily Nation*, Barbados, 1 June 2002
13. *The How to be Jamaican Handbook*, Kingston, 1992, p.40
14. Cecilia Karch and Dann, Graham, 'Close Encounters of the Third World', *Human Relations*, vol 34, no 4, 1981
15. Neil Price, *Behind the Planter's Back: Lower-Class Responses to Marginality in Bequia Island, St Vincent*, London, 1988, p.231
16. *The Guardian*, 24 August 1995
17. *El País*, Madrid, 8 November 1993
18. *New Internationalist*, May 1998
19. *Cuba Business*, London, June 1994
20. Quoted in Mette Louise Rundle, 'Tourism Social Change and Jineterismo in Contemporary Cuba', Society for Caribbean Studies annual conference papers, Vol 2, 2001
21. *Time*, New York, 6 December 1993
22. Mark Connolly, 'Sex Tourism and Children in the Dominican Republic', paper for Defense of Children International, New York, 1992
23. Cited in *Sun, Sex, and Gold, Tourism and Sex Work in the Caribbean*, edited by Kamala Kempadoo, Rowman & Littlefield, 1999
24. Gillian Clissold, 'Divergent International Perspectives on the Caribean', Caribbean briefing paper, Georgetown University project, April 1998
25. Bureau of International Narcotics Matters, 1994, op. cit.
26. Ibid.
27. Philip Cash, Gordon, Shirley and Saunders, Gail, *Sources of Bahamian History*, London, 1991, p.300
28. *Sunday Times* Magazine, London, 29 September 1985
29. Regional Conference on the Socio-Cultural and Environmental Impact of Tourism on Caribbean Societies, 'Recommendations', Grenada, 1979
30. *Caribbean Week*, Barbados, 7-20 January 1995
31. La Nacion, online newspaper, Miami, lanacioncubana.com, April 2003
32. *Barbados Advocate*, Barbados, 15 February 1994
33. Klaus de Albuquerque and JL McElroy, 'Visitor Harassment: Barbados Survey Results', *Annals of Tourism Research*, vol 28, no 2, 2001
34. CANA, 14 September 1994
35. CANA, December 6 1996

36.   Jean Holder, 'The Caribbean Tourism Organisation's Role in Caribbean Tourism Development' in Dennis Gayle and Goodrich, Jonathan (eds), *Tourism, Marketing and Management in the Caribbean*, London, 1993, p.215

37.   Orville Durant, paper delivered at conference on Crime and Tourism in the Caribbean, St Lucia, 1993

38.   Klaus de Alburquerque and JL McElroy, 'Research, Tourism and Crime in the Caribbean', *Annals of Tourism Research* Vol 26, No 4, 1999

39.   Hopeton Dunn and Leith Dunn, *People and Tourism, Issues and Attitudes in the Jamaican Hospitality Industry*, Arawak, 2003

40.   Kim Thurlow, Social Capital and Tourism in Dominica, unpublished paper, 2002

5

GREEN CRIME, GREEN REDEMPTION: THE ENVIRONMENT AND ECOTOURISM

When Christopher Columbus went ashore on Crooked Island, Bahamas, in October 1492 he wrote:

> Here and in all the island everything is green and the vegetation is like April in Andalusia. And the singing of the birds is such that it would seem that a man would never wish to leave here. And the flocks of parrots that darken the sun, and birds of so many kinds so different from our own that it is a marvel! And then there are trees of a thousand kinds all producing their own kind of fruit, and all wonderfully aromatic...[1]

Four hundred years later, a Victorian traveller, E.A. Hastings Jay, described his first sight of a tropical beach at Hastings, Barbados: 'There were the cocoa-nut palms, with clusters of green cocoa-nuts, growing all long the sea-line out of the soft, white sand, with beautiful rainbow colours in the water as it moved lazily backwards and forwards, glittering in the brilliant sunlight.'[2]

And so it remained. Accounts by visiting Europeans, whatever their purpose in the region, continued to marvel at the Caribbean's pristine physical beauty in diaries, letters, travelogues and novels, straining for the words to describe that beguiling landscape. Even by the 1940s, when the US war correspondent Martha Gellhorn passed through the British Virgin Islands, little had changed. Despite 400 years of European exploitation, the coasts were largely untouched: it was the flat hinterlands that had been transformed, in the 18th century, into prairies of cane and slavery. Gellhorn came across a cove which was 'a place where nothing had changed since time began, a half circle of white sand, flanked by huge squarish smooth rocks, the rocks overlapping to form cool caves and the water turquoise blue above the furrows of the sandy sea-bed.'[3] Returning many years later, she found her cove 'full of sun-tanned bodies and ringed by boats, from swan yachts to rubber Zodiacs, and there were bottles and plastic debris on the sea-bed and picnic litter on the sand for the rich are as disgusting as the poor in their carelessness of the natural world.'[4] The magic had become tainted.

Yet it is that Caribbean canvas, brushed blue for the sea and sky, green for vegetation and yellow for sand, so conveniently splashed with hummingbirds and hibiscus, coconut palms and sunsets, that tourists have come to expect. Those well-edited images of the Caribbean environment are available to consumers. For tourists have traditionally been lured to the Caribbean for its climate, sea and beaches, not for its mountains or rivers, its cities or ruined battlements. Such demand has put those coastlines under enormous pressure.

The sort of tourism that now dominates the Caribbean, as Martha Gellhorn noted, has redefined its physical landscape. Tourism brought about the region's second invasion of land-snatchers. First it was the planters who changed the natural environment when they cleared the land for sugar (islands now almost treeless, like Barbados and Antigua, were once shaggily forested). In the past half a century, it has been the coastline which has been cleared – for however much Europeans admired the Caribbean paradise, they could not resist claiming it and 'improving' it.

The Nobel prize-winning poet Derek Walcott, who was born and brought up in St Lucia, has been a stern critic of the way tourism has changed his homeland. In his acceptance address for the prize, he made his view clear in eloquent terms.

> But in our tourist brochures the Caribbean is a blue pool into which the republic dangles the extended foot of Florida as inflated rubber islands bob, and drinks with umbrellas float towards her on a raft. This is how the islands from the shame of necessity sell themselves; this is the seasonal erosion of their identity, that high-pitched repetition of the same images of service that cannot distinguish one island from the other, with a future of polluted marinas, land deals negotiated by ministers, and all of this conducted to the music of Happy Hour and the rictus of a smile. What is the earthly paradise for our visitors? Two weeks without rain and a mahogany tan, and, at sunset, local troubadours in straw hats and floral shirts beating 'Yellow Bird' and 'Banana Boat Song' to death.[5]

Such passion has an intensity that few should attempt to imitate. Witness an academic saying roughly the same thing: 'Conflict is most evident in small, ecologically fragile islands that have restructured their colonial export staple economies towards tourism by establishing transformational infrastructure and large-scale resort complexes along delicate coastlines.'[6]

Those coastal clearances have been along white sand beaches, on ancient and ground-down coral, predominantly on the sheltered coastlines away from the rougher Atlantic shores. Large concrete hotels have been built close to the high-water mark, groynes and piers erected, marinas for yachts and deep-water harbours for cruise ships constructed. The great wetlands of the Caribbean have been grubbed out by developers eyeing their proximity to some of the region's best beaches. In Jamaica, Montego Bay's international airport was built on a wetland, while at nearby Ocho Rios, 40 acres of swamp was turned into a resort with 4,000 beds and a cruise ship pier.[7] More recently the extension to the airport on Beef Island, British Virgin Islands, has meant the destruction of the largest grouping of the rare lignum vitae trees in the islands. Critics of plans for a megaport at Punta Caucedo in the Dominican Republic have said that dredging would endanger the coral reefs and beach of Boca Chica. Still the clearances continue.

In a generation, land and seascapes have been transformed: the bays where once local fishermen pulled in their seine nets, where villagers went for a sea bath or where colonies of birds nested in mangrove stands now provide for the very different needs of tourists.

These transformations have been superimposed on an environment vulnerable to change. The CTO's Jean Holder warned in 1988: 'Our tourism product is our environment. We therefore destroy our environment at our economic peril.'[8] Others have also warned of the dangers. In the mid 1990s, Calvin Howell, the then director of the Caribbean Conservation Association (CCA), talked about the Caribbean's fragility and how the environment was 'tourism's resource'. He went on to say that there were 'countless examples throughout the region to suggest that the tendency is to overlook the well-being of the environment in order to maximise the tourist dollar. Significantly, he added, 'it is hard to find examples of good practice.' The critical thread has continued. By 2000 a member of the natural resources management unit of the Organisation of Eastern Caribbean States stated: 'There is a limit to how well one can develop one's tourism infrastructure, if the natural resource on which that infrastructure is being built is itself destroyed.'[9]

A Catalogue of Destruction

'The problems causing coastal resources degradation in the region [the Caribbean] have not changed significantly over the past decades, though the scope of the problem appears to have increased,' reported the United Nations Environment Plan in 1997.[10] The catalogue of coastal and marine destruction directly or indirectly attributed to the growth of the tourist industry is long. It includes erosion of beaches, breakdown of coral reefs, marine and coastal pollution from watersports, dumping of waste and release of raw sewage, sand mining, and destruction of wetlands and salt ponds. In many cases, the impact is interrelated, locked into a chain of tourist development where short-term gain takes precedence over long-term protection. For example, a hotel cuts down coastal trees to improve the view from its rooms; this accelerates coastal erosion and sand loss. A jetty is then built for a new dive shop and even more sand is lost because sand from the newly shaped beach is washed onto the coral reef. The result is two-fold: the sandy beach has become smaller and the marine environment has been spoiled. And both land and sea are more exposed to damage from hurricanes. What originally drew the tourists no longer exists in its pristine condition.

The impact of tourism is not only multi-faceted, it also depends on the size of the tourist sector, the growth rate of tourism and the style and content of the tourism facilities themselves. For many of the Caribbean's smaller islands and communities, the greater the number of tourists, the greater the pressure on the physical environment and the demands on those limited natural resources. Even without tourists, Barbados, for example, is densely populated, with over 250,000 people on an island 21 miles long by 14 miles wide. The majority live along the narrow coastal strips of the south and west coasts (roughly one-sixth of the island). These two coastlines are also the heartland of the tourist industry, packing in more than half a million stayover visitors and the same number of cruise passengers per year. The result has been an overwhelming pressure on the tourist zones.

Yet in the bid to keep the tourists coming, and especially the rich, Barbados fell in love with golf. It is a game which requires space; it also uses 600,000 gallons of water per course per day. The Royal Westmoreland Golf and Country Club, a US$400 million residential and tourist resort, is the island's largest private investment, but its 27-

hole golf course was completed without an environmental impact assessment. According to objectors led by the Caribbean Conservation Association and the Barbados National Trust, the problem was that despite laws which addressed environmental problems, there was 'considerable lack of political will to enforce them.'[11] The Barbados government appeared not to question the problem of water shortages or the pesticides required to maintain golf courses; by 2002 Barbados had four 18-hole courses.

This is just one example of how the region as a whole pays lip service to the environment, but – with some important exceptions – it has allowed its degradation to continue largely unchecked and unmanaged, so long as tourist arrival figures look good. One of the worst offenders has been Antigua and Barbuda. This twin-island state, which is heavily dependent on tourism, promotes itself as 'the heart of the Caribbean'.[12] As the official blurb has it: 'With 365 powdery white sand beaches (one for every day of the year), a wide variety of hotels and other accommodation, a fascinating history and warm, friendly people, the islands offer an exotic and unspoilt paradise in the Heart of the Caribbean.' Yet the growth of its resorts has been at the expense of the environment. The creation of the Jolly Beach hotel and marina, for example, involved the destruction of 'large areas of mangroves (by filling them in), part of a nearby beach (by dredging) and seagrass coral habitats (by creating siltation).'[13] Local communities lost beach access, opportunities for crab hunting and coconut gathering and the absence of the mangroves increased vulnerability to flooding.

North of Jolly Beach, on one of the busiest stretches of coast, is the sandy sweep of Dickenson Bay and nearby Runaway Bay. There, hotels (including the all-inclusive Sandals) and restaurants edge the beach, facing seas used by scuba divers and snorkellers, windsurfers and waterskiers. Locals familiar with the recent history of the area are reluctant to swim in its murky waters, have complained of itchy skin and, during some months of the year, peculiar smells. The cause may lie close by. Behind the beach, on a spit of land that divides Dickenson Bay from the more southerly Runaway Bay, is a former salt pond, part of an expanse of wetland called McKinnons Saltpond. Wetlands such as salt ponds, lagoons and mangrove stands have several important functions: they are wildlife habitats and provide nesting grounds for birds; mangroves also act as nurseries for reef fish and lobsters; they collect and filter the rainwater run-off which damages coral reefs and sea grass meadows. The tangled root structure of mangroves also holds the land together and so functions as the last line of defence against the sea, providing protection against land erosion, sea surge and storm damage.

McKinnons Saltpond in Antigua was no exception, even if it had earlier been subjected to damage from oil spills from a now abandoned refinery. Yet like thousands of other stretches of mangrove throughout the Caribbean, the attractions of unused land close to stretches of fine sandy beach were too great a temptation for developers to ignore. In the mid 1980s the St John's Development Corporation, a statutory government body, and an Italian investment company planned to build condominiums and a marina on land that included the salt pond. Before this could happen an environmental impact assessment was made which recorded, among other things, that the condition of the reef at that point was 'fair' and that the salt pond prevented the outflow of polluted fresh water into the two bays. It recommended various remedies to limit the environmental damage that would be incurred by the Marina Bay Condominiums project.[14]

The report was shelved and the project went ahead. Part of the pond was reclaimed by dredge-and-fill methods and the condominiums were built. Within a few years the impact of these changes had been felt: divers confirmed that there was dead coral on the reef, together with fewer fish, turbid water and patches of dead sea grass around the dredge channel. The salt pond, which had become a swamp, also suffered. Its mangroves began to die because untreated sewage from hotels was periodically emptied into the swamp. For several consecutive summers following the draining of the pond, thousands of fish died from lack of oxygen, their bodies rising to the surface of the rotting swamp. To solve this problem, the government pumped sea water into the swamp. The 'diluted' sewage spilled out of the swamp and ran down onto the beaches before escaping into the sea to join the frolicking tourists. There were also reports of raw hotel sewage being pumped directly into the sea that laps at its frontage and so, as one observer noted: 'dispersing offal among the tourists, who are so happy to be in the sun, they do not notice what else they are in.'[15]

Antigua is not alone. According to a 1994 study commissioned for the CTO at the request of Caricom governments, the treatment facilities of water waste in many hotels were of 'limited value with regard to the treatment of micro-biological and nutrient removal.' The report added: 'It was found that few hotels operated treatment plants that complied with the US Environmental Protection Agency recommendations.' While conditions in the larger resorts have now improved (see below), at that time 80 to 90 per cent of sewage was disposed of in near-shore coastal waters, near hotels, on beaches and around coral reefs and mangroves, without adequate treatment, according to the report.[16]

It is not just the creation of big resorts that threaten the environment: small hotels often do not score as high as the bigger complexes in terms of sewage control. Island Resources Foundation pointed out that Grande Anse beach in Grenada had been contaminated by a proliferation of small hotels. The reason? None of them could afford adequate sewage treatment. Housing for hotel staff and ancillary workers also sprang up in the same area, but these homes too had no proper sewage.

Sand mining is another cause of environmental degradation in coastal areas; the removal of sand from beaches for use as construction material has a long-term impact beyond the specific act of vandalism. The worst incidences of sand mining have been in Barbuda, according to Edward Henry, a founder of the Environmental Awareness Group, the island's only environmental watchdog. Where there used to be miles of 'pristine sand', said Henry, beaches disappeared, their sand shipped to places like the Virgin Islands to build other beaches.

In Tobago, a surge in sand mining coincided with the expansion of tourism. Both the airport extension and the deep-water harbour at the island's capital, Scarborough, were constructed with the use of sand from local beaches. As local naturalist David Rooks pointed out, 'The beaches are Tobago's tourism mainstay, take them away and your tourist goes away... Furthermore, the sand contains micro-organisms, so without the sand another part of the food chain has gone.' Goldsborough beach, for example, had already shown the effect of mining: the sand is black, the beach has narrowed and it is littered with dead and rotting plants and trees. 'No one, tourist or local, goes there any more,' reported a local newspaper.[17]

A Sick Sea

Beaches are destroyed not only by sand mining and careless construction but also by coastal erosion. Wave motions move sand along coastlines and replenishment occurs naturally. But this equilibrium has been disrupted on many Caribbean beaches by groynes and piers, built to trap the movement of sand. On the west coast of Barbados, some beaches have been reported as receding at a rate of 1.5 metres per decade.[18] Those sandy beaches are made up of coral, thrown up on the coastline from the continuous erosion of the reefs which ring Caribbean islands. When the Caribbean archipelagos were created, colonies of corals were formed just below the surface. The coral comprises millions of living polyps which depend on specific environmental conditions to survive; these include warm, clear and unpolluted water, strong wave action, oxygen and plenty of sunlight. In return, coral reefs provide an important barrier against coastal erosion and in themselves create a source of food for both humans and marine life. Without the reefs, the sand eventually disappears to expose a mass of jagged limestone, the antithesis of the desirable beach.

Approximately 14 per cent of the world's coral reefs are found in the Caribbean region. Globally, some 90 per cent of all reefs are considered damaged and those in the Caribbean are no exception. Tourism is one of the causes. All over the Caribbean, environmentalists and divers have reported tales of reef abuse: snorkellers and scuba divers break branching coral with their flippers and kill marine life by spearfishing; tourists destroy the shallow, exposed coral by walking on it in plastic sandals (the Buccoo Reef in Tobago); anchors of cruise ships, dive-boats and yachts drag over the coral, ripping it to shreds (the US Virgin Islands and Cayman Islands) and dump their garbage overboard, further damaging the reefs (the Grenadines); fishermen either dynamite the reefs or overfish them, their catches of lobster and conch going to feed tourists (US Virgin Islands); souvenir shops loot the reef for stock, loading their shelves with shells, dead coral and seahorses (Bahamas); beach vendors sell the rare black coral made into earrings (Grenada) and backs of endangered turtles (Barbados).

From the land, the reefs have also been under threat as they become smothered by sediment from run-off caused by destruction of mangroves and salt ponds for hotels and marinas (Jamaica); from airport construction (Bequia) or dredging to build marinas (Rodney Bay, St Lucia); from sewage plant leakage (Buccoo Reef, Tobago); or from soil erosion and excessive use of agricultural chemicals (most territories).

All these factors have chipped away at the Caribbean's reefs, including its finest and most prestigious reef, the 150-mile long Belize Barrier Reef, the second largest in the world after Australia's Great Barrier Reef. Belize has rapidly expanded its tourist business, from under 100,000 visitors in 1985 to more than 250,000 cruise and stayover visitors in 2000. The damage to the reef, including rapid depletion of its fauna and well-being, has occurred within the timespan of the tourist boom.

Yet neither the beaches, the reefs, nor the wetlands of the region can be separated from the Caribbean Sea itself, which has become increasingly polluted. Oil tankers and other ships passing through the Caribbean have dumped oil and garbage. There has also been anxiety over the transshipment of hazardous nuclear substances in ships passing to and from Europe and Japan by way of the Panama Canal.

It is the dumping of cruise ship waste, however, which has been the focus of most concern. The cruise ship industry (see Chapter Seven) has grown and grown: an average of 200 cruises take 400,000 cruisers to Caribbean ports every month. Each passenger, says the International Maritime Organisation, generates up to 2 kg of waste per day. But it is not how much that is necessarily the problem; what is problematic is where cruise ships put all that waste.

The Marpol Convention, the international treaty on pollution by ships (1978) prohibits the dumping of food waste and sewage in coastal waters and of plastics anywhere at sea. Most Caribbean countries have now ratified this convention although all must ratify it before the 'special area' status of the Caribbean can be enforced. Despite Marpol, for many years the Caribbean remained a readily available dustbin. 'There can be little doubt that hitherto cruise lines have been somewhat negligent in this area,' wrote a cruise industry analyst in 1994 .[19]

This was illustrated in 1993 when Princess Cruise Lines was fined US$500,000 after pleading guilty in a US court to violating anti-pollution laws. A passenger had made a video of crew members of the Regal Princess dumping plastic bags stuffed with rubbish into the seas off the Florida coast during a Caribbean cruise in 1991. Two years later, another cruise company, Kloster Cruise Lines, was fined US$4,000 by a Cayman Islands court for allowing harmful waste products to be discharged from one of its ships in George Town harbour. The Cayman Islands maximum fine is now US$592,400, in line with US penalties.[20] This was the first time a Caribbean country had imposed heavy fines for violating waste-disposal laws.

The prosecutions continued, but with fiercer penalties. In 1999, Royal Caribbean, one of the largest cruise companies, admitted to dumping oil and hazardous chemicals into the sea; it was fined US$18 million by the US government. A year earlier, it had been fined US$9 million for dumping oil off the coasts of Miami and Puerto Rico and falsifying its records.

The Center for Marine Conservation Organisation has noted that some cruise lines have adopted a much 'greener' approach to waste disposal. The Princess line, for example, after its fall from grace, had done 'an excellent job by focussing on waste reduction and recycling,' it was reported. The Princess Line now has a 'zero discharge programme' which has become the industry standard. New cruise ships have elaborate modern waste-processing facilities, which means that no waste needs to be discharged at sea (this excludes processed food waste which is allowed to be dumped outside the 12-mile territorial water limits). 'We do the compacting and separating the waste. All plastics are discharged in the US,' Bob Stenige of the giant Fantasy cruise ship has stated, 'but foods and so on are discharged in the Bahamas.' In 2001, the industry as a whole, through its International Council of Cruise Lines (ICCL), announced that its members had adopted mandatory environmental standards for its cruise ships. 'These environmental standards,' said the president of ICCL, 'show the cruise industry's commitment to the environment by developing new technologies and practices that minimise the impact of cruise ships on the oceans upon which our vessels sail.'[21]

This attempt to clean up the ocean has put extra strain on the land-based disposal facilities of the islands. Signatories to Marpol are obliged to provide waste disposal facilities for cruise ships. However, small islands have found it hard to provide appropriate sites for its own rubbish, let alone the rubbish cruise ships produce. Progress in the provision of facilities has, according to IMO, 'not been satisfactory.' All over the region garbage from all sources accumulates, usually occupying landfill sites such as wetlands, causing health and environmental hazards to adjacent residential, agricultural and tourist sites. On small islands, space is at a premium. Tourists increase the waste problem. The US Virgin Islands – with its high density and high energy-consumption style of tourism – had particular waste problems. According to the Island Resources Foundation, local pressure and a 'dump' fire on the island of St John caused the government to close all public dumps on St John. Rubbish was then taken daily to St Thomas and deposited on another overflowing dump, Bovoni, first created 30 years ago, where underground and surface burning caused smoke, fumes and flies close to a school, resorts and residential areas. The problems at Bovoni have continued despite the threat of a US$6.5 million fine and attempts to transform waste into solid energy.

Of course, it is not only tourism that creates rubbish. The region's elite has thrown out old ways (associated with backwardness) in favour of modernity, thus making their own careless contribution to environmental degradation, while its poor have also damaged the environment in their struggle to survive. They have collected coral to sell, killed wildlife, cut down vegetation, littered the beaches and thrown their own garbage into the sea. Although land has a specific cultural, economic and religious role in Caribbean societies, it has not traditionally been 'appreciated' in a European sense. Change has come with better education and a more European attitude, including the idea that natural beauty is to be admired for itself. Among those who have taken a lead in environmental awareness are the Rastafarians with their emphasis on the value of what is natural or 'irie', their knowledge of and care for the land, and their rejection of materialism. 'Better a piece of land than a big Cadillac,' according to a St Lucian Rasta elder.[22]

If the Rastas' words are heeded, sound environmental management would include education of local people about the environment and how to safeguard it. Caribbean children are now encouraged to participate in 'beautifying' the environment, to conserve plant and animal life, to understand how their environment works and how not to destroy it. The wider population has also slowly become engaged in understanding about sustainability through campaigns about litter control, pesticide use or building practices and so on – all part of a wider tourism awareness education programme (see Chapter Three).

Planners and Politicians

'The tourist who has a choice will not put up with litter, beach erosion, water pollution, dead coral reefs and other fallout from environmental neglect,' said Jean Holder of the CTO. Invoking the Butler tourism-cycle model (see Chapter One), Holder was referring to the last phase of that model – the point of self-destruction. 'As the place sinks under the weight of social friction and solid waste,' he said, 'all tourists exit, leaving behind derelict tourism facilities, littered beaches and countryside, and a resident population that cannot return to its old way of life.'

In the face of such a warning, who and what groups are working towards environmental sustainability and mitigating the negative impacts of tourism on the environment? And how effective are they? For, as the West Indian Commission's Time for Action put it: 'We cannot assume automatic victory in our battle against environmental degradation of our tourist destinations in the region.'[23]

One of the problems for the Caribbean is that many of the institutions and mechanisms that are required to best prevent the region from destroying what it most needs are either absent or faulty. This situation stems in part from a lack of trained people, scientific technology and funding in the public sector. Such problems have been exacerbated by, in some countries, a political dedication to short-term gain rather than long-term sustainability. This continues to plague the Caribbean's decision-making processes. Klaus de Albuquerque, an American academic who wrote extensively about the Caribbean, concluded: 'The hard reality is that the majority of Caribbean governments are the worst regional environmental offenders, and even in the most liberal of democracies, the kinds of participatory planning processes necessary for sustainable utilisation of resources are often absent.'[24]

Antigua again provides a template for how the cavalier behaviour of politicians can render environmental legislation almost meaningless. The story of the Coconut Hall development project shows how the interests of a developer (backed up by the government) were only thwarted by the efforts of a handful of local people concerned about another attack on the island's coastline. The events illustrate how weak environmental legislation and enforcement coupled with government collusion and neglect allow developers to take control of other people's environment.

Foster Derrick is an Antiguan businessman who has watched the way in which developers have influenced government, which in turn colludes with the interests of the developer. 'The government has wreaked havoc with the environment,' he says. 'We have allowed this to happen. The developers are inconsiderate and wield influence over the government. Developers will buy a tract of land, they get it at a good price because they are seen as facilitators. The quickest way to make money is to build as cheaply and destroy as much as possible. They have no feeling for the place.'

Foster Derrick's home faces an inlet of sea, Mercer's Creek, on the north coast of the island in a village called Seatons. On the other side of Mercer's Creek is a peaceful, uninhabited area of low-lying hillside and waterfront. The land is forested with thorn and loblolly trees and, at the water's edge, part of the last stretch of mangrove in Antigua, 50 per cent of which has already been destroyed. This is the site where the Italian developer, Canzone del Mare, planned to develop a tourist complex. In a one-page proposal submitted to the Antigua Development Control Authority for approval in 1992, Canzone del Mare described the scope of the 86-acre complex. It was to have a hotel with swimming pool, housing for some 120 people, shops, casino, open-air theatre, marina, yacht club, roads, tracks for cycles and pedestrians and a parking area for 310 cars.

The Development Control Authority is nominally responsible for planning approval, but its work, according to Derrick Foster, was hampered by staff shortages and governmental interference. As an environmental profile of Antigua and Barbuda (commissioned by the CCA and regional environmental bodies) reported: 'Inadequate development planning and control represent the greatest environmental threats' to the twin islands. [25]

Then the developers started bulldozing, clearing the vegetation from the hillside. It was the first time any local person had been aware of plans to develop Coconut Hall. Furthermore, it was difficult to learn who was behind the project and what was planned. Foster Derrick alerted the local Environment Awareness Group and looked for support from the villagers. This was difficult, he said: 'The majority are afraid to take sides because they are afraid their families could be victimised.' When four back-hoe excavators began to dig up the mangroves, the DCA issued instructions for this to stop. Foster and some colleagues defied the bulldozer by sitting down in front of it putting up a flag saying 'Respect our Laws, Defend our Laws'.

The DCA wrote to the developers to complain. 'I have found that the state of work currently undertaken is environmentally unfriendly,' wrote Tyrone Peters, the Town and Country Planner. 'Your earth-moving methodology has demonstrated that you care very little about the environment in which you propose to construct your project.' Peters instructed them to stop work immediately until an environmental impact assessment had been carried out. Later, the then minister of agriculture, Hilroy Humphries, wrote to the developers on DCA paper giving them permission to go ahead. Peters of the DCA was subsequently fired.

The bulldozers never returned. The resort was never built. But by then erosion from the bare hillsides of Coconut Hall had damaged the inner reefs of the creek. The mangroves have gone for ever, breaking the 18-mile stretch of Antigua's last stands of mangrove, an important hatchery for the lobsters that tourists crave.

Some years later, another developer arrived. This time a Malaysian businessman, Dato Tan Kay Hock, wanted to create an Asian Village in the same area. The resort was to include 1,000 rooms, a casino and golf course. Mindful of the earlier furore, the government required an environmental impact assessment to be made. Its report argued that the 'scale of the project was incongruent with the nature of the site.' It concluded: 'Due to Antigua's poor performance in mitigating adverse effects from tourism projects and major budgetary and other existing constraints to effective environmental management, we doubt that a project of this scale can be accommodated in the environment without major long-term damage, despite good intentions.' It was not what the government of Antigua would have wanted to hear. For a time, Dato Tan went away, a victim of the Far East financial crisis, but in 2002 the Antiguans were still in discussion with him.

A more controlled example of tourist expansion has been the South-East Peninsula development project on St Kitts. Even so, there were difficulties. The project was spearheaded by a new 10 kilometre road from Basseterre to the south-east tip of an uninhabited 4,000-acre peninsula. The peninsula has some of the island's best beaches in an area of dramatic beauty, and the new road twists along the sweeping and still empty peninsula with views of beaches and salt ponds at every turn. The US Agency for International Development (USAID), a major donor, stipulated stringent controls. A board was established, with representatives of both the public and private sector to act as the development control authority and to report to the minister.

Patrick Williams, then manager of the Development Board, expressed his caution (and the dilemmas facing Caribbean governments) when he said: 'We have attempted not to duplicate the mistakes of other islands. Other destinations have allowed developers to get away with too much. We are being careful; sometimes we wonder whether we are being too strict. But my feeling is that five years on when others have destroyed their beaches, we will still have ours.'

Williams was accurate in one sense: the beaches were still there, five years on; development, except for a resort at Frigate Bay, had been negligible. A US company, Casablanca, had started work on a hotel only to abandon its work when it went bankrupt, although by then it had spent US$2.5 million filling in a salt pond to erect a storage structure, while its bulldozers had damaged the landscape. Apart from this one project, which was alleged to have had the personal support of powerful interests in government, things moved slowly.

In Belize, environmental management strategies have been under pressure in another direction: keeping up with the enormous expansion in tourist arrivals. The Half Moon Caye Natural Monument, for example, is now a UNESCO world heritage site. Acclaimed for its biological diversity, its future is assured. However, before UNESCO stepped in the increase in tourism had already taken its toll: 'sparse supplies of fresh water, inadequate waste disposal facilities and a lack of electricity have led to environmental degradation,' while unregulated fishing offshore had diminished the stock of a number of species, it was reported in 1989.'[26]

But not all marine reserves become World Heritage sites. The Hol Chan Marine Reserve, for example, set up in 1987, is close to a rapidly expanding tourist centre on the southern tip of Ambergris Caye and a massive and long-proposed development on the northern part of the caye. By 1997, 35,000 tourists a year were visiting the reserve, and despite the area's protected status, its coral reefs had been infected with black band disease, an algae which attacks corals that have been knocked and broken. By then experts feared that 'carrying capacity' had been breached.[27] The issue was then whether to close the reserve to allow the coral to recover or to open new sites on the reef in order to spread the tourist load. It was a typical dilemma for management of environments under threat.

Beyond the conservation of the environment is the matter of the survival of people living within that environment. The creation of the Virgin Islands National Park on St John's illustrated how conservation created conflict between local needs and conservationists schooled in North American perceptions about natural wildernesses. Firstly, the landscape of the park, which reverted to 'nature', alienated the local residents, who had been used to cultivating the land; secondly, according to one study, the scheme's economic benefit to them was limited. 'The park service has not sought to stimulate local business outside the park, but rather seems to have circumvented it whenever possible,' reported an anthropologist.[28]

Whereas the Virgin Islands National Park is part of the US Park Service, a government agency, the well-being of most national parks in the Caribbean is often dependent on voluntary contributions or funding by outside agencies, such as the World Wildlife Fund. Both the El Yunque Tropical Rain Forest in Puerto Rico, a 28,000-acre bird sanctuary with a rich and rare variety of trees, and the Asa Wright Nature Reserve in Trinidad, which attracts naturalists and ornithologists, depend in part on visitors' receipts. Again, many of the most important protected sites in Belize, such as the Half Moon Caye and the Cockscomb basin wildlife sanctuary, are not managed by the Belize government but depend on the voluntary Belize Audubon Society for funding and management. The costs of running sanctuaries and maintaining national parks are high; the introduction of user fees and merchandising sales all contribute to management problems.

Managing the environment is a complex business. Protected status sometimes creates conflict between old and new functions, and managing these new relationships requires both a flexible and a holistic approach. It is one that has been adopted in St Lucia. There, the Soufrière Marine Management Area (SMMA) in the south of the island was formed in 1994 in acknowledgement of conflicts between local fishermen and divers and yachting people, who were the newer users of the same waters. A mechanism is now in place for dealing with the problem with different zones delineated for different purposes. The declaration on the SMMA's website tells the story.

> In this rich area, we find superb scenery, healthy and diverse coral reefs, valuable fish stocks and attractive beaches. Unfortunately, in recent years, these marine and coastal areas have been under increasing pressure from competing human activities. In response to these threats, local fishermen, hoteliers, divers, yacht operators, government agencies, and community groups came together and negotiated an agreement... Parties to the agreement believe that, with harmonious management and development, all economic activities can prosper without damaging the area's resources, now and in the future.

The SMMA, made up of all the stakeholders in the area, has found a way to manage conflict. 'You can not resolve conflicts for ever. What you must do is to manage conflicts,' said Yves Renard, former head of the Caribbean Natural Resources Institute in St Lucia. In its study on tourism and coastal degradation, the Island Resources Foundation identified the potential for such partnerships. 'These protected systems are becoming increasingly flexible as planners realise the benefits of exploring real multiple uses for an area, while seeking to preserve environmental amenity values.'[29] The SMMA is one of a handful of such schemes in the Caribbean which are 'people centred' and demonstrate an inclusive strategy for development. With an increase in revenues, collected from yachts and divers, and an increase in fish stocks, the SMMA is seeing the results for its members. 'The

SMMA has acted as a mobilising institution for the enhancement of wider civil society,' according to one study of Soufrière's coastal zone management. [30]

The Private Sector Wakes Up

In the wake of so much environmental destruction, the Caribbean's private sector has begun to recognise the problem and has started to engage in some damage limitation. There have always been some individual examples of good practice but, more significantly, the Caribbean Hotel Association (CHA) has begun to address its responsibilities to the environment. All these initiatives, however, remain in line with the World Travel and Tourism Council (WTTC) guidelines which state: 'Travel and tourism companies should seek to implement sound environmental principles through self-regulation, recognising that national and international intervention may be inevitable and that preparation is vital.' Such a position is what Martha Honey, in her book *Ecotourism and Sustainable Development*, has called 'a clear call for pre-emptive action to stave off outside regulation.' [31]

Within this framework, the CHA set up the Caribbean Alliance for Sustainable Tourism (CAST) in 1997 aimed at supporting Caribbean hotels to be better environmental managers. In 2002, CAST won the International Hotel Investment Forum's sustainable tourism pioneer award for 'their longstanding commitment to the sustainable development of Caribbean tourism.' The organisation provides member hotels with training and technical assistance and also involves them in the international Green Globe certification programme; the Caribbean has the most Green Globe certified properties of any region in the world. Various offshoots of CAST have been spawned to address particular environmental needs. The Caribbean Hotel Environmental Management Initiative (CHEMI), funded by USAID, for example, is aimed at small hoteliers 'to introduce [them] to the concept of environmental management.' CHEMI sells itself with a three-point 'win-win' situation: saving money, promoting recognition and customer satisfaction and helping with long-term sustainability. 'We are starting with everything on a voluntary basis and hope that people adopt it,' said a CHEMI official.

In Jamaica, a CHEMI programme embraces Environmental Audits for Sustainable Tourism (EAST), funded by USAID. Sea Splash Resort is one hotel helped by this initiative. An environmental audit was undertaken to identify how this 15-room hotel on Negril beach could improve its efficiency and reduce its environmental impacts. Sea Splash claims that, thanks to the programme, it has cut its water and electricity consumption and reduced the volume of its garbage sent to the landfill. It reported a saving of US$38,000 in its first three years – an average of US$800 per room per year.

At the other end of the hotel spectrum, the giant Sandals Resorts has also made an effort and spent money on environmental management. Its list of 'what we have done' for the environment includes: no disposable plastic plates and cups, no tree cutting, no aerosol products, a reduction of energy, use of recycled paper and so on. Its list of 'what we will do' includes increased solar power usage, yearly environmental audits, the recovery of water and energy from laundry effluent and so on. Sandals Negril was the first to get its Green Globe certification and by December 2003 Sandals became the first chain in the English-speaking Caribbean to be totally certified.

One interesting survey commissioned by British Airways and British Airways Holidays looked at the environmental impact of the hotel sector in St Lucia, now home to three Sandals Resorts. In particular it compared all-inclusives with conventional hotels. It drew attention to the fact that all-inclusives, by their nature, can 'stand alone,' often in remote areas of high ecological value. Thus the environmental impact is greatest at the point of planning. In terms of environmental management, however, the survey found that all-inclusives offer 'the ability to achieve economies of scale and operate coherent management systems.' Their sewage disposal systems, for example, were found to be operating efficiently, with attention paid to treatment plants. 'There is an opportunity for all-inclusive resorts, which have the capital and human resources to operate advanced environmental management programmes and to help raise the environmental standards of other tourist accommodations.'[32]

The Green Globe certification scheme was launched in 1992 by the WTTC at the first Earth Summit in Rio de Janeiro to oversee implementation of the Earth Summit's Agenda 21. Like the voluntary regulation supported by the WTTC, Green Globe has its critics: one tourism analyst has described it as 'PR fluff'. Part of its problem is that anyone can become a member of Green Globe: by paying a fee and promising to 'aspire to environmental improvement', any member can use the logo. While there is a standard of certification and regular auditing, commentators have pointed out that there is too much of a vested interest to allow for independent verification. CAST has become heavily involved in promoting Green Globe and, for some critics, this has meant an overemphasis on certification, which is sometimes a deterrent for small hotels. There are different ways to promote environmental responsibility and good practice other than certification, said one expert in the field. The Caribbean is also working on an alternative certification programme called Quality Tourism for the Caribbean, which concentrates on health and safety.

A short-lived initiative by British Airways Holidays in 1997 (in partnership with the International Hotels Environment Initiative) went down a more demanding route. Following an audit of 100 Caribbean hotels used by British Airways Holidays, 16 of them were awarded an environmental logo. The idea was to set a benchmark, to indicate good standards of practice. The audit covered nine areas, including waste, water and energy management, and less obviously, community relations and purchasing policy. Hotels such as Half Moon Club in Jamaica, Galley Bay in Antigua and Le Sport in St Lucia attained the standard. However, this interesting programme was not continued after 2001. While the hotels were keen on it, customer awareness was not so evident (see Chapter Six).

The Blue Flag scheme for working towards clean beaches is also soon to be implemented. This scheme, providing a voluntary certification for beaches and marinas, has worked effectively in Europe for a decade. CAST has become part of the planning programme to look at how it might be transferred to the Caribbean, and a pilot scheme was launched on selected Caribbean beaches in 2002. The right to fly the prestigious Blue Flag might encourage competition for cleaner Caribbean beaches.

All these private sector initiatives are part of the Caribbean's recent thrust towards environmental reform. Karen Fletcher, director of International Hotels Environment Initiative, has commented that the Caribbean is one of the most enthusiastic regions in terms of interest and effort on the part of a growing number of hotels. CAST, she said, had been very effective in raising awareness and in providing practical help. Although the programmes have to be paid for, hotels have access to some effective ideas, such as 'rent an engineer' and packages of computer materials showing the way to better practices.

One different sort of initiative was developed in the Dominican Republic following an outbreak of food poisoning among Airtours customers. Ineffective water and waste management combined with poor hygiene and public health standards were to blame – the tourism industry had grown massively but without the infrastructure to support it. To protect their customers, reputation and share price, Airtours developed a risk management programme with a British hygiene company Cristal. A hygiene audit system was put into place alongside the training of local workers in hygiene. Benjamin Carey, at that time marketing manager of Airtours, said that 'the result was a major contribution to public health because staff were gaining important skills that were then being distributed out into the wider local community. There were long-lasting social and political benefits for the whole host community.' However, critics of this scheme argue that the reforms were led by consumer demand rather than the needs of a community whose own sanitary and cooking conditions remained as inadequate as ever.

While all such programmes involve much work and represent an important thrust towards greater environmental consciousness, ensuring sustainability of the environment remains an elusive goal. One anecdotal indicator came from the CTO's second sustainable tourism conference in 1998. Three workshops, composed of representatives from the region's three geographical blocs, were asked to list the key issues and challenges. Each group came up with an almost identical list. Of these, the most significant were: a need for better legislation, regulation and enforcement; a lack of planning (including the role of all-inclusives and cruise ships) in developing a strategy for sustainable development; a lack of public awareness about the environment; and a lack of community involvement.

What this points to is a continuing public sector indifference about the 'greening' of the Caribbean and what one observer called its 'mindbogglingly' unsupportive behaviour. The difficulties involved in good environmental practice are especially acute in countries that market the attractions of 'ecotourism'. For as Vincent Vanderpool-Wallace, director general of tourism of the Bahamas, noted: 'You have to be an eco-nation first before you can start talking about ecotourism.'

Not everyone agreed. The concept of ecotourism has been too attractive a concept to waste and like any 'good' new idea, it has been embraced and 'implemented' without a great deal of thought. And although it was shown to be a complicated business, this was not necessarily understood by all of those who claimed it for themselves.

Ecotourism Time

The Ecotourism Society's definition of ecotourism is: 'Responsible travel to natural areas that conserves the environment and improves the well-being of local people.' The one cannot exist without the other. Many other sorts of tourism, however, such as nature tourism or adventure tourism, are often swept up in the definition. Hiking, white-water rafting or scuba diving may bring no benefit to the local population nor do they necessarily contribute to sustainability. Likewise, pristine management of and respect for the environment is not enough to ensure economic benefit to ordinary people. Critics of Maho Bay resort in the US Virgin Islands, for example, say that despite its ecological credentials – recycled materials, low-impact design and renewable energy resources – it does not practice ecotourism. What is missing, say critics such as Martha Honey, are ecotourism principles such as involvement of the local community, and conservation and tourism education. [33]

The result of effective ecotourism benefits the host communities through such things as better linkages and a reduction in leakages. It can also be a tool for learning – for both guests and hosts. Addressing the first Caribbean Ecotourism Conference in Belize in 1991, Jean Holder said that ecotourism could present the last chance for the region 'to find the formula which does not at one and the same time entice the visitor, while alienating the local residents.' Adding that not all tourists may be eco-tourists, he said that 'even those, who come primarily to laze on our beaches can by the provision of creative programmes' learn about their hosts and their cultures and so indirectly about themselves. [34] Holder here broadened the idea of ecotourism to include its social aspects. Ecotourism, he believed, could minimise the negative social impacts of traditional tourism (see Chapter Four).

Alarm at the damage tourism had already inflicted on the environment was one reason why the Caribbean began to talk ecotourism. Another was the trend in North America and Europe for 'green' holidays, away from sunbathing and duty-free shopping. The statistics began to pile up, from the early 1990s onward, about the demand for an alternative to the beach and an alternative to mass tourism. The WTO, for example, reported that the demand for ecotourism had grown by approximately 20 per cent annually in the five years up to 2000. Based on the Ecotourism Society's definition, around 5 per cent of all international tourist arrivals in 1998 took what they perceived to be an 'ecotourism trip'. The growth is set to continue. It is, therefore, no wonder that the Caribbean is talking ecotourism and promoting it in its marketing plans (see Chapter Six). At the very least, it has become a tool to sell more than a beach. But how much is it just ecotourism 'lite' or 'greenwash', a convenient add-on to conventional tourism? And how much does it implement the criteria and thus deliver an ecotourism which integrates environmental conservation with economic benefit, respect for and engagement of peoples and culture?

One discussion around ecotourism has been about its definition and the abuse of this definition. Another has been that the use of ecotourism as an alternative tool to traditional mass tourism misses the point. Ecotourism, it is said, is one sector of the tourist industry. It is one part of a whole – all of which should engage in sustainability. As Agenda 21 put it: 'Focussing attention on ecotourism alone will fail to realise the industry's huge potential for worldwide improvements. The real benefits lie in making travel and tourism sustainable.' In tune with that thinking, the CTO changed the name of its annual conference on ecotourism, started in 1991, to that of sustainable development. This first Caribbean Sustainable Tourism Development conference was held in 1997, in Dominica.

The labels, however, remain. Ecotourism – with its emphasis on the environment – is generally the term in use in the Caribbean alongside nature tourism, adventure tourism and green tourism. Community and heritage tourism – defined as a subsector of ecotourism – takes the definition further and makes more rigorous demands at all levels of its development and delivery (see Chapter Nine). This chapter, however, with its emphasis on the environment and how tourism affects it, concentrates on how ecotourism has been adopted (at a range of levels) in response to the threat to the environment.

When the UN Caribbean environmental programme first looked at ecotourism in the Caribbean in 1993, it found that ecotourism was considered as a mechanism to increase the number of arrivals; it appeared to focus more on economic development than environmental conservation. Its evaluation concluded: 'The majority [of countries] do not consider ecotourism as a section of the framework, but only as a part of their programmes.' There was also a lack of expertise, said the report, in addressing the issue at all levels.

In 2000 the CTO came to its own conclusions as to how ecotourism had developed in the region. Its 2000 annual report stated: 'Despite the growing importance of ecotourism and a general concern for the protection of the environment, the Caribbean region has, with the exception of a few countries, not made any serious efforts to examine the potential which this type of tourism may hold to the region or to capitalize on any advantages which the region possess.' It went on to say that despite 'a decade of discussions on ecotourism' progress was slow, 'given the enormous potential that ecotourism represents for the region.' It also came to the conclusion that ecotourism was mainly geared towards 'economic development rather than preservation.'

The CTO identified the factors affecting the development of 'real ecotourism policies and products.' They included the difficulties in distinguishing the ecotourists and thus making it impossible to ascertain the economic benefits of ecotourism; the lack of qualified staff and institutions to look after the development of ecotourism and the lack of policies to support it. It then went on to describe some ecotourism projects that appeared, according to the CTO, to be working well and integrated into the national plan. These included Bonaire for its award-winning Marine National Park, Belize for its research findings into its visitor attractions, the Cayman Islands for Cayman Brac heritage site and nature tourism development initiative, St Lucia for its heritage tourism project and Cuba for its Las Terrazas tourism complex (see Chapter Nine).

Cuba's spectacular return to the tourism fold is largely associated with its 1.9 million tourists who head for cheap holidays in resorts that have little to distinguish themselves from anywhere else in the Caribbean except, for the tourists, the enticement of Cuban music and vague associations with revolution. Ecotourism has, however, begun to feature in Cuba's tourism plans. On a wider front, ecotourism has become of growing importance to Cuba's tourism policy. With its large landmass and the greatest diversity of plant and animal life in the Caribbean, Cuba is an ecotourist's dream. Although mass tourism is what drives the industry, ecotourism is emerging as a key ingredient with more and more areas being developed for ecotourism. In 2000 some 50 areas of the country covering 12,000 square kilometres were identified for 'nature tourism', with 116 tour circuits and trails. Thousands more hotel rooms are projected for these areas.

In Cuba, ecotourism is being initiated and planned from the top, with a battery of development programmes, institutions, environmental legislation and a new ministry of science, technology and environment. As such, it is paying greater attention to the principles of ecotourism than any other country in the Caribbean, and its showpiece, Las Terrazas, also demonstrates a commitment to community tourism within a Cuban framework. The debate within Cuba – and between Cuban experts – is if and how ecotourism can co-exist with mass tourism and whether the commitment will become watered down by the demands of multinationals and the process of globalisation.

While Cuba struggles to forge a balance between the 'two tourisms', a handful of Caribbean destinations have publicly adopted ecotourism as the base of their tourist industry; Belize and Dominica fall into this category. Does the practice of ecotourism, however, match the theory?

With their stunning landscapes and marine environments, Belize and Dominica claim to be ecotourism destinations. Both avoided conventional mass-tourism development by default because of poor communications, both internal and with the outside world, poor infrastructure, and, in the case of Dominica, because of a lack of white sand beaches. However, both these predominantly agricultural countries have turned to ecotourism for classic reasons: to diversify the economy (in Dominica's case to offer an alternative to bananas), to generate foreign exchange and to provide jobs.

Belize: Green Dilemmas

Belize, in Central America, boasts rainforest, the second-largest barrier reef in the world and Mayan ruins. It is also only two hours' flying time from Miami and some other US cities to Belize City's international airport. During the 1980s arrivals soared and Belize became fashionably synonymous with ecotourism. Results have been mixed, with examples of both good and bad ecopractice. The pressure on prime tourist sites such as the reefs has led to a series of environmental problems, but it is in the structures of ecotourist enterprises that the hidden contradictions of ecotourism are best seen.

One of the first effects of the dash to promote Belize as a 'natural attraction' destination was that foreigners arrived to buy land. An estimated 90 per cent of all coastal developments were bought up by foreigners.[35] 'Own your own piece of paradise... Prices start as low as US$9,950... Values are starting to soar,' ran the blurb of an advertisement in a US publication *Belize Currents*. It was no different to what happened in 'mass' tourism countries where the most attractive, easily accessible land was snapped up by outsiders, beyond the means of most locals.

Foreign ownership of land and businesses (in partnership with wealthy Belizeans) has led to the emergence of a powerful expatriate group, who now own and manage many of the country's ecotourism lodges and small hotels. The presence of foreigners has, from time to time, created conflict with local communities which feel that the foreigners manage to bypass legislation in league with local elites. This happened on Ambergris Caye, where a small number of US citizens owned large chunks of the island. A government report showed that several foreign resort owners had avoided compliance with legislation in the construction and management of piers. At a more profound level, the development of an ecotourist resort at Caye Chapel – its development includes an airstrip, casino and golf course – was seen to exemplify the way the owner could side-step environmental legislation, such as sand dredging, because of his relationship with highly-placed local elites. Speculation centred on the accusation that the owner 'was allowed to undertake such activities because he was protected by the highest political authorities in the country.'[36]

Southern Belize has developed a different sort of ecotourism, well away from the cayes of the barrier reef. There, tourism has centred around conservation projects and local, mainly Mayan, communities.

Rosaleen Duffy's *A Trip Too Far* provides a review of how such schemes have worked – or not – and why. The original attempt at community-based conservation, according to Duffy, was the Cockscomb Basin Jaguar Preserve, the first such sanctuary in the world. Its creation required the displacement of various local communities to what was called the village of Mayan Centre. The Mayans lost access to hunting and agricultural ground but were promised that they would gain from ecotourism revenues and eventually participate in the management of the preserve. This, however, failed to happen.

In view of the mistakes made at Cockscomb, the Tourism Strategy for Belize recommended that in future all stakeholders involved in community-based tourism should be consulted and that the benefits should be shared equally by all. The Toledo district has been at the centre of such initiatives. In Toledo, Mayan villagers who are members of the Toledo Ecotourism Association (TEA) provide basic accommodation for tourists who are interested in experiencing village life and customs (see Chapter Nine).

Indeed, the small-scale, community-controlled ecotourism of the TEA was in stark contrast to the ecotour operators, who assembled at the CTO's first Caribbean Ecotourism Conference in 1991, held at the US-owned, luxury Biltmore Plaza Hotel in Belize, built on a former mangrove swamp. One representative from the American Society of Travel Agents declared that there were 'millions of Americans just waiting to come' to Belize, while investors promised large-scale loans with a 25 per cent US stake attached.[37] In such ways ecotourism can appear to be all things to all people.

The exclusive haven of Blancaneaux Lodge, owned by Francis Ford Coppola, the film director, represents a coda to Belize's tourism profile. Overlooking rapids and waterfalls and small-scale it may be, but this place provides 'modern comforts in an entirely self-sustained jungle sanctuary.' Coppola has taught his Belizean cooks how to make pizza and pasta according to his own recipes (perhaps with sun-dried tomatoes flown in to the lodge's own airstrip). Yet Blancaneaux Lodge has its place in the new 'niche' tourism; it responds to the needs of those who like a corner of chic wilderness. As such, it adds to the diversity of Belize's ecotourism product. As such, it also subverts the concept of ecotourism into something surreal.

Belize remains particularly affected by foreign investment and control. As Osmany Salas, executive director of the Belize Audubon Society, wrote in the society's newsletter: 'In Belize, there is a fundamental need to address the question of who owns the resources and how responsible stewardship will be effected to the benefit of all.'

Dominica: Fragile Future

In contrast, Dominica, the largest of the Windward Islands, is not subject to such overt foreign control. An even later arrival in the tourism business than Belize, its 'under-development' stemmed from a set of classic constraints such as the absence of white sand beaches, no major airport, and an under-developed infrastructure. These constraints acted as a protective mechanism, ensuring that tourist development remained low-key and small-scale. Indeed, until recently, the wildness and relative remoteness of Dominica (its Morne Trois Pitons National Park is now a UNESCO World Heritage site), was considered a disadvantage by the tourist establishment. This changed when it was realised that a landscape of waterfalls, rare indigenous parrots, the second largest boiling lake in the world and the best rainforest in the Caribbean could become assets and were 'marketable'. Calling itself 'the Nature Island of the Caribbean', Dominica steadily began to attract more nature-loving, 'adventure-seeking' tourists during the 1980s, in the wake of the Kastarklak report (1975) which had proposed that Dominica was a suitable destination for the development of what would eventually become known as ecotourism.

Since then there has been a steady rise in tourist arrivals, increasing from 24,400 stayovers in 1986 to 73,000 in 2003. Cruise ship arrivals also rose, far more substantially, from 11,500 in 1986 to 177,000 in 2003.[38] These two arms of the tourist industry, developing at the same time, have become a cause of heart-searching between those who see a conflict between the two brands of tourism and those who argue that the two are compatible. Another conflict – between those who support whale watching and those who have supported the government's pro-whaling position in the international arena – has become a political issue, which has attracted negative publicity.

It was the government of Dame Eugenia Charles which, when faced with the start of the collapse of the banana industry, began to push tourism strenuously in the early 1990s. As a result of an improved infrastructure, a marketing push and Dominica's appearance at trade shows, tour operators began to feature Dominica in their brochures. This was considered somewhat pioneering for Dominica has no typical 'resort' accommodation and that which does exist is almost entirely owned by Dominicans. By the turn of the century, there had been a proliferation of small guest-houses and cottages and a couple more hotels, but only a handful had more than 50 rooms. Foreign investors – relying more on fantasy than finance – occasionally arrived on the scene with promises of marinas and condominiums, golf courses and time-shares but usually disappeared, leaving behind white elephants and deflated government ministers.

Despite – or perhaps because of – the failure of outside investors, tourism in Dominica had the opportunity to forge its own character and take its place in the forefront of sustainable tourism. In fact, policy and practice have delivered a confused bag of benefits and blemishes. One guest-house that has demonstrated a sustainable style of local ownership and management, small-scale development and links with the community is Papillote Wilderness Retreat. Its long-term commitment to ecotourism was rewarded in 1994 when it won third prize in the Islands Magazine ecotourism award, behind the well-established Bonaire National Park and the Turks and Caicos National

Museum. The citation was 'for combining a small, low-key resort with a programme that highlights local flora and fauna on an island that's already well known for nature tourism' (see Chapter Nine).

However, the well-being of this small, eco-dominated establishment and other places like it ultimately depends on the 'eco-quality' of the surrounding environment, for it is the island and the immediate environment that attract guests to Papillote. A potentially disastrous development was the construction of a hydro-electric power station nearby; its humming generator can be heard on occasion. Its presence somehow suggested an official indifference to the very principles that Papillote embraced. 'If you take nature away from Dominica, what is there? We have to preserve the rainforest and rivers; otherwise there is nothing more to sell,' said Ken Dill, a local tour operator who specialises in hikes to the interior and nature tours.

As Dominica has boosted its tourism profile, increased its tourist numbers and modernised its infrastructure, the fragile relationship between *any* sort of tourism, the environment and local people has been highlighted. One of the first effects of the increase in tourist numbers, especially the cruise-ship visitors, was, as happened in Belize, increased pressure on the sites, with the most accessible ones the most affected. 'Our main concern is about the carrying capacity of the island as a whole and some sites in particular,' stresses Dill, a former president of the Dominica Hotel and Tourism Association. 'At the moment, the physical effect on the sites is still negligible, the effect is on the tourist.' Even so, more trails were opened up to take the pressure off the well-established ones while the existing ones were 'upgraded'. Geared to the cruise ship market, the sites, once lost in the rainforest, have themselves become almost an adjunct of the toilets, café, interpretation centre, vendors' stalls and so on that were built to service them.

The increase in tourist numbers has also increased the costs of managing the environment. The introduction of user fees (with locals exempted) in 1997 to seven key sites was a way of generating funds for their management and conservation and, importantly, as a way of determining optimum use without degradation. One criticism of the scheme, however, is that the cash goes into the general treasury and is not used specifically for environmental management.

While most stayover visitors to Dominica fall into some kind of ecotourist category, its cruise ship tourists have a very different agenda. They are the closest thing to mass tourism that Dominica has experienced. There are two berths on the island: one at Cabrits National Park, in the north of the island and is little used; the other is the deep-water facility that opened in 1995 in the capital, Roseau, where up to 1,000 people per day pour off the cruise ships. Ken Dill makes sure his own customers do not bump into the cruise tourists when they visit the Emerald Pool, a nature trail in the Morne Trois Pitons National Park leading to a small waterfall. 'No one hates tourism more than a tourist,' he said. 'If you promote ecotourism and then go to a site and find 250 other people there, our sort of ecotourist gets annoyed.'

It is the cruise ship tourists (and their highly visible profile) who some critics believe compromise the government's commitment to ecotourism. 'The concept of nature tourism has not been translated into reality,' claims Atherton Martin, a local hotelier and former minister of the environment. 'The contradictions are in developments like cruise tourism, high-input agriculture, voting with Japan against the whale sanctuary and promoting Dominica at conventional travel fairs. The goal must be the whole country as a destination.'

The government, however, does not see a conflict between cruise and nature tourism. Minister of Tourism Charles Savarin has said that his perception is that Dominica 'is not a national park in which we live.' He added: 'It has got to provide for the people to enjoy a quality of life. Tourism has to be a tool for development.' And this includes the cruise market. The government believes that cruise ship tourism helps to get the island talked about. The economic argument drives the political perspective. However little the cruise ship tourists spend – a drink here, a Carib basket there – a dependency has developed, with the cruise ship passengers providing the extra dollar for a range of the ancillary services, in particular for the taxi drivers (see Chapter Seven). Any shift against the cruise ships would create a substantial political opposition.

Other aspects of government policy have also worried conservationists, such as a hydroelectric power project which reduced the flow of water into the Trafalgar Falls, while a road was extended to give more convenient access to the falls themselves. Dame Eugenia, had also, when prime minister, favoured building a road to within a mile of the remote Boiling Lake so that non-hikers could reach it. Such a development 'to provide motorable access to tourist sites' was, in fact, part of an action plan prepared by the National Consultative Committee in 1991. Such moves were under consideration for some time despite the views of those like Dill, whose customers come to

Dominica especially to experience the arduous hike to the Boiling Lake with not a T-shirt stand in sight.

Another proposal was for a cable-car from the village of Laudat to the Boiling Lake. In the late 1990s the government bought into this plan, promoted by a company called Sea to Sky: it was to be a one-way, five-mile circuit through the rainforest held in place by 36 lift towers made of reinforced concrete. It was specifically conceived as an attraction for the cruise-ship market: 'Even the most hurried cruise ship passenger can experience... within a three-hour window' a visit to the Boiling Lake. While the original scheme was blocked by the UNESCO heritage site, an aerial tram opened under new ownership in 2004. The villagers, those most affected by the scheme, had not been consulted. Opinion in the village was divided between those who saw opportunities for jobs and those who felt threatened by this scheme.

A plan for an extensive hotel resort in the Layou Valley emerged out of the introduction of the controversial Economic Citizenship Policy, a government-initiated programme in which businesspeople from the Pacific Rim were invited to invest in tourist and other approved projects in return for a passport. The Caribbean Shangri-La Hotel was planned to have 250 rooms, 400 time-share units, a convention hall and a shopping centre. This project, described as a misplaced folly by many, was defended by Tourism Minister Charles Savarin as the means to help with Dominica's marketing. 'You need to create a hotel that will help with promotion,' he said. 'We don't benefit from airlines, hotel chains or tour operators, so it places strain on public finances to market Dominica.' By the late 1990s, however, although the land had been cleared, the foundations built and walls half finished, the project had been abandoned: the concrete was the wrong sort, financial difficulties ensued and the bush began to grow back to reclaim the Caribbean Shangri-La. These events did not deter Savarin. 'One or two hotel chains would... serve as a flagship in terms of quality, in terms of the range of services offered, and help generally to enhance our country as a destination,' he said in 2000.[39]

All these difficulties do not seem to dim the enthusiasm of Dominicans in general for tourism – they have been told it is an important future ingredient of economic growth in the wake of the collapse of the banana industry. Many, however, argue that it does not bring enough benefits to local people. However, within a range of responses, there are some common threads: Dominicans see the cruise tourists pass through without spending money, they think the facilities aren't good enough, the craft is too expensive and not distinctive enough, they believe that there's not enough marketing. Some want mass tourism because it would bring jobs; others are not so keen because they don't want 'tourism to become an irritant for the locals.'

Those villagers who live far away from the usual tourist circuit are hoping for business despite knowing little about how to go about it. 'How would the tourist dollar come to the grassroots man?' asked one man at a meeting in a remote northern village. 'We are concerned we have nothing to offer – only the beauty. We can't take advantage of tourism. Nothing is left behind with us,' said Adeleine Detouche, of the Scotts Head Improvement Committee, a village sometimes visited by cruise ship passengers who admire the jutting headland attached to the mainland by a narrow isthmus that separates the Caribbean Sea from the Atlantic. The neighbouring village of Soufrière has had a similar experience despite a foreign-funded development at its sulphur springs. The calypsonian, Mico, encapsulated the views of many local people with his lyrics: 'They pass on a bus/They don't make a stop/Don't stop at a hop/All they know, they pass on a bus!'[40] There is a sense in which Dominicans outside the privileged grouping do not understand what drives tourism; nor are they, in general, getting a chance to be part of that process.

In 1994, a national environmental action plan had declared that 'the island's natural resources are not only the base of its economic mainstay – agriculture – but also the essential assets for its future as an ecotourism destination.' In 1997, Prime Minister Edison James addressed the CTO's annual ecotourism conference – held in Dominica. It was an opportunity to show off Dominica's dazzling potential and demonstrate his commitment to ecotourism. Yet his speech was equivocal. 'No, we cannot delude ourselves into believing that all our development needs will or can be satisfied solely by a well defined and implemented ecotourism programme. We are seeking to benefit from mass tourism too.' That sort of political ambivalence has plagued Dominica for a decade, exacerbated by a lack of trust and cooperation between the public and private sectors. This has reduced the capacity to build appropriate institutions to sustain and nurture ecotourism.

The conflict that arose over Dominica's support for Japan's pro-whaling stance at the International Whaling Commission (IWC) is part of this tension. Dominica has some of the best whalewatching in the Caribbean and has built up this aspect of its ecotourism product, alongside its reputation for scuba diving. Yet its government has

continued, with other eastern Caribbean countries, to support Japan's
position at the IWC, voting with Japan, in return, so say Dominica's
critics, for aid. Indeed, Dominica has received US$12 million aid for a
fisheries complex in its capital, Roseau, with promises of larger sums
to come. This contradiction, publicised by international organisations
such as Greenpeace as well as by Dominica's own conservation
association, did little to help Dominica's 'green' reputation. It also
brought about the resignation in July 2000 of Atherton Martin,
Dominica's minister of the environment, planning and agriculture.
The row divided Dominica with many local people supporting the
government. Attempts by local conservationists, such as Martin, failed
to convince despite the fact that the Japanese aid appeared to many to
be inappropriate and unsustainable.

One project, still at the very beginning of its life, is the Waitukubuli
National Trail. The idea is to create a great hiking trail linking the
extremities of the island from north to south. It would be a model for
the new concept of pro-poor tourism providing an income for the
island's rural people. It has grassroots support, indeed, consultation
and partnership have been integral to its thinking. It has had some
government support and international support from the British
government, which funded a feasibility study. Yet its development has
already shown signs of the weaknesses endemic in the story of
Dominica's tourist industry.

The mixed messages of the government towards ecotourism have
undermined those who have a clear view of a holistic ecotourism
future. The task for Dominica is to have the political will to make it
work and not to be deflected by short-term gain or superficially
attractive schemes which deliver little. The entry of the wild card,
cruise ship tourism, continues to jeopardise its reputation. The
objective for the Waitukubuli national trail is to practise successful
community tourism (see Chapter Nine). That will be Dominica's
sternest test in its aspirations to be 'the nature island of the Caribbean'.

Guyana: Promise and Threat

Guyana, the last Caribbean territory to join the tourist game, raises yet
more interesting questions about the viability of 'green' tourism, with
somewhat similar patterns of development as in Belize. A vast country
of forest and savannah on the northwest shoulder of South America,
Guyana has some of the tallest waterfalls in the world, and an interior

of great beauty and mystery populated largely by Amerindians. Before 1991 it had no minister of tourism, no tourism association, no tourist literature, few hotels, even fewer tourist facilities and, of course, no tourists.

The absence of white beaches is one explanation for Guyana's lack of tourists; the other is political. President Forbes Burnham, who died in office in 1985, promoted a 'no dependency syndrome'. So tourism, with its alien influences and foreign money, was considered inconsistent with Burnham's vision of 'cooperative socialism' and was actively discouraged. Burnham's successor, Desmond Hoyte, however, reversed the anti-tourism policy, announcing that tourism was to be part of a new thrust to revitalise the sagging economy through the private sector and foreign investment.

By 1987, a National Tourism and Development Policy of the Cooperative Republic of Guyana had been drawn up. This stated that the new government believed tourism could 'offer significant contributions to national revenue and foreign exchange earnings indefinitely.'[41] The ministry of trade became the ministry of trade and tourism, and a tourism department within the ministry was set up to promote Guyana's natural attractions (staffed by two people, it was once described as 'about the smallest tourism organisation in the world'). Subsequent governments have also continued to back ecotourism.

In a sense, Guyana has had no choice in the matter. The only sort of tourism that could be developed, at least in the immediate future, is ecotourism. Guyana's recent politics, its economic crises and its extraordinary topography make for a country with a poorly developed infrastructure, few roads, poor air links, erratic electricity, water and telephone supplies and restricted financial facilities. A 1989 consultancy report was blunt: tourism was impossible to develop if transport was not improved and if Timehri Airport (Guyana's only airport of international standard and size) could not improve its capacity. Its suggestions for upgrading the infrastructure ranged from licensing boat services ('transport by steamer or ferry is uncomfortable, dirty and dangerous') to erecting road signs and establishing a casino.[42]

Yet even without a sophisticated infrastructure, by the mid 1990s there had been a surge of interest in tourism. At the first national conference on tourism, organised by the University of Guyana in 1993, it was suggested that the government needed to establish codes and laws, especially in relation to the Amerindians, and to ensure proper monitoring of tourism operations. No environmental assessment studies had been carried out, it was said, and there was insufficient manpower and finance. The government, however, appeared to be taking a back seat. Indeed, it remains in the back seat of the industry, which is run by the Tourism Association of Guyana (TAG), formed in 1992 to represent the private sector. At first, TAG, now called the Tourism and Hospitality Association of Guyana, was not very well supported. One of the reasons, said one hotelier, was that it was perceived as 'a white people's organisation with the big hotels running it.'

Indeed, Guyana's new-born tourist industry has been dominated by those with investment money, the knowledge to put together attractive 'eco-packages' and the contacts to market them. Timberhead, the closest resort to Georgetown, is part owned by the Le Meridien Pegasus Hotel, Georgetown's most prestigious hotel. A three-hour journey from Georgetown by road and river, Timberhead is 'a collection of three native jungle lodges', overlooking the extraordinary black waters of the Pokerero Creek and within the boundaries of the Amerindian Santa Mission. 'At night you can lie on crisp white linen sheets under mosquito nets and look out across the savannah,' says the brochure. It is beautiful, simple and comfortable. Visitors go jungle walking, swim, canoe, fish and bird-watch.

The Amerindians have been at the sharp end of the ecotourist boom. They have been promoted as one of the main 'attractions' of Guyana's tourist package. In the past, visits to the interior were closed to foreigners or required special permission; this is still true in some areas. However, the recent opening up of the interior to foreign loggers and mining companies has already exposed the vulnerable Amerindians. 'Tourism is an added pressure,' said Desrey Fox of the Amerindian Research Unit at the University of Guyana, who is concerned that in the talk about ecotourism the Amerindians once again have not been consulted. Janette Forte, also of the Research Unit, believed that Amerindians should become involved in the tourist industry, 'not just as the guides and camp hands – and certainly not as the destination for curious sightseers – but with training and support, as entrepreneurs who also provide ecotours.' It might, she added, even help to reverse their present powerlessness and be a tool for sustainable development in preserving natural areas. By providing alternative employment, tourism could be a buffer against unregulated logging and mining, against the illegal hunting of animals and birds and against the drug trade.

Meanwhile, at Timberhead, part of the tour incorporates a short stop at the Santa Mission. 'We try to minimise the effect on the village; we only spend half an hour there,' said one tour operator. The Mission is the most 'exposed' of all Indian communities and its people travel regularly to Georgetown to shop. Even so, tourists have caused some disruption to the community. The young woman teacher at Santa Mission said: 'We don't want to be seen as "antique things". It's OK to have visitors twice a week but when they come and swim in the river here, changing their clothes, we are not happy about that. We try to teach our children a moral way.'

Timberhead, however, has given some employment to the people of the Mission; it also provides community support and has helped to train women to resurrect their craft-making skills to supply the Mission's craft shop. Timberhead's land was originally a 'gift' from the Mission in exchange for financial help; later a 25-year lease was renegotiated. While the Amerindians have begun to learn about the benefits and perils of tourism, the grandees of the private sector have begun to market their new 'product'. This seems closer to Belize's ecotourism - moulded by a wealthy elite into an up-market product.

Ecotourism has become a central platform for tourist development in three countries in the Caribbean – Guyana, Belize and Dominica – as well as being incorporated as an alternative 'niche' within the more mass markets of other destinations. It has provided a sort of lifeline. But while it can help conserve the environment, it also makes demands on it, and while it can offer sustainable development and empower local people, it can also alienate them – almost as easily as mass tourism. As Erlet Cater, a British geographer and commentator on Third World ecotourism, has written: 'There is a real danger that ecotourism may merely replicate the economic, social and physical problems already associated with conventional tourism. The only difference... is that often previously undeveloped areas, with delicately balanced physical and cultural environments, are being brought into the locus of international tourism.'[43] If that happens, ecotourism in the Caribbean, or indeed anywhere else, no longer has any specific meaning.

NOTES

1.   Christopher Columbus, *Journal of the First Voyage*, California, 1990, p.51
2.   E.A. Hastings Jay, *A Glimpse of the Tropics*, London, 1900, p.38
3.   Martha Gellhorn, *Travels With Myself and Another*, London, 1983, p.70
4.   Ibid. p.107
5.   Walcott, Derek, *The Antilles, Fragments of Epice Memory, the Nobel lecture*, Farrar, Straus and Giroux, 1992
6.   McElroy Jerome, *Island Tourism: A Development Strategy for Biodiversity*, INSULA magazine, September 2001
7.   Peter Bacon, 'Use of Wetlands for Tourism in the Insular Caribbean', *Annals of Tourism Research*, vol 14, 1987, pp.104-117
8.   Jean Holder, 'Tourism and Environmental Planning: An Irrevocable Commitment', Caribiana, Caribbean Conservation Association, 1988
9.   CANA news agency, September 13 2000
10. United Nations Environment Plan, 'Coastal Tourism in the Wider Caribbean Region', Technical Report No 38, 1997
11. Graham Dann and Robert Potter, 'Tourism in Barbados', in Drakakis-Smith D and Lochart D (eds), *Island Tourism: Problems and Perspectives*, London and New York, Mansell, 1997, p 205-228
12. Antigua & Barbuda Tourist Office, press release, 1994
13. Paul Lorah, in David Barker et al (eds), *A Reader in Caribbean Geography*, Ian Randle Publishers, 1998
14. Klaus de Albuquerque, 'Conflicting Claims on Antigua Coastal Resources: the Case of the McKinnons and Jolly Hill Salt Ponds' in Norman Girvan and Simmons, David (eds), *Caribbean Ecology and Economics*, Barbados, 1991
15. Lorah, op. cit.
16. CANA, 2 October 1994
17. *Caribbean Week*, Barbados, 16-29 April 1994
18. Roger Hamilton, 'Joining the Coastal Erosion Battle', The IDB, Washington, September-October 1992
19. Lloyd's Ship Manager, Cruise and Ferry Supplement, London, August/September 1994
20. Ibid.
21. Caribbean Cruising, Florida Caribbean Cruise Association, Third Quarter, 2001
22. Yves Renard, 'Perceptions of the Environment', Caribbean Conservation Association, Barbados, 1979, p.53
23. West Indian Commission, 'Time for Action: Overview of the Report of the West Indian Commission', 1992
24. De Albuquerque, op. cit.
25. Caribbean Conservation Council and Islands Resources Foundation, Antigua-Barbuda Environmental Profile, Barbados, 1991
26. Ibid., p.76
27. Erlet Cater, 'Profits from Paradise', *Geographical Magazine*, London, March 1992
28. Karen Fog Olwig, 'National Parks, Tourism and Local Development: A West Indian Case', Human Organisation, vol 39, no 1, 1980
29. Island Resources Foundation, Tourism and Coastal Resources: Degradation in the Wider Caribbean, 1996
30. Robert Potter, 'The Changing Face of Coastal Zone Management in Soufrière, St Lucia', *Geography*, 2001, vol 86
31. Martha Honey, *Ecotourism and Sustainable Develoment, Who Owns Paradise?*, Island Press, 1999

32. Louise Dixey, An Environmental Assessment of Tourism in St Lucia, UK Ceed Bulletin, Autumn 1998

33. Honey, op. cit.

34. Jean Holder, paper delivered at first Caribbean ecotourism conference, Belize, 1991, mimeo

35. Cater, op. cit.

36. Rosaleen Dufy, *A Trip Too Far, Ecotourism, Politics and Exploitation*, Earthscan, 2002

37. Egbert Higinio and Ian Munt, Belize: Eco-tourism Gone Awry, NACLA Report on the Americas, New York, vol 26, 1993, p.10

38. Caribbean Tourism Organisation, Caribbean Tourism Statistical News, Barbados, 2001.

39. CANA news agency, September 2000

40. Louise Dixey, Ecotourism in Dominica, disertation, 1996

41. Festus Brotherton Jr, 'The Politics of Tourism in a Caribbean Authoritarian State', *Caribbean Affairs*, Trinidad, vol 3, no 2, 1990, p.51

42. CHC Consulting Group, 'Developing Tourism for Guyana', Dublin, 1989

43. Cater, op. cit.

6
THE HOLIDAY AND ITS MAKERS:
THE TOURISTS

Late afternoon, Grantley Adams International airport, Barbados. The American Airlines flight to New York has left and long queues form at the British Airways check-in desk for the overnight flight to Gatwick. Many of the passengers are white tourists, their skins rosied and bronzed by sunshine; some of the women and children have had their hair braided, a souvenir of 'native' style; the men carry outsize straw hats and are still wearing brightly-patterned shorts and T-shirts with slogans such as 'Life is a Beach' or 'Jammin' Barbados'. Some hold duty-free Cockspur rum or gift-wrapped packs of flying fish, the Barbadian speciality. The final holiday jokes and good-byes have been said to taxi drivers, couriers and the representatives from the large tour operators.

The departing tourists are a mixed bunch: middle-aged couples, young honeymooners, a sprinkling of friends and family groups; only a few look seriously wealthy, older perhaps with deeper tans, linen suits, golf clubs or tennis racquets. But for the most part, the tourists, like most visitors these days to the Caribbean, are ordinary folk on a two-week package holiday. They have had, for the most part, a great time.

Barbados, one of the earliest Caribbean holiday destinations, now attracts a broad tourist base: from south coast cheap and cheerful, US$30 a night for a double room at the Firholme Hotel and Studios, Maxwell, to west coast, super-luxury snobbery at the Sandy Lane Hotel, US$2,000 a night for a double room, probably the most exclusive 'property' on the island.

Opened in 1961, Sandy Lane was built on a former sugar estate (another example of how history links the old plantocracy with the new), a two-storey Palladian creation built in local stone. It re-opened in 2001 after another refurbishment – more marble, more ersatz stately home. Both old and new money hole up at Sandy Lane: European aristocracy, American financiers, sports stars and a showbiz line-up of names such as television presenter Cilla Black, singer Julie Andrews, and film director Michael Winner.

Luciano Pavarotti and family members have stayed at Sandy Lane with a suite (or two) on the ground floor which looks out between mahogany trees to the beach. Meals were served for them in a white tent-like structure that rose protectively like a giant parasol over a table stiff with linen and crystal. Meanwhile, other guests relaxed on the small gently curving beach tended by friendly, elderly attendants. At Sandy Lane, sunbathers are given a towel, asked whether they want to lie in sun or shade and told to display the yellow flag when they require service. Security guards with walkie-talkies hover discreetly. Long, hot mornings end at the ocean-fronted restaurant where a 'sumptuous lunch buffet' is served. The days drift by amidst attentive service and courtesy.

The west coast tourists like their luxury in bucketfuls. They stay in places such as Sandy Lane, tucked away from normal life behind heavily guarded perimeter gates, with private drives of royal palms sweeping down to marbled reception halls, swimming pools and fountains – and always beyond there is the Caribbean Sea. (Some of these hotels, although not Sandy Lane, are called 'clubs', a legacy of the days when you did not have to be a member but just the right colour to be admitted.) Even more exclusive are the private homes – like Heron Bay, the US$20 million holiday home of Sir Anthony Bamford, whose family made its fortune from steel beam supports. Guests such as Joan Collins drop in to stay in a cottage in the grounds for New Year and to party with the likes of Rocco Forte (whose family own Sandy Lane), while David Frost and Robert Sangster entertain at the cliff top 'no shorts' Carambola Restaurant. For those who care, 'winter in the Caribbean' retains its snobbish ring.

They do it differently on the south coast at places like the Firholme Hotel, where the clientele is about as likely to tuck into a Sandy Lane sea-food buffet with 'fine wines' as a Barbadian cane-cutter. The south coasters pour off the charter flights on the cheaper package tours. They stay in modest self-catering hotels and condos (not all on the beach), nip across to the supermarkets for tins of spaghetti hoops, have a day out on the wild east coast in their hired mini-mokes, eat at Chefette's takeaway facing a turquoise sea, sunbathe at Rockley Beach, drink rum punch at a pirate party aboard the Jolly Roger, dine on ribs and pasta, burgers and garlic bread, and have cocktails called Thousand Flushes or Bajan Silk Panty. At night, they go to disco and karaoke at the Reggae Lounge, the Ship Inn with 'the feel of an old English pub' or Harbour Lights ('exclusive open air beachfront club with top live entertainment').

Between these extremes of holiday style are middle-class families with children or older people escaping the northern winter. At Worthing, a Canadian widow sunbathes by the pool of an 'apartment hotel', overlooking Dover Beach. 'This is my eighteenth visit. I come for four weeks every year and have already put my deposit down for next year.' She finds Barbados congenial and 'very British'; the sandwiches are made of nice thin bread and the tea is good. Over the years, things have changed, she says. 'The beaches are emptier but the supermarkets are better stocked and the roads and pavements have improved.' A British couple with two children who stayed on the west and south coasts ('They assume you're richer on the west coast') in self-catering accommodation had found the island friendly and safe. 'We were never made to feel uncomfortable. We hired a car, shopped locally and felt very much at home. Everyone was very helpful.'

Tourists to Barbados represented 2.6 per cent of all stayover visitors to the region in 2002. They come from all over the world. That year there were just under half a million of them (compared to 432,100 in 1990). Some 38.7 per cent came from the UK; 24.8 per cent from the US; 9.4 per cent from Canada; 18 per cent from the Caribbean itself; and 5.1 per cent from mainland Europe.[1]

For the Caribbean as a whole, a different pattern emerges. In 2002, 53.1 per cent of stayover tourists came from the US and 6.7 per cent from Canada compared to 23.7 per cent from Europe and 6.8 per cent from the region.[2]

While the US clearly remains the most important market, the European market has expanded. Whereas more than 2.25 million Europeans visited the region in 1993, their number increased to 4.5 million in 2002. The largest group (nearly 1.5 million) were the French, although this included large numbers of French West Indians travelling back from metropolitan France. The second largest concentration was the British (more than a million arrivals, representing 24.6 per cent of the European market). The Germans (510,000), Italians (347,000), Spanish (320,000) and Dutch (244,000) provided another growing market, with tourists from Switzerland and Spain putting on a considerable increase in just a few years.

National preferences for destinations are products of geography and history. Americans, the majority of whom come from the Atlantic seaboard states and the Midwest, in 2002 favoured Puerto Rico (28 per cent of all US stayovers) and the Bahamas (13.5 per cent), with 9 per cent going to Jamaica and 7 per cent to the Dominican Republic.

Europeans spread themselves more widely although their

destinations, to a certain extent, still echo the old colonial pathways. In 2002, the British, for example, liked Barbados best (192,000) – an old favourite – followed by the Dominican Republic (146,300). The next most popular destinations were Jamaica (126,000) and Cuba (108,000). These four destinations accounted for more than 50 per cent of all tourists visiting the region from the UK. The least visited destinations by the British were the Dutch Antilles and the French Caribbean.

For the French, more than two thirds went to the French Caribbean départements of Martinique and Guadeloupe while 85.6 per cent of Spanish visitors went to Cuba and the Dominican Republic. Four-fifths of all German visitors to the Caribbean visited the Dominican Republic (241,000) and Cuba (153,000).[3]

Traditionally, most visitors arrived during the long northern winters. This was the pattern set by the super-rich before the arrival of long-haul jets. Now the Bahamas can be reached from Florida in under an hour while New York is only four hours from Jamaica. Even for Europeans, travelling times are manageable, with the eastern Caribbean only eight hours flying time away. This has changed the profile of the Caribbean holiday-maker; now those with average incomes and short holidays (Americans average around one week in the region and Europeans nearly two weeks) can afford it.

The other change that accessibility has brought is that the Caribbean is no longer an exclusively winter destination. The busy 'high season' from December to March remains the fashionable time to be in the Caribbean, but arrivals are now much more evenly spread over the year. The summer is also popular, especially with first-timers and honeymooners, with July and August in particular doing well.

Up-market, Down-market

These changes have broken the elitist mould of the Caribbean tourist. As in Barbados, the region now receives a cross-section of visitors. The rich, however, remain loyal to the Caribbean as part of the winter calendar. The traditional destinations such as Barbados' west coast and some smart hotels in Antigua pick up such a clientele, who have now also spread out to chic resorts on smaller islands like Anguilla and Virgin Gorda or to private islands such as Mustique. Caribbean cool – if there is such a thing – is now associated with models and rock-stars. Once, artists, writers and well-heeled drop-outs visited the Caribbean: it had its own colonial 'happy valley' enclaves. There is no longer Hemingway in Cuba or Graham Greene in Haiti or Noel Coward in Jamaica although for a few years in the early 1980s radicals of Europe and North America made the trip to Grenada to express their solidarity with the regime of Maurice Bishop. Cuba, too, became attractive for 'study tours' and those interested in Castro's revolution, until its tourism policy widened the profile of its visitors.

Traditionally, the Caribbean has not featured much in up-market advertisements for specialist tours to 'adventurous' places. More typically, tourists to the Caribbean are like mass tourists anywhere, conservative rather than radical, seeking suburban security in the sun. They have responded to the tired old slogan of the "three Ss" – sun, sand and sea (with a fourth for sex often thrown in, see Chapter Four) which has defined the Caribbean typical holiday. Nowadays, however, there has emerged a new sort of tourist who looks a little further than the beach for satisfaction.

North American tourists to the Caribbean are no longer particularly rich nor particularly well-educated, although some specialist tour operators still attract a more moneyed clientele. British tourists remain somewhat more up-market. More than 85 per cent of the customers of the UK-based company Caribbean Connection, for instance, are between 35 and 60, company directors and professionals, and more than 60 per cent of them have an income of £80,000 or more. Patrick Leigh Fermor's lament in *The Traveller's Tree* that Barbados (or more precisely white Barbados) reflected 'the social and intellectual values and prejudices of a Golf Club in Outer London'[4] would probably still suffice today as the intellectual snob's verdict on tourists to the Caribbean.

Whatever their tastes, however, it is the wealthier tourists who find favour with the region's tourism establishment. Islands remain anxious 'not to go down-market' or 'not to get like Barbados and the Bahamas', now identified as over-developed and catering for the masses. The up-market visitor makes the best tourist, according to local wisdom and tour operators, hoteliers and tourism officials all agree. This is partly because they spend more, but it is also to do with lifestyles and attitudes. 'The independent traveller fits in better,' said Drew Foster, chairman of Caribbean Connection. 'They tend to be well travelled, cause fewer problems and are not trying to change the local ways.' The older, quieter, wealthier (if paternalist) guest is in a traditional mould.

Another UK tour operator stressed that clients must have respect and understand that the environment and culture belong to the host communities. 'My type of client wants to meet Caribbean people and eat Caribbean food. That works very well in some places; but others such as St Thomas and Puerto Rico have just been overwhelmed.' An up-market tour operator, Caribtours, which has been operating in the Caribbean for nearly a quarter of a century, has noticed an increase in the demand for family holidays. 'It's an interesting development. Families flying long-haul – even for a week at school half-term – is no longer considered a big deal. So there's a demand for family friendly resorts and for places with lots to see and do,' said Catherine Leech, managing director of Caribtours.

The downmarket tourists, who are seen as graduates from the Costa Brava, have had a mixed reception. They tend to come on a charter with a 'room only' booking and, whether true or not, they are seen as penny-pinching, young and more likely to create social problems: 'the tattoo-bearing biscuit and cheese brigade' as one minister of tourism said. The influx of what was perceived as 'yobbo' English to Barbados, for example, when the charters first started to arrive, caused concern around reports of racist behaviour. The Dominican Republic and Cuba, cheaper and charter friendly, now attract the less well-off tourists from Europe.

In Jamaica, a new category of tourists, the 'spring breakers', students from the US taking their Easter holidays in the Caribbean, has emerged. These visitors are particularly attached to Negril, the cool, laid-back resort, where they occupy the cheaper hotels and guesthouses. They do not spend as much as more mainstream visitors but local opinion reckons that they are worth cultivating as potential future visitors – when their pockets will be fuller and their tastes more mature.[5]

In general, young backpackers have also traditionally been identified as downmarket. The Caribbean establishment has a certain suspicion of scruffy visitors who travel on local buses, buy food from the market and probably stay in humbler guesthouses. Without couriers, reps and tour agents to supervise them, they are free agents and sometimes viewed as potentially troublesome, as liable to wander off the beaten track, become involved in drugs and get caught up with locals. As a result, non-package tour visitors sometimes receive a less than friendly welcome from customs and immigration.

But what attitudes do the consumers hold about their Caribbean hosts? Do they care about the environmental degradation, the social impacts, the unequal distribution of wealth, the overall control by foreign interests? There is no specific information relating to visitors to the Caribbean. What information is available indicates a mixture of attitudes. A UK survey of more than 2,000 adults found that 48 per cent were 'completely apathetic' and a further 22 per cent 'were generally unconcerned about ethical issues and just wanted to relax on holiday, believing they were not causing any harm, but were actually benefiting the local economy.'[6] However, there are also findings from surveys undertaken by Tearfund, the Christian charity, and the Association for British Travel Agents and Tour Operators. Such surveys have found the majority of holiday-makers would pay more if their holidays supported better wages and working conditions and sound environmental practice. As Tearfund concluded: 'Holiday-makers are beginning to realise that their visits to exotic, sun-based paradises have an impact on local people and environments.'[7] Whatever the case – whether ethical tourism is a turn-on or a turn-off – holidays have to deliver, turning expectations into reality. For the Caribbean, those needs are high on the agenda.

Heaven on Earth

Europeans and North Americans search out the Caribbean for all the classic reasons: climate, beaches and landscape. It is also safe from disease and, for the most part, dangerous beasts, and someone somewhere speaks the language (English, French, Dutch or Spanish). For European first-timers, it is the next stop after the Mediterranean for those who want to go further afield. They visit the Caribbean for 'a holiday in a lifetime', to 'make a dream come true'.

The visitors' book at Bluff House, Green Turtle Cay, on the Bahamanian island of Abaco, is filled with passionate thankyous from guests, penned as they leave their holiday haven for the journey back home. The messages read: 'This surely must be paradise. Can't wait to come back.' And 'Another day in paradise for two weeks. Glorious holiday. Kind and friendly people.' And, simply, 'Heaven On Earth.'

It is the fortune, and the misfortune, of the Caribbean to conjure up the idea of 'heaven on earth' or 'a little bit of paradise' in the collective European imagination. Although in pre-Columbian Europe it was originally the east with its wonders and riches that enshrined images of paradise, the west offered the mythical 'blessed islands', symbolic and timeless places of gentle fruitfulness and harmony. That utopia was to some extent reinforced by Columbus who speculated that he had encountered a terrestrial paradise. In his footsteps were countless travellers bringing back news of its natural physical beauty. Thus the region, whatever the brutality of its history, kept its reputation as a Garden of Eden before the Fall. The idea of a tropical island was a further seductive image: small, a 'jewel' in a necklace chain, far from centres of industry and pollution, a simple place, straight out of Robinson Crusoe.

Not only the place, but its people too, are required to conform to this stereotype. The Caribbean person, from the Amerindians whom Columbus met in that initial encounter to the 20th century taxi-driver whom tourists meet at the airport, is expected to satisfy those images associated with paradise and Eden. The images are of happy, carefree, fun-loving men and women, colourful in language and behaviour, whose life is one of daytime indolence beneath the palms and a night-time of pleasure through music, dance and sex.

What academics call 'a search for authenticity' involves the labelling of Caribbean peoples according to the needs and presumptions of the tourist. The thesis goes something like this: locals are not 'allowed', as it were, to be part of global society. Lives which are concerned with daily chores – jobs, banks, cars and so on – which preoccupy many people in the Caribbean as much as in the developed North are not seen as appropriate for the tourists' gaze. Thus local peoples are, it is argued, 'twice fetishised': first as objects of discovery, and then 'as being so close to nature that their dispositions are derived directly from the climate,' which sounds as if it were written by a 16th-century conquistador rather than a post-modern academic.[8]

In the Caribbean, the mythology of blackness reinforces the focus on play and partying. Those still powerful representations stretch down the years from the plantocracy, through the racism of the 19th-century English historian J.A. Froude's observations on the black peoples of the Caribbean ('they are naked and not ashamed... they are perfectly happy')[9] to the more careless clichés of the modern travel brochure. The two aspects of place and people come together in a riot of exotic fun and sun-soaked escapism where tourists can 'go native' by which they mean indulge in a kind of mental torpor. (A *New Yorker* cartoon of a middle-aged couple talking over drinks bears the caption: 'Let's go to the Caribbean or someplace and give our brains a rest.')

The fantasy is reinforced by two factors. Ordinary people are transported to luxury, to live 'like royalty' in a style they never experience at home; alternatively the rich can afford to 'slum it' on holiday. At the same time, everyone, both rich and poor, leaves behind everyday life, 'adult' duties and professional labels, when they put on their shorts and T-shirts, bikinis and sarongs, and clutch their cameras and beach bags. They are far away from home, in an unfamiliar environment where no one knows them and where, so the brochures have told them, hedonism is the key quality of the place.

The brochures traditionally concentrated on the hotels, beaches, landscape and fun. The introduction to the Caribbean section in a Thomson's Faraway Shores brochure states, for instance: 'Our Opinion: A Caribbean holiday is what Thomson Faraway Shores is all about – clear blue seas, golden sands and gently swaying coconut palms. Whichever island you choose you are sure to receive a warm welcome.' Or, the verdict of Kuoni: 'offering everything from lush landscapes to golden coral beaches, from calm turquoise waters and above all a tropical climate to entice you to swim, sunbathe, dive and relax.'

By the beginning of the 21st century, however, there had been a slight shift in the way such brochures projected the Caribbean. Virgin, in 2002, stated: 'The Caribbean offers a mixture of history, culture, fantastic weather and of course some of the most beautiful beaches in the world.' Or Thomas Cook: 'If you've never visited the Caribbean, you could be forgiven for thinking its all sun, sea and sand – these it certainly has in good measure, but they are only half the story.' The point that is being made is that there's more to a holiday in the Caribbean than lying on the beach (for beaches can now be found all over the world).

What the advertisements do continue to sell, however, are enduring visions of the Caribbean as a place of sex and romance. As the sun sets in a thousand photographs, couples embrace, and as waters lap the sand, they walk barefoot hand in hand. The Caribbean market is mainly couples; some all-inclusives are even for couples only. Sandals, for example, has as its slogan 'Where Love Comes to Stay'. Its brochure boasts: 'Couples in love always stay at Sandals, because they always fall in love with the resorts as much as they do each other… At Sandals, couples can do it all or nothing at all. But most of all, they'll experience the most romantic and exciting vacation ever.'

The Issa group even has an all-inclusive called Couples. Its blurb says: 'Enter Couples, a world bounded by romance. A white sand beach skirted on one side by clear blue Caribbean water, on the other by a lush, flowering tropical jungle. This is your hideaway, a perfect latitude to do nothing but satisfy your desires for food and play and love...'

Weddings and honeymoons are now big business for Caribbean hotels. Sandals, for example, organised 10,000 weddings in 2001 on its premises. Virgin Holidays promises that 'the Caribbean is an almost incomparably romantic place to say "I do".' Hotels will provide the services of a minister or registrar, a wedding cake, a bottle of sparkling wine, a decorated gazebo, a bouquet and buttonhole, a best man and maid of honour (if required), a professional video, photographs and a fruit basket. The wedding extras on hand include a calypso band, classical harpist, helicopter transfer, and a lace-covered wedding photo album. For a nurse from Devon, her wedding was on the beach in St Lucia. 'My husband had said, if you want to marry me, it'll be on a beach in the Caribbean. We've got photos of my husband dropping me in the sea in my wedding dress. It was our day and an hour after the wedding I was back in the pool with a glass of champagne and my husband was off waterskiing.'

The Caribbean can still delight Europeans and North Americans just for its sand and sea and its laid-back reputation. 'It was a holiday promise we had made to ourselves,' say an elderly English couple enjoying Grande Anse beach in Grenada. 'The classic Caribbean holiday. We stay on the beach, we're not adventurers. We just want to sleep and get used to the sun.' 'When you think of the Caribbean, you think of Jamaica,' says a 30-year-old naval serviceman who has spent two weeks in Montego Bay. He went to have a beach holiday, to see the island and meet the people in a 'very relaxed atmosphere'. A middle-aged couple holidaying in Dominica said that 'you have the feeling that you have stepped back in time, the way God intended it to be. The ugly, demanding tourist would be an insult to this country.' They compared this experience to going to St Lucia which they felt 'had lost the Caribbean flavour. It's as if the tourists had not gone to another country but just somewhere on a beach.'

Besides the brochures, the travel pages of newspapers and magazines are another source of information about the Caribbean. Much of this coverage is worthy, respectful if uninteresting, and replete with chewed-over clichés. This may be as much the fault of the tourist boards, which give journalists free trips in exchange for the hoped for piece of 'product endorsement', as of the writers themselves. The search for new niche markets, however, has encouraged tourist boards to sometimes offer journalists the opportunity to experience something a little less conventional. Even so, many of them still push the sun-and-sand image of the Caribbean with writers extolling luxury and a cult of doing nothing because there's nothing to do; or a frenzy of activity at all-inclusives with wall-to-wall cocktails and canned calypso. When writers do discover somewhere different, such as Guyana or Dominica or the hinterland of Jamaica, the results are far more interesting.

In 2000, the up-market British newspaper, the *Observer*, published a special 24-page supplement on the Caribbean entitled 'Islands of Dreams'. It contained a package of pieces about individual islands and a map showing 'the islands at a glance' with two-sentence summations of the islands. Here then – in a collection of the summaries – is what the well-read Brit might be expected to think about the Caribbean at the turn of the 21st century. Jamaica: 'Hangs on to its identity – Rasta and reggae – while catering for most tastes and budgets.' Cayman Islands: "British crown colony with a north American flavour. Clean, safe and well-developed." Dominican Republic: "Mass-market operators were quick to spot the potential of this Spanish-speaking island, now packed with cheap, all-inclusive resorts." Dominica: "Pack binoculars for rainforest treks in search of boiling lakes, wild orchids, waterfalls and 100 species of birds. Great diving." St Lucia: "Friendly people, golden beaches and beautiful landscape dominated by the twin peaks of the Pitons." Grenada: "Cinnamon, nutmeg and cloves, cocoa and bananas are the main exports of the charming Spice Island." It showed that worthwhile if soundbite-like distinctions could be made in a region that has often suffered from a homogenised image.

Fantasy and Reality

Meanwhile, those largely romantic 'desert island' images of the brochures and the magazines triumph over the real and painful complexities and paradoxes of Caribbean life and culture. The fantasies mock the history of the Caribbean: from the almost complete annihilation of the Amerindians, through slavery and the plantation system, to migration, the difficulties of nationhood and the forging of new identities and economic strategies.

Most tourists know little of all this. Until recently, the fantasies projected by brochures and travel agents also failed to distinguish between one island and the next, building on the impression of nothing but sand, sea and sun from the Bahamas to Bonaire. 'Most of them don't know anything about the island,' admitted a Kuoni tour rep in Antigua. 'Nowadays they've heard about Antigua because of the TV programme Blind Date. They might know of a famous person who has stayed here, and the unifying factor is Viv Richards – everyone knows about him.' Or, as an Airtours manager in Barbados said: 'They have high expectations, they have an image that the Caribbean is all white beaches and green waters like the Bacardi ad. They expect it to be like the Grenadines and the ones that don't like it complain about the pavements and buildings, that it's dirty.'

A Yorkshire secretary and her builder boyfriend have been to Barbados four times: 'It's like our second home now.' However, her first impressions made her feel uncomfortable. 'All I could see in the brochures were golden beaches, but on the way from the airport it looked so different. The sheep and cows looked so thin; everything looked brown and bleak and all those wooden shacks... But then we got to the hotel and everyone was very friendly.'

Understandably, tourists like the locals to be friendly, whether engaged in tourism or not. This 'friendly' requirement is a problem for many Third-World countries grappling with tourism (see Chapter Four). The Caribbean, in particular, defined largely by outside forces and with the shape of its tourist industry laid down by external demands, has to conform to this warm-hearted image.

It is this image that sells holidays at the expense of the reality of its people's needs. Many tourists to the Caribbean are aware at some level of the discrepancies between their own holiday standards and the environment outside the resorts. At the most basic level is a response that acknowledges, but shrugs off, local poverty. 'They live in shacks like hen houses. It makes you feel guilty but we were told there was no starvation,' said a woman to a fellow tourist on her way home from St Lucia. At a somewhat deeper level, some tourists make the connection between economic inequalities. 'Sometimes it made me uncomfortable,' admitted the Devonshire nurse. 'Compared to them we were millionaires. Sometimes I would take off my jewellery, not wear my engagement ring because people would look at it and I would feel guilty. We felt this particularly in Jamaica. In St Lucia people were better off and the women looked so elegant.'

A tourist to Jamaica had tried to explain to people that he and his friends were not well off. 'We said that we are not rich. When our holiday money is gone, it's gone. We said we had to work 50 weeks out of the year to save up for this holiday. It was an expensive holiday for us, but it was hard to get through to people and we spent a fortune on tips to get anything done because it was assumed that we were rich.'

Tourists want to believe that the hosts are 'friendly' because 'meeting' other people is seen as a good thing. In the 1960s, when the least known corners of the globe (for the most part the Third World) were being 'discovered' by tourists, travel was seen as desirable, not just for the old cliché about 'broadening the mind'. The new theory was that travel could be an equal encounter between locals and visitors. It was even pompously described by an international body of travel organisations as 'a most desirable human activity deserving the praise and encouragement of all peoples and all governments.' Since then, much of this thinking has been discredited, for the evidence suggests that such interactions are plagued by complications that anthropologists have yet to disentangle.

For June Jordan, the African-American writer who died in 2002, the layers of race, class and gender were laid bare during a holiday in the Bahamas. Jordan recorded her thoughts in an essay from her book *Moving Towards Home*. Observing the women traders in the straw market whose wares are haggled over by tourists, she noted: 'This is my consciousness of race and class and gender identity as I notice the fixed relations between these other black women and myself. They sell and I buy or I don't. They risk not eating. I risk going broke on my first vacation afternoon. We are not particularly women anymore; we are parties to a transaction designed to set us against each other.'[10]

Most tourists have a limited view of the Caribbean: the airport, the hotel, the beach and the sights. Their encounters with local people and their everyday life are limited. This is particularly true if the tourists stay in an all-inclusive where the resort becomes the centre of the holiday. There is little inclination for tourists to move out of the commercial environment of hotel, duty-free shops, gift shops and restaurants. The more developed the tourism, the less possibility there is for a social rather than an economic exchange.

In many instances, the only locals whom the tourists meet are the hotel staff and the tour operator rep (who is sometimes an expatriate), the taxi-driver, the beach vendor and the hustler. Thus the tourist's impression of 'local' is defined. This narrow definition tends to reinforce stereotypical images.

Tourists who want to 'meet the locals' express the greatest of pleasure at encounters that do not involve money: to be invited to a private party; to be given fruit from a yard or help with directions; to be shown round a school or join in a game of dominoes. Tourists praise holidays where 'The people just seemed delighted to see us and to show us around. They were so proud of their country and wanted us to have a great time.' Such needs prompted the Jamaican Tourist Board to introduce a Meet the People programme in which visitors are teamed up with Jamaicans of similar tastes and backgrounds and given an opportunity to talk, get taken around and discover different aspects of Jamaican life. 'It was good to see the other side of Jamaica – and go beyond the walls of a well-laid out resort... Thanks and here's hoping that Meet the People remain alive and well for others to enjoy,' wrote a visitor from Washington DC.

A 1991 visitor satisfaction survey of tourists leaving Barbados found that 'what they most enjoyed' were: beaches and climate (60 per cent); friendly people (27 per cent) and scenery (10 per cent). A similar judgement emerged from 300 Americans on their way home from Montego Bay, Jamaica. Their list of positive factors was as follows: scenery (60.4 per cent); people (20.8 per cent); hotels (9.4 per cent); culture (7.5 per cent); everything (1.9 per cent). And would they recommend Jamaica?: 85.1 per cent said 'yes'. And would they return?: 83 per cent said 'yes'.[11]

Crime and the fear of it limit the sort of casual encounters one might expect to have on holiday. One man who had hoped that he would have a chance to 'meet the locals' in Montego Bay recalled: 'On the first morning we decided to go for a stroll but near the craft market we were told to empty our pockets and lost J$400. The courier later told us that it was best to go out in a group and then only in the day. The holiday was worth it but we did have problems that I hadn't expected.'

Those sorts of experiences make the arguments for the success of all-inclusive resorts all the more understandable. All-inclusives are sold partly on the basis that they are safe. A survey done for Sandals in Jamaica in 2002 reported a huge endorsement for all-inclusives. According to the poll, guest ratings gave 91 per cent for the all-inclusive against 76 per cent for normal hotels. All inclusives scored 95 per cent in hotel security, 94 per cent for quality of service and 91 per cent for efficient management; they outscored conventional hotels in all categories.

What tourists dislike is harassment by vendors and other unofficial hustlers (see Chapter Four). While almost one-quarter of visitors said that nothing displeased them about their visit to Jamaica, the majority complained about vendors, poverty and begging, drug dealers, crime and a general sense of being unsafe. Harassment, crime and violence and high prices were 'consistently reported as the most important deterrents' by US visitors to Negril in Jamaica in two surveys conducted in 1994 and 2001.[12] The problem most often mentioned by the respondents in a Barbados survey was also harassment. 'Beach harassment seems to be the most outstanding of the negative features of the Barbados tourist product. It is the aspect with the largest potential for having adverse repercussions on the tourist industry among those things over which local control can be effected.'[13] What Dunn & Dunn called the 'scourge of harassment' continues on occasions to create tensions between visitors and hosts and taints all those positive images that find favour with the holiday-makers who were sold that dream holiday back home in the everyday environment of western culture.

Selling Sunshine

Tourist satisfaction depends on the 'product'. What is called 'product development' is the responsibility of tourist boards throughout the region, usually in partnership with the private sector. Selling the region to potential tourists is seen as a fundamental function of the industry, and governments are charged with this key remit: to market what their particular destination has to offer. Large sums of money are spent by national tourism organisations, largely on administration and what is known as 'destination marketing': for high-profile islands the budget runs into tens of millions of dollars.

Holiday choices are often made on very random information, based on hearsay rather than knowledge. 'We had heard Antigua was very expensive, that Jamaica had a "wild fun" image, but that Grenada was quiet,' said an elderly Englishwoman. 'Barbados sounded like it had the most to do, was the cleanest and the safest,' recalled a social worker from Sheffield, while a midwife from Lancashire said, 'As a once-in-a-lifetime holiday I thought Jamaica was like the heart of the Caribbean – beautiful scenery, relaxed, easy-going, good music.' And according to a young English woman, 'We expected the Dominican Republic to be a paradise island, all sand, with no industry and no proper roads.' An up-market British tour operator said that her clients know what style of hotel they want to stay in but which island is a matter of less consequence.

In the past, each Caribbean country has been responsible for its own marketing programme (echoing the Caribbean's overall difficulties in moulding a regional dynamic, whether economic or political). The marketing and advertising has often, as we have seen, been piecemeal and unfocused. 'No one is thinking big enough,' claims Drew Foster of Caribbean Connection, who has long campaigned for a 'Caribbean Centre', promoting the region's assets, to be set up in a major western capital.

But for the islands themselves, differentiating one from another has been one of the region's problems. As John Bell, of the Caribbean Hotel Association, wrote: 'For the last 30 years, the Caribbean has been fragmented in the market, an unrelated patchwork quilt of mini-destinations, mostly with limited budgets. The average North American or European can no more tell them apart, or in some cases whether they are in the Caribbean or Micronesia, than fly to the moon.'[14]

The CTO, with its membership of 34 states of the Caribbean Basin along with powerful private-sector organisations, such as American Express and the Florida Caribbean Cruise Association, works both to promote the Caribbean 'as one destination', and also as a research resource, providing the region with its major source of information for the industry. Its research wing was started in 1974 as the Caribbean Tourism Research Centre, instigated by the Caribbean Conference of Churches which questioned the kind of tourism suitable for the region, and was taken over by Peter Morgan, a former minister of tourism for Barbados. It was launched, said Morgan, 'in order to find out if our grandchildren would curse us.' In 1989, it merged with the Caribbean Tourism Association to become the CTO. It holds the strands of both public and private sector interests together as well as having close links with the Caribbean Hotel Association, the University of the West Indies and so on.

It was not until 1993 that the region launched its first ever co-ordinated print and television advertising campaign in response to wavering arrival figures. The US$12 million cost of the campaign was financed by the private sector (hotels, airlines, cruise lines, tour operators and so on) and the member states of the CTO. Twenty-eight member countries participated (only three countries were absent: Haiti, too poor; Cuba, forbidden by the US trade sanctions; and St Vincent and the Grenadines, which chose not to be involved). The campaign was launched with a 60-second television commercial to the sound of the Beach Boys' song 'Kokomo'. Its aim was to promote 'image awareness' and, most importantly, to show variety. According to Michael Youngman, director of marketing for the CTO, 'The

Caribbean has always had a problem because except for a few places it is not well known – and the truth is that it's more than just a few places.' This regional 'branding' was a way in which the member states, however small, could "project their voices amid the clamour of the marketing noise,' said the CTO. The idea was seen as a great success – with others, such as Florida, copying the model – although under-financing meant that the Caribbean was unable to make the most of its own initiative.

The commercial was followed up with a glossy book, Caribbean Vacation Planner, 'the only guide put together by the peoples of the Caribbean,' designed both for the trade and the consumer. The Caribbean Vacation Planner, which now appears as often as governments provide the funds, reflects the concept of promoting the region as a whole. Country by country, from Anguilla to Venezuela, it is its people and architecture, mountains and rivers that are highlighted rather than merely beaches. And where beaches are featured, it is the sporting dimension that is dominant. As Youngman pointed out in 1994, 'The beach will always be the number one attraction but what has changed is that more and more people are looking for alternatives.' That has become more and more the case as the response of the 'trade' to the 'market' has shown.

The Caribbean also focussed its marketing efforts in Europe. In 1993, a three-year US$10 million Tourism Development Programme for the Caribbean began, funded by the European Development Fund. Two-thirds of its budget was aimed at European market development, with the rest going in 'product' development. It aim was to attract up to 90,000 more European tourists a year to the Caribbean. New markets such as Italy, Spain and Germany were being particularly targeted, as well as improved promotion in the more established countries. European marketing committees were formed to bring together tour operators, national tourism organisations, airlines and other travel industry groups. Traineeships in marketing and language skills for Caribbean nationals working in the tourist industry were also set up. Travel agents were also a priority, with a correspondence course launched in 1993 aimed at up to 10,000 agents from the European Union and Switzerland.

While the whole of the Caribbean was a beneficiary of the programme, a second European-funded programme concentrated on the seven-nation Organisation of Eastern Caribbean States (OECS). It, too, looked at the Caribbean 'product' end, while the marketing component involved the training of three OECS nationals based in

London, Paris and Frankfurt. Its task was to develop new programmes with tour operators, participate in promotional activities and maintain effective links with the travel press. High-quality glossy brochures were produced to inform the travel trade of the specific attractions of each OECS country and other promotional material was geared to potential hotel investors.

This much needed activity preoccupied Caribbean marketing energies in the mid 1990s. However, much to the dismay of many elements within the Caribbean tourist industry, there was not another major regional marketing campaign until 2002, following the September 2001 attack on the World Trade Centre. Caricom's strategic plan of 2002 draws attention to the 'weak approach to the marketing of the region.' To be effective a sustained advertising campaign is required. Yet, the 2002 marketing campaign had a major funding problem. Jean Holder admitted, 'getting a critical mass of funds had been extraordinarily difficult.' The problem – as ever – was to get the region to operate as a bloc; attempts at first met, as Holder said, 'with remarkably little success.' One proposal of the strategic plan is to set up a fund to pay for regional marketing and other tourism development programmes. This would be funded by a head tax on all tourism arrivals in the region.

In the end, the 2002 campaign was more modest than that of 1993 and limited to the US market. A television campaign was launched in September 2002 under the theme 'Life Needs the Caribbean'. Filmed in the Bahamas, Dominica and New York, the commercial juxtaposed urban stress with Caribbean tranquillity. Its aim was to 'brand the region' and recover some of its lost US market. Largely funded by the Caricom Caribbean countries (the Dominican Republic, Puerto Rico and the Cayman Islands pulled out of the consortium pleading economic reasons), only US$8 million was raised out of an anticipated US$16 million. In the end, only about half of the CTO's member nations contributed to the commercial.

Promoting the Caribbean in the traditional markets of North America and Europe takes much of the region's marketing budget. However, there are occasional attempts to break into new pastures. In the mid 1990s, Latin America's middle class was eyed as a potential customer. But the rhetoric of ministers of tourism to encourage Colombians or Argentinians to Barbados, for example, did not really materialise – there were no appropriate air links.

Critics, who have remarked that attempting to lure these non-traditional markets to the Caribbean has largely been a waste of time and money, argue that more interest should be shown in markets closer to home – to the Caribbean region itself, which already provides a substantial percentage of arrivals. It is, for example, the third largest provider of visitors to St Lucia, accounting for 30 per cent of all tourists to the island in 2001. Special events, such as music festivals and sport, can lure the local tourist, who is more likely to fill the beds at the smaller hotels and spend money in local restaurants than the long-haul visitor. One difficulty in attracting this market is that there is no automatic freedom of movement through the Caribbean for its nationals. 'The intra-regional traveller is by and large looked upon with suspicion by immigration authorities of sister Caricom territories,' complained Ralph Gonsalves, prime minister of St Vincent and the Grenadines, who described such travellers as 'unwanted strangers at the gate' of many immigration desks. This was also the opinion of focus groups in Jamaica who felt that black Jamaicans and other visiting black people received 'distinctly inferior treatment in many hotels.'[15]

One other market that was traditionally ignored by much of the Caribbean was the African-American market. According to Lebron Morgan, regional advertising sales director for the Afro-American magazine *Essence*, the Caribbean chased every other market, including Latin America and Asia, but it ignored his readership. 'When I think about vacations, about exposing my family, my children, my wife to a situation, I'm very sensitive about where I take them.' He believed that the marketing people 'need to be sensitised that I don't think like the general market in America. They think they know black America but they really don't.'[16] It was not enough to have images of black tourists in promotional literature, argued Morgan, 'we need to get the invitation... to come on down.' A similar point was made by the president of the US Black Travel and Tourist Association, Lloyd Williams. 'It's unfortunate that while Caribbean destinations are failing to tap into the estimated US$43 billion black travel market in the United States, European nations and places like the Pacific rim are promoting themselves among blacks.'[17]

Non-resident returning nationals are also a category that has until recently been ignored by tourist boards. They go to the Caribbean for weddings, family gatherings and also for holidays, as do growing numbers of black British. Among the conclusions of the OAS analysis of Jamaica's tourism economy was that 'non-resident Jamaicans, whom the Jamaica Tourist Board does not even consider tourists, represented 9 per cent of total visitors and contributed 7.4 per cent of total expenditure.' This represented a considerable amount, given that returning nationals usually stay in private homes.[18]

Apart from these groups, the travel industry now analyses tourists far more minutely, breaking down demand into sectors and sub-sectors. No potential need can be overlooked. The key shift for the Caribbean has been to identify a growing number of tourists for whom the beach is not enough. There is, for example, an increased interest in health spas and, at the top end of the market, a great attention to pampering. As one British product manager commented: 'If [people] can lie on a beach, use a state-of-the-art gym and have a seaweed wrap, then the destination will be that much more attractive.'[19]

Hotels now have to pay attention to the details. Out with the chintz and in with stylish minimalism. Bathrooms, for example, are important features. 'They need to be large, luxurious, and have two basins,' said Catherine Leech of Caribtours. For another sort of client, there is a demand for 'soft' adventure – for mountain bikes, hiking trails, scuba-diving and whale watching. 'Some of the Caribbean islands are well geared up to this,' said Leech. 'They should be proud of what they have and promote it.' The emergence of ecotourism (see Chapter Five) is an essential part of this 'product diversification'.

The customer in his or her dazzling variety is what marketing departments have to seduce and satisfy. Most Caribbean countries support national tourism offices overseas in the same way as they do embassies or high commissions. The alternative is to hire a local marketing company to do the job for them. The quality of the service in these tourism offices, in places like New York, Toronto and London, varies. Smaller, poorer islands are sometimes staffed with under-trained nationals who have lived overseas for many years and do not know much about the country they represent; in reality, the offices operate as little more than in a brochure envelope-stuffing capacity. At the other end of the scale, some islands can afford a large and well-trained staff. The Bahamas, for example, has 106 employees in overseas tourism offices, with Barbados, Jamaica and Puerto Rico hovering just under the 50 mark.

To attract tourists, industry officials involved in marketing are constantly on the move, to trade shows, seminars for travel agents and travel business conferences. To have a presence is the thing. At the annual World Travel Market in London, for example, a whole area is turned into a 'Caribbean Village', part-funded by the European Community. The largest tourist destinations, such as the Bahamas,

Jamaica, Barbados and Cuba, build gingerbread-fashioned enclosures, decorated with armfuls of anthurium, tables and parasols, and generously dish out rum punches. There, the minister of tourism, scores of blazered tourist board officials, hoteliers, public relations officials, marketing managers, hotel owners, diving operators and time share reps do business in an endless round of meetings with tour operators and travel agents.

For the smaller hotels or tour companies with less muscle and marketing financing, it is hardly worth it. 'The tourist board pay part of the package, but you have to sell your hotel in the five minutes you have with a tour operator and travel agent. They can't even remember you or your hotel at the end of the day,' said one Barbadian hotelier from the south coast. Other small hotels approach it differently and often more effectively by contributing to 'familiarisation' trips made by travel agents, tour operators and journalists.

The internet is another – and new – marketing tool. Its existence means that, in theory, even the smallest hotel has a chance on the global market. It is certainly true that most Caribbean hotels and tour operators, however small, now have their own website; and for some small hotels, especially those catering for independent travellers, this is now the way much business is done. However, a website can not solve all promotional problems, and even putting your hotel or restaurant on a high profile site is a high price to pay.

Every aspect of marketing shows how it now has to rest on some sort of partnership (and not always an easy one) between the public and private sectors. Yet tensions remain between the two sectors, and the private sector claims that governments neither understand marketing (a claim that the professionals would endorse) nor spend enough money on it.

The Dominican Republic was unique in leaving the private sector to shoulder all the promotional side of the industry. In 1993, it spent less than US$100,000 on promotion, compared with US$15 million in Jamaica and US$25 million in the Bahamas. By 2001, however, the government had joined the big spenders, committing US$53 million to tourism in that year.

Even so, the private sector is quick to complain that the marketing budget is never enough, that the tourism offices are inefficient and that its personnel spend taxpayers' money on expensive jaunts to the shopping capitals of the world rather than engaging in hard sell. Small hotels and guest-houses in low-profile destinations feel particularly vulnerable. According to one OAS survey: 'The ineffectiveness of destination marketing for small properties is seen as a major constraint to acceptable small hotel sector performance.'

The small hotel sector is not, however, the only group to complain. Here, in 2002, is Butch Stewart of Sandals suggesting that the Jamaican Tourist Board (JTB) and the ministry of tourism are run by people who 'are either inept or have no sense of what their duties are.' He went on to say that given that the JTB had failed to draw up a strategic plan for the island's main markets, he would not 'support any further allocations to the JTB' unless 'every single tax dollar allocated to the JTB' was approved and monitored. The row exploded in the wake of the suspension of Jamaica's overseas advertising programme. The JTB responded by saying that the ministry of finance had not provided the cash for the board to pay its US advertising agency.

The all-inclusive sector is seen to take its marketing seriously; it is one indicator of its success. Indeed, the marketing budget alone of the Sandals chain exceeds that of many individual Caribbean destinations. Certainly, all-inclusives spend more than conventional hotels as the CTO's 1993 survey of all-inclusives indicated. It pointed out that, in St Lucia, all-inclusives spent some 80 per cent more on marketing on a per room basis than a sample of conventional hotels.

The relentless enthusiasm and energy of the Sandals chain is reflected in its chairman's response to September 2001 attacks saying there was no question of retreating. Stewart sent a 60-strong team to sell Sandals in the United States. He said: 'We certainly do not get into a bunker, we do the opposite as, while some people might still be travelling, we need to encourage others to do so by spreading the word that the Caribbean remains a safe zone.'

Jamaica has the Caribbean's largest individual advertising budget. The Jamaica campaign is extensive and sophisticated, with slogans such as 'Heavenly Jamaica, Hell for the Indecisive' and '500 years ago, Columbus Logged Jamaica. Now It's Your Turn.' Its print advertisements use high-class colour photography to appear in up-market newspapers and magazines.

Like the rest of the Caribbean, but very much a pioneer, the Jamaican tourist industry has wanted to get away from the idea of the island-as-beach. The slogan, introduced during Michael Manley's first administration of the late 1970s, was 'We're More than a Beach, We're a Country'. This was both a nationalist appeal to Jamaicans to have pride in their own identity and also a way of introducing tourists to the island's rich culture and hinterland. It was an affirmation of Jamaica and Jamaicans.

Jamaica's advertising had also fundamentally shifted from the 1960s message which portrayed white tourists 'being served' by blacks as an intrinsic attribute of the holiday. In 1968 the Jamaica Tourist Board had advertised its villas for rent as 'The Life You Wish You Led'. The villas, said the advertisement, come 'equipped with gentle people named Ivy or Maud or Malcolm who will cook, tend, mend, diaper, and launder for you. Who will "Mister Peter, please" you all day long, pamper you with homemade coconut pie, admire you when you look "soft" (handsome), giggle at your jokes and weep when you leave.'

In the 1990s advertising mode, tourists did things for themselves: explore, hike, ride, raft, windsurf, golf and so on. 'I don't think we've had images of waiters in our advertising material for a very long time,' said David Winter, who looked after the Jamaican Tourist Board's UK account in the 1990s. 'We want to show variety, that Jamaica is more than beach and palm trees. No other Caribbean island has such a contrast. Hence the shots of people. We have to identify the product in its most viable form for our market.'

The agency's 1995 campaign for television (some of which was a joint public/private sector promotion with Sandals) used images in which Jamaicans feature more often than tourists. There are reggae musicians, dancers, artists, children, country people; the faces range over age, gender and colour. The strong representation of Jamaicans is almost incidentally intercut with tourists riding horses, rafting on rivers, ending in romance and a good sunset. The music is Bob Marley's 'One Love', which provides the main message of the advertisement. 'Some of the more conservative elements in Jamaica didn't want us to use reggae because they didn't think the connotations were suitable,' Winter commented.

By 2002, a new television campaign for Jamaica was still promoting the island with Marley's 'One Love', with the concept 'It's a journey we both take together'. The agency emphasised that showing images of towns and countryside and Jamaicans of all ages, gender and colour underlines the idea that Jamaica is not just a sanitised beach experience. Both the new umbrella approach and a more diversified image for the region have been helping to sell the Caribbean. As the Caribbean Hospitality Training Institute's newsletter said in 2001: 'There is a new consumer out there, and we need to reach each one with a more personalised product in order to effectively compete in the world.'

A holiday now needs a focus, a special effect. That is one reason why the original 'niche' holiday – the floating hotel on every horizon, the cruise ship – has always been the region's greatest challenge.

NOTES

1. Caribbean Tourism Organisation, Caribbean Tourism Statistical Yearbook, 2000
2. Ibid.
3. Ibid.
4. Patrick Leigh Fermor, *The Traveller's Tree*, London, 1984, p.132
5. Hopeton Dunn and Leith Dunn, *People and Tourism*, Arawak Publications, 2002
6. In Focus, Tourism Concern, Autumn 2001
7. A Tearfund Guide to Tourism, Don't Forget Your Ethics, Tearfund, 2000
8. Gavan Titley, 'In the Compound of their Skins: Island Identities and the Global Market', Society for Caribbean Studies annual conference papers, vol 1, 2000
9. J.A. Froude, *The English in the West Indies*, London, 1888, p.43
10. June Jordan, *Moving Towards Home, Political Essays*, Virago Press, 1989
11. Dennis J Gayle, 'The Jamaican Tourist Industry' in Dennis Gayle and Goodrich, Jonathan (eds), *Tourism, Marketing and Management in the Caribbean*, London, 1993, p.53
12. Ibid.
13. Dunn & Dunn, op. cit.
14. John Bell, 'Caribbean Tourism in the Year 2000', in Gayle and Goodrich, op. cit., p.233
15. Dunn & Dunn, op. cit.
16. Caribbean Week, Barbados, 25 June-8 July 1994
17. *The Gleaner*, Jamaica, 15 April 1995
18. Organisation of American States (OAS), Economic Analysis of Tourism in Jamaica, Washington DC, 1994
19. *Travel Weekly*, July 2 2001

7

SAILING INTO THE SUNSET:
THE CRUISE SHIP INDUSTRY

The first journeys across the Caribbean Sea were made by Amerindian canoeists who settled the island chains, paddling north from the river systems of the Orinoco and the Amazon. Hundreds of years later the Spanish explorers arrived, and when other European powers joined the fight for control of the Caribbean it was the sea, not the land, which saw their greatest battles. Then the sea became an economic highway: for slavers, traders, buccaneers and fishermen; or it became a passageway for escaped slaves, indentured labourers and settlers, and later still a watery flight path for emigrants and boat people.

These shipping channels (except for those traditionally used by Caribs and fishermen) were linked with the economic and political power blocs of Europe and North America rather than with each other, for each harbour was a juncture of imperial arrival and departure. Caribbean ports are still working places. Container ships arrive with imports from tableware to tractors, mostly from the US, or cars from Japan, and they depart for Europe with bananas from Martinique or St Vincent. Now, however, by far the biggest vessels in port are cruise ships, also from the US, on pleasure journeys that no longer pay attention to those old colonial lines.

Crisscrossing the Caribbean Sea, these great white whales come and go quicker than the banana boats loading up alongside them. There is time though for seven hours or so on land – arriving in the morning and departing late afternoon.

Down the gangway come the cruise ship passengers, straight into a purpose-built, duty-free shopping mall, or into streets packed with tourist shops. Just like at the last port of call, most terminals have pizza joints, ice cream parlours, souvenir shops, perhaps a casino or two and hoardings with familiar transnational names: Dollar Rent a Car, Colombia Diamonds, Benetton, Gucci and Little Switzerland. There is time to fit in shopping, an island tour or a trip to a beach or to the cruise line's private island. Ranks of minibuses line up to whisk the tourists away on their pre-booked, pre-paid tours arranged by the cruise lines with chosen ground operators. Those who have failed to book can take their chances and get a cheaper deal with the many freelance taxi drivers and tour guides.

The most popular ports of call are the ones with the best duty-free shopping and casinos. The shops are ice-cold and imitate Fifth Avenue: the gifts, under glass, are much the same whether in Ocho Rios or Antigua – jewellery, perfumes, or china figurines of pastel-coloured cottages or simpering milk maids. Each destination is in competition with the next to provide a shoppers' paradise. St Kitts, for example, with its modest duty-free mall in Basseterre, must try to compete with St Maarten, its flashy Americanised neighbour, stiff with shops and casinos. 'We would like to see a greater turnover so we are upgrading our duty-free outlets,' said an official from the St Kitts division of tourism.

Armed with leaflets on shops recommended by the cruise ships, cruisers know which are the best and cheapest destinations. Not St Kitts, for sure, and even Antigua is not a star attraction. A young couple in Antigua's duty-free Heritage Quay did not plan to spend much money there. They were saving it for St Thomas, in the US Virgin Islands. 'We might as well go back on board and get some breakfast.' They had heard that shopping was better in St Thomas where the average expenditure in 2002 was US$260.77 compared to US$25.47 in Grenada.[1]

By afternoon, the passengers drift back to the ship with their purchases to eat (food is included in the cruise price) or to join those who have never left, preferring to glimpse the island from the rails. The last somewhat drunken stragglers, with T-shirts reading 'Drink Till You Sink', are scooped up the gangway. Soon, the quayside will be almost empty, as shopkeepers count their takings and taxi-drivers give up for the day. Only beggars and scavenging dogs remain as the ship disappears over the horizon, lights twinkling, on its way to another sunset at sea.

The Cruise Boom

The Caribbean cruise business is booming; it grows still larger as the numbers and sizes of ships visiting ever-bigger terminals increases. 'The untapped potential in the Caribbean – where we're putting more tonnage over the next several years – is vast,' claimed Julie Benson of Princess Lines, a subsidiary of P&O Cruises in the early 1990s.[2] A decade later that boast seemed well founded with the industry running at a remarkable capacity of more than 90 per cent, far higher than land-based tourism.

The 1990s saw particularly spectacular growth. At least 28 new ships were delivered to the cruise companies; most were destined for the Caribbean. The biggest companies, Royal Caribbean Cruise Line (RCCL), Carnival Cruise, Holland America and Princess, led the way. RCCL had three ships on order, all with a capacity for more than 1,800 passengers; Princess had spent almost US$1 billion on three ships, one, Grand Princess at 105,000 tonnes, the biggest liner ever. Carnival also had added 11 ships to its fleet by 1996, and spent US$400 million on the Italian-built boat Tiffany. Disney Corporation also entered the cruise market, with its first ship in operation in 1999. Even the smaller companies had increased their fleets, building vessels for 300 hundred or so passengers for the luxury market or for the even more select sail-ship market.[3]

The emphasis, however, is on size – and the bigger the better. Of the new ships built between 1995 and 2001, nearly 80 per cent had 1,500 or more berths. The largest, Mariner of the Sea, built for Royal Caribbean International at a price of US$520 million has a tonnage of 140,000, and a capacity for 3,835 passengers and more than 1,000 crew. Another giant, Carnival Glory, which was due to launch its seven-day cruises in mid 2003, boasts 14 passenger decks with 22 bars and lounges, a 15,000 square foot health club, four swimming pools and three restaurants, including an upscale 'steakhouse-style' supper club serving prime US beef.[4]

The Caribbean has nearly half of the world capacity of cruise 'bed days'. However, its share of the cruise business has declined from a peak of 60 per cent of all bed days out of North America in 1991 to 48 per cent in 2000. According to the CTO this is because the cruise industry has 'sought to add itineraries for the burgeoning capacity.' Even if its share has decreased, its awesome volume of business continues to expand. In the Caribbean itself, it has grown much faster than land-based tourism – from 7.8 million passenger arrivals in 1990 to an estimated 20.5 million in 2004. The Bahamas, a traditional cruise destination close to Florida, was the busiest port of call, with nearly 3 million cruise ship passenger arrivals in 2003. Next most popular destination was Cozumel (2.7 million) on the Mexican coast, the Caymen Islands (1.8 million), the US Virgin Islands (1.7 million), followed by Puerto Rico (1.2 million), St Maarten (1.1 million) and Jamaica (also 1.1 million).[5]

Many destinations have recorded spectacular growth. St Lucia, for example, had 58,000 cruise arrivals in 1986 but 393,000 in 2003, when Dominica recorded 177,000, up from 11,500 in 1986. Other islands with an expanding cruise ship market were St Kitts and Nevis, Aruba and Curaçao.[6] Belize and the Dominican Republic were late, but expanding, entries and even Haiti, abandoned by the cruise ship industry in 1993 when sanctions against its military regime were announced, was back on the itinerary by 1995. Only Trinidad, perhaps, with an industrial rather than a tourist base to its economy, has not seen a massive rise in cruise visitors, along with some of the very small islands that do not have cruise facilities, such as Anguilla, Saba, and St Barthélémy.

Most cruises begin in either Miami or Port Everglades in Florida or in San Juan, Puerto Rico. Of non-US bases, Aruba, Antigua and Martinique also play their part, all being significant airline hubs for the European market. From these starting points, the ships crisscross the Caribbean Sea, dropping into islands here and islands there as they see fit, depending on the duration of the cruise and the range of attractions that the destinations can muster.

Rocking the Boat

Yet while the cruise lines steamed ahead, unloading more and more passengers off bigger and more luxurious ships onto the docksides of small Caribbean states, fundamental questions began to be asked by the mid 1990s about the benefits of the cruise industry to the Caribbean and its people, and its long-term effect on the region's own land-based tourism.

Taxation has been a thorny issue. Departure taxes for both airline and cruise passengers have traditionally been set by individual governments. This head tax is one way in which the cruise industry contributes to the expenses involved in providing appropriate port or airport facilities. In the case of the cruise tax, this ranged in 2000 from US$1.50 in Guadeloupe and St Maarten (an increase from zero in the mid 1990s) to US$15 (Jamaica and the Bahamas). Inter-country rivalry and what are considered to be differences in the quality of facilities offered to cruise ships by each destination were said to explain such a discrepancy.[7]

To eliminate these discrepancies, in January 1992 the Organisation of Eastern Caribbean States (OECS) had agreed to adopt a standard head tax of US$10 to take effect in October of that year. The decision did not please the cruise lines. 'To solve the hotel problem by raising taxes on cruise ships is stupid and punitive,' said Bob Dickinson, president of Carnival Cruise Lines.[8] Retaliation was not long in coming. The RCCL announced that it would drop St Lucia, one of the seven OECS states, from its itinerary; the Nordic Prince, which had made 18 calls to St Lucia in 1991, also decided to go elsewhere. The boycott of St Lucia resulted in calls of solidarity from other CTO members, but in the event they were empty promises.

The OECS position was, however, strengthened when Caricom, the wider regional organisation, also came up with a plan to adopt a unified tax (Jamaica had already taken the lead). It was to be set at US$5 in April 1994, to be raised to US$7.5 in October that year and to US$10 by 1995.[9] For the Caribbean this was a major step forward, since earlier discussions about increasing the head tax had only taken place bilaterally, giving the cruise operators the in-built advantage. The operators could play off one country against another by threatening to skip one destination for another with a lower tax. This time the region as a whole seemed to be flexing its muscles. As Jean Holder said: 'The concept of the minimum tax, set at a reasonable level, was intended to enable the weak destinations to earn a little much needed revenue, to create some Caribbean solidarity and thus effect an adjustment to the strategic advantage which is held largely by the cruise lines. Its success is dependent entirely on each country keeping the agreement.'[10]

Caricom's move raised the possibility of a regional approach, not just about the head tax but about other important issues surrounding the cruise industry. John Compton, St Lucia's prime minister, expressed the opinion that the region would 'no longer accept mirrors and baubles for the use of its patrimony.'[11]

The tax issue was symptomatic of the tensions between the cruise ships and the region's land-based tourist industry. Those on the side of the cruise ships express barely disguised contempt for the Caribbean's hotel industry. Without the cruise industry, said Joel Abed in Travel Trade News, 'to both promote and present its attractions and facilities to potential vacationers, the Caribbean resort industry, as we know it today, would all-too-quickly become a virtual tourist desert.'[12] Bob Dickinson of Carnival expressed his position only marginally less aggressively. 'They're not only biting the hand that feeds them, they're yanking off the whole arm.'[13]

The tax row provoked similar outbursts of passionate rhetoric from the region. There was a general distrust of what was considered to be imperious behaviour by the cruise lines. Yet despite this, and the agreement made at the highest level in Caricom, the unified passenger head tax was not achieved within the agreed time span. (St Lucia even aborted its decision to raise the head tax in 1994 according to the OECS decision.) Indeed, as has been seen, it has yet to be achieved.

Royston Hopkin, then president of the Caribbean Hotel Association, conceded in the wake of the row: 'The cruise ship lobby is very strong and the governments have been very weak. The cruise lines sweetened the governments who were not united. We gave our best shot, but by the time the heads of government got to it the three-tier system was introduced and this weakened our position.' The Caribbean's failure dismayed many sections of its tourist industry. It demonstrated the inability of the region to take a unified stand and also showed just how powerful the cruise industry's grip was.

Peter Odle, then president of the Barbados Hotel Association, was another aggrieved hotelier. 'I was against cruise ships from the beginning,' he said. 'The Caribbean will not realise the cruise business is a disservice until it's nearly too late. The cruise ships are using our most precious asset – the sea – polluting it like hell and not making any significant contribution to our economy. And instead of taking a firm stand, the governments are all over the place; there is a lack of political will.' Similar sentiments were expressed by Allen Chastenet, a former Director of the St Lucia Tourist Board: 'If anyone is sucking the Caribbean dry it is the cruise ships.'

A further row developed in 1997 when the Organisation of Eastern Caribbean States, representing seven islands in the eastern Caribbean, decided to impose an environmental levy of US$1.50 per capita on all visitors, including those from the cruise ships, entering its member countries. The fee would help pay for a waste management project, partly financed by the World Bank and aimed at improving the collection of waste from sources such as cruise ships. The Florida-Caribbean Cruise Association objected, saying that its ships had 'zero discharge' and that each vessel 'usually' had 'about US$10 million worth of waste disposal facilities, including incinerators, pulpers and compactors'. It argued that an across-the-board levy was not needed. Finally, the FCCA agreed to pay. It was a rare victory for regional unity.[14]

The CTO has continued to take the position that Caribbean governments have the right to take action to make the competition between land and sea tourism more equitable.[15] On the other hand, it has also recognised that the Caribbean doesn't hold many cards in relation to the cruise industry. 'The cruise lines have the ability to move their ships and they do move them when they are not happy,' said Jean Holder in 2000.[16]

From the shore, foreign cruise lines are seen as having built-in advantages over land-based tourism – which generates greater local revenue and employment per passenger – and these advantages are used, it is argued, at the expense of the Caribbean, in a particularly rapacious manner.

Despite the row over head taxes, cruise ships do not pay as many taxes as the land-based industry, where taxation either doubles the price of many purchases or restricts the hotelier to buying regional products only. Hotels must also pay corporation tax and casino tax profits. In contrast, cruise ships are seen as moveable feasts which sail away into the sunset, their bars and casinos untaxed. Secondly, raising money to build hotels is problematic even though construction work employs local labour and supports local financial institutions. In contrast, cruise ship contracts go to overseas shipyards largely in Europe, where long-term, low-interest loans are also available. Thirdly, more and more hotels are now owned by Caribbean nationals; no cruise ships are owned by Caribbean nationals.

The contrast continues. Caribbean hotels provide jobs for locals, with work permits required for the employment of non-nationals. Cruise lines operating in the Caribbean, on the other hand, are free to employ whom they wish. Their ships are not registered in the United States, their home base, but use flags of convenience to avoid its labour laws, taxes and regulations. Thus, as the president of the Carnival Corporation, whose ships are registered in Panama, wrote in his book, *Selling the Sea*: 'Of course, ships registered in these flag-of-convenience nations pay lower wages and taxes on an aggregate basis than those registered in the United States (or Norway or Italy for that matter). But that makes it possible for them to offer cruises at a much lower cost than if their ships were registered in countries with restrictive hiring policies.'[17]

Many lines employ European officers, with North American and western European staff in areas like business and entertainment , supported by a Third World crew. Around 50 countries may be represented as cruise employees. The officers on the Carnival's *Fantasy*, for instance, are Italian, while what is called its 'international' crew is drawn from Latin America, India and the Philippines. Crew members, often from the poorest parts of the Third World, are paid low wages, labour in shoddy working conditions and endure an authoritarian management code, according to a 2002 study. 'Conditions for workers below deck haven't improved in decades,' said Tony Sasso, a Miami-based inspector with the International Transport Workers Federation. 'Many are reluctant to come forward and complain. To most people, workers on cruise liners are nonentities. They have an almost invisible existence.'[18]

In contrast, work in the land-based industry may seem more attractive with many employees being paid union rates and enjoying trade union representation. This may be one reason why so few Caribbean nationals have jobs on cruise ships. Meanwhile, other nationals – from the Philippines or Bangladesh, for example – find the wages better than at home.

The proportion of Caribbean products purchased by cruise lines also remains small. Caribbean supplies to the cruise industry are estimated at between one and five per cent of total requirements. According to the FCCA, member cruise lines spent US$51.2 million on Caribbean supplies in 1993. Technical inputs such as petroleum products, parts and chemicals represent US$30 million (59 per cent of total expenditure), while handling services such as warehousing and stevedoring at ports account for US$7.1 million or 14 per cent of total expenditure. Just over a quarter of the cruise lines' expenditure in the Caribbean was on food and drink (US$13.8 million), of which half was on beer and liquor. Foods included fruit and vegetables, dairy products, bread, water, spices, seafood, coffee and sugar. If this figure is at all accurate, only US$6 per passenger was spent on food and drink grown and produced within the Caribbean.[19]

The list of significant Caribbean suppliers is short: Bico Ice Cream and Pine Hill Dairy, both of Barbados; Dominica Coconut Products; Commonwealth Brewery of the Bahamas; Tropical Beverages of Trinidad and Desnoes & Geddes; Red Stripe Beer, Jamaica.[20] Toilet paper from Trinidad and Tobago also joined the list after what the managing director of Savvy Traders Ltd called 'a long and frustrating battle'. The result is that not only are most cruise ships supplied by US companies, but that fresh produce from outside the region is also flown or shipped into the Caribbean during a cruise. Thus, in one ludicrous example, a barge from Venezuela filled with bananas was seen to supply the cruise ships in St Lucia, one of the Caribbean's major banana producers.

Since the tax row, however, the FCCA has been seen to play a more sensitive role. There have been opportunities for purchasers and

Caribbean producers to talk to each other at trade shows and conferences. Such meetings, said the FCCA, enabled these companies 'to strengthen their contacts within individual cruise lines, make new contacts and learn from other successful suppliers of cruise lines.'[21]

The difficulties (quantity, quality, regularity of supply, delivering on time) faced by Caribbean producers are similar, and even greater, to those they face in supplying the land-based industry (see Chapter Three). In a commitment to high standards, the cruise lines make tough demands on their suppliers. Part of the RCCL's mission statement, for example, pledges 'to locate, buy and deliver the highest quality of specified goods and services at the fairest overall cost possible in a timely manner.'[22] The supplies must be competitive with products from Hong Kong and Taiwan; they must be on time and they must be delivered in an appropriate condition. They must also fit US tastes. According to RCCL's head of purchasing, American cruise passengers expect steak from grain-fed cattle and brand-familiar products, such as yoghurt and cereal. Such demands are beyond most Caribbean producers.

From this low base, selling Caribbean goods to the cruise lines has proceeded painfully slowly. It began in the early 1990s with a CTO initiative which, according to Jean Holder, brought together the Caricom Export Development programme and cruise lines to discuss their needs. Even the successful and efficient Dominica Coconut Products, now a Colgate-Palmolive subsidiary, took three years to sign a contract with the RCCL to supply three million bars of soap a year.[23] Most producers and tourist boards have been only vaguely aware of the needs of the cruise lines and even less able to deal in the quantity and the quality required. The small scale of many producers and the lack of developed regional exporting and marketing groupings have further limited the opportunities.

One successful link-up between producers and cruise ships shows just how small – and rare – are such occasions. In 2001 up to 10,000 tons of tomatoes from St Kitts-Nevis found their way each week onto the dining tables of Royal Caribbean International ships. The contract was the result of collaboration between the producers, shippers, cruise lines and the Republic of Taiwan's agricultural mission on St Kitts-Nevis. It was trumpeted as a major achievement, with further opportunities for other crops to reach the cruise shippers sometime in the future.[24]

Yet the cruise lines have always made it clear that servicing their ships is 'no easy task' and 'cannot be taken lightly'. 'This is a very price competitive business, often with very little differentiation in price. The key difference is who has what we need and who can deliver it 100 per cent accurately,' said the director of purchasing for Carnival Cruise Lines in 1998.

Despite what appears to be an uneven match between sea and land tourism, regional governments continue to give the cruise ships their blessing, boasting of the increase in passenger arrivals over the years. Responding to the needs of bigger ships, for example, the host countries have to expand and improve port facilities. The FCCA is in no doubt as to its requirements: 'Ports must be welcoming, modern and comfortable in order to effectively accommodate upwards of 3,000 "guests" and crew arriving at the same time. Services must be first-class, and ground excursions must be efficient, dependable, and offer visitors the best of the destination,' is the FCCA's line. In an article, 'Keeping Up With The Megaships', it continued: 'When the passengers disembark they should receive the same seamless attention and service that they do on board the cruise ship.'[25]

The ships tie up at ports which have been especially deepened, widened and modernised by local governments. To be able to offer a home porting facility (using a cruise destination as an arrival and departure point, as in San Juan, Puerto Rico, for example) is another reason behind port improvements. But San Juan has faced criticism from the cruise industry. While Puerto Rico had spent money on land-based facilities, similar developments had not taken place at the port, the FCCA complained. The cruise industry had been treated with 'an astonishing indifference' with the infrastructure lagging behind the needs of the ever-increasing size and numbers of cruise ships and San Juan had become 'unappealing'. This remained the case until early in 2001 when a new administration had, according to the FCCA, decided to stop the drift to indifference and to begin a 'new sense of welcome' for all those future cruise ship visitors.[26]

This sort of criticism from the FCCA makes both old and new cruise destinations scramble to invest millions of dollars on new facilities. In the eastern Caribbean, all the islands have sprung into action to improve their cruise facilities. Dominica spent US$28 million on a dock extension at its Roseau port and a wharf and terminal building at the Cabrits, a national park on the north of the island, to boost its cruise ship arrival figures. The facilities opened in 1991, and in that year alone cruise arrivals increased from 6,800 to 65,000. St Kitts, too, has sought to expand its cruise business. In 1994, a US$16.25 million loan agreement was signed with the Bank of Nova Scotia to construct a new cruise ship berth, separate from the dust and cargo of the old port.[27] In 2002, it opened later than planned, the construction twice having been demolished by hurricanes. In 1995, St Vincent also announced a cruise ship berth development at its capital, Kingstown, to be funded by the Kuwaiti Fund and the European Investment Bank.[28] The latest destination to publicise a major upgrade of what is called its 'cruise-tourism product' is the US Virgin Islands. A US$30 million expansion of its second pier was announced in 2002. 'If it is not built, St Thomas, which is now number 4 in the world in cruise ship destinations, within a decade will drop to number 10,' said Gordon Finch of the Virgin Islands Port Authority.[29]

Even larger islands with established cruise ship facilities sometimes have to run to keep up. The logistics of providing such facilities and service for these mega-ships is an enormous challenge. Ocho Rios in Jamaica, a popular cruise ship destination, was, by the beginning of the 21st century, considered to have an inadequate port for the forthcoming mega-liners. A lack of cleanliness at St Vincent's capital, Kingstown, and harassment of visitors led to cruise cancellations; similarly, the Princess Line decided to drop Jamaica from its itineraries in the 2001 to 2002 season citing 'very poor comments from visitors'. The Caribbean is constantly addressing such problems – many of which require massive investment to overcome. It's not easy being a host to the cruise ship industry.

Big Spenders?

The cruise lines also have another winning card: their very own islands. Cruise lines can reduce the number of days in port by buying or leasing their own island or by anchoring off a deserted stretch of beach. As *Caribbean Travel News* noted: 'Increasingly, the trend is for cruise lines to go one step further from taking their passengers around the Caribbean islands – and to give them one all to themselves.'[30] This policy was begun in the early 1980s by Norwegian Cruise Line, which owns Great Stirrup Cay in the Bahamas, now 'remodelled' with a wider beach, a barbecue area and water sports. A key point is that the islands are uninhabited. Holland America's 1997 brochure about Half Moon Cay, also in the Bahamas, paints an appropriate picture for the cruisers. 'Half Moon Cay recalls the idyllic Caribbean of 30 years ago. There are no hassles. It's just you and a balmy island with a white-sand beach, coral reefs and a clutter-free arrangement of attractive facilities designed for casual roaming.' One inference is that it's desirable because it has no inhabitants – no needy locals to get in the way of the fantasy. By the end of the 20th century, six out of the eight major cruise lines operating in the Caribbean owned their own private islands.[31]

On these islands, the cruise lines show off their private beaches, where what is called 'cruise-style service' is on hand with barbecue and bar provided by cruise staff. Princess Cruises owns Princess Cay on Eleuthera, Bahamas, ('For total tropical tranquillity, it's hard to beat this land of lotus-eaters') and Saline Bay, Mayreau, in the Grenadines ('every castaway's first choice'). The RCCL owns Coco Cay, also on the Bahamas, and leases Labadee in Haiti, an isolated promontory on the north coast where tourists spend a day on a beach surrounded by a high wall patrolled by guards. When cruise lines create their own version of paradise, they avoid port fees and passenger head taxes while protecting their customers from the less than paradisical reality of much Caribbean life.

Desert-island days, days at sea, island tours booked through the cruise ship: all are ways in which cruise lines can persuade customers to buy their services and thereby control the quality and quantity of the holiday experience. Another way is to attract customers to spend money on board in the shops, boutiques and bars, available at all times (except when the ships are in port) and often at competitive prices compared to goods sold on land. The Princess Line brochure states: 'There's no need for you to be in port to go shopping. Both Canberra and Sea Princess carry a remarkably comprehensive selection of goods...' As an Economist Intelligence Unit report on the Caribbean pointed out: 'On board shopping, which by definition is duty-free, is being promoted increasingly aggressively as a means of maximising their share of a passenger's overall holiday expenditure.'[32] This continues to affect the land-based duty-free outlets, which find that the outlets on the cruise ships can outbid them.

The Fantasy of Carnival Cruise Lines is a typical giant cruise ship that provides its customers with just about everything they could desire. Sailing out of Cape Canaveral bound for Nassau and Freeport, its 2,634 passengers have paid as little as US$249 in 2002 for a three-day cruise. It has two dining rooms, nine bars and lounges, including Cleopatra's Bar (decorated with hieroglyphics and Egyptian statuary) and the Cat's Lounge with its tables in the shape of bottle tops and cats' eyes glinting from the ceiling. There is a casino and concert hall for 'Las Vegas style revues', and 1,022 'accommodation units', most of which convert to 'king-size beds', while 28 have bathtub whirlpools.

There are three outdoor swimming pools, a 500-foot banked and padded jogging track and a health club. The belly of this gleaming ship boasts two glass elevators that surround the Spectrum, a twirling lump of coloured geometric kitsch.

The cruise industry continues to introduce more elaborate and more unusual attractions in its ships. Appealing to a broader market of cruisers – away from the stereotypical image – cruise ships have introduced ice-skating rinks, rock-climbing walls and basketball courts. No Caribbean island can compete with such an array of delights.

'This is a tremendously dynamic industry. It's great value for money; everyone can afford a cruise. Everything is done for you and the marketing is tremendous. The passengers see the ship as the destination,' claimed Robert Stegina of the Fantasy. Or as a Carnival spokesman said: 'People do not come to us to visit the Caribbean, but to be on our boats.'[33] If this is so, what then is left for the land destinations? How much do customers spend on land if the ship becomes the economic centrepiece of the holiday?

Cruise lines argue that they make a major contribution to the economic well-being of the region. Their reasoning is affirmed in periodic reports commissioned by the FCCA. The Economic Impact of the Passenger Cruise Industry on the Caribbean, for example, drew its material from surveys of passengers and crew undertaken in the first quarter of 2000. It reported that passengers and crew accounted for a total annual economic impact of US$2.6 billion throughout the Caribbean of which US$1.4 billion was in direct spending and US$1.2 billion in indirect. It estimated that a typical ship, carrying 2,000 passengers and 900 crew members generated almost US$259,000 in passenger and crew expenditure during a port visit. In a survey of 10 ports, average spending per passenger per call totalled US$104 ranging from US$173.24 in the US Virgin Islands (USVI) to US$53.84 in San Juan, Puerto Rico. Crew members spent an average of US$72 per port and were similarly most attracted to goods and services in the USVI. Other figures showed that cruise-related indirect expenditure generated 60,000 jobs throughout the Caribbean.[34]

The CTO's own figures for passenger spend at various ports in 2002 shows a different pattern. The USVI scored highest in passenger spend, with an estimate of US$260.77. At the bottom of the CTO's scale is St Vincent with a passenger spend of US$15.36. Whatever the statistics, most of passenger on-shore expenditure went on duty-free shopping, with much less on tours and attractions and little on food.

In 2000, however, the CTO reported on 'the gradually increasing economic contribution from the cruising sector.' It commented that while cruise passenger expenditure was just under 6 per cent of all visitor expenditure at the beginning of the 1990s, this had increased to 12 per cent in 2000. Statistics threw up an infinite variety of claims in that decade; the EIU similarly plumped for a total cruise ship contribution of 6 per cent in 1990.[35] The Bahamas, the largest of the cruise destinations, put the industry's contribution at 10 per cent in 1993, while Jamaica's 1994 OAS report concluded that cruise ship passengers contributed only 3.6 per cent of tourist expenditure, 'more than a quarter of which was for goods at in-bond stores which contribute little to the economy.'[36]

Big Business

Conflicting statistics, major leakages of spending, especially of duty-free goods, and a generally low contribution to the overall income generated by tourism in the Caribbean are themselves indicators of the economic limitations of the cruise industry. But even more fundamentally, who earns the money spent by the cruise industry? Who benefits from the government's expenditure on port and shopping facilities and such expenses as extra police security?

The cruise ship disembarkation points, with their car rentals, taxi services, helicopters, and tour-operator booths all under one roof, are largely controlled either by transnational chains, by local elites or by established expatriates. These groups make private contracts with the cruise lines to act as their agents; they also own many of the retail outlets.

The Bridgetown Cruise Terminal, for example, which opened in January 1994 is a joint venture between the port authority, three local companies (Cave Shepherd, Harrison's and Beer & Beverage Ltd) and the public (25 per cent of the shares). Its financial structure was criticised by commentators including Professor Hilary Beckles of the University of the West Indies at Cave Hill, who commented: 'Those three companies have used their position to franchise to the duty-free outlets. They have restructured the white corporate structure of Broad Street [the capital's main shopping area] and duplicated it at the cruise terminal.' Indeed, there are replicas of local streets and a chattel-house village – all accessible without leaving the terminal. While the chairman of the Port Authority, Edmund Harrison, denied any such monopolisation of the terminal, opportunities for the smaller entrepreneur appeared to be limited.[37]

The extent of the interlocking of interests between cruise ships and local big business at the expense of local small business is at the heart of the debate about the cruise industry's economic contribution to the region.

Complaints by small businesses in the Cayman Islands, for instance, illustrate this issue. Some years ago, taxi drivers, watersports businesses and tour operators threatened to hold demonstrations against cruise ships if their grievances were not addressed. The main complaint of the Committee against Cruise Ship Abuse of Local Watersports/Taxi Owners was that cruise lines pre-booked passengers on island and watersports tours with a few, foreign-controlled companies. 'Small operators like us do not have the financial resources, marketing infrastructure or contacts to approach the cruise lines in Miami,' said the committee's chairman, Ron Ebanks. Cruise passengers were charged US$30 by the cruise ships for a snorkelling trip that was minutes from the cruise dock, where equipment could be rented at the site from local suppliers for US$8. Ebanks also charged that cruise ships told passengers not to use local taxis but to take a tour sold on board.

There have been similar complaints from small retailers in Nassau and Freeport in the Bahamas, where T-shirt sellers claim that cruise ship staff accompany cruisers on shopping trips, recommending certain stores which pay for advertising space or are big enough to offer concessions. The retailers allege that shopping is controlled by the few large outlets which have made financial deals with the cruise lines.

Such difficulties, together with occasional insults and patronising behaviour from some cruise officials, have further reinforced suspicions that the cruise industry is a foreign-controlled body that seeks to make deals to its own advantage rather than in partnership with the Caribbean. While the immediate bitterness sparked off by the tax row has simmered down, even the CTO's diplomatic Jean Holder remarked that while some cruise lines seek a partnership in cooperation, others 'seem to see the Caribbean simply as an area of exploitation for profit.'[38]

On the other hand, many of the islands now have a population that has come to depend on the cruise ship visitors. In Dominica, for example, where by the end of the 1990s the banana industry was in disarray, many people in the informal economy had turned to finding a source of income in tourism, and, in particular, the cruise ships. The CTO recorded average spending per cruise visitor to Dominica of US$27.70 in 2002, the third lowest of all reported destinations after St Vincent and Grenada. During the tourist season, four boats a week tie up in the capital, Roseau. Across the road, at the converted old market place, vendors' booths are crammed together selling craft that varies little from one booth to another. If the tourists only buy sporadically, it is better than nothing and 'better than staying at home', according to one vendor. For other vendors, like the Rastafarian who sells attractively printed T-shirts and incense sticks, every little dollar counts as it does for the women who provide the ice for the vendors at the entrance to one of the island's main sites. Whatever the tourist brings, however little, makes a difference.

Whatever the temperature of the relationship, cruise companies remain fierce and powerful competitors. They also spend large sums in promoting themselves. Behind the campaigns is the 'concept', spelt out by Bob Dickinson of Carnival Cruise Lines when he listed six aspects of the cruise 'product' which, he said, were superior to a land-based holiday: value for money; a 'trouble-free' environment; excellent food; the 'romance of the sea'; superior activities and entertainment; 'an atmosphere of pampering service.'[39]

These factors are emphasised in cruise advertising, a constant presence on North American television and in magazines and newspapers. Indeed, cruise ship brochures dazzle with descriptions of a life of luxury on board. As the FCCA's executive director, Michelle Paige, told Caribbean Week, the passengers require excellent service on land because they are accustomed to the high standards on board. The Caribbean, she said, 'could do a better job of providing a better service.'[40]

The Princess brochure, for instance, exudes self-congratulation: pampering includes a 'fluffy white bathrobe' and 'delicious petit fours to welcome you to your cabin and a foil-wrapped chocolate left on your pillow each night.' Then there is the gala buffet, which, according to the same brochure, is an 'ingenious display of gastronomic artistry that's a tribute to the skills of ice-carving and sugar-sculpture... But for sheer flamboyance, nothing can match the Champagne Waterfall, a glittering pyramid of 600 glasses with bubbly cascading from top to bottom. Magnifique! And the perfect introduction to the night ahead.'

Such flourishes have little to do with the Caribbean but if the ship is the destination, the Caribbean itself loses relevance except as a vague and shimmering backdrop. Or, as Carnival's Bob Dickinson, put it: 'The limited number of countries and ports offered is not a deterrent to Carnival customers; after all the ship is the attraction, not the port of call.'[41]

Both the covert message of the cruise industry and its upfront promotional material compare cruise tourism favourably to land-based tourism. 'Should anyone be in doubt that the cruise ships are in competition with us, the attached photocopy of a Royal Caribbean advertisement should set their mind at rest,' was the curt memorandum sent by John Bell, executive vice president of the Caribbean Hotel Association, to his board of directors and member hotel associations. The advertisement was headed 'Why A Hotel Should Be Your Last Resort', and the introductory blurb began:

> There's not a lobby on earth that can stack up to the Centrum on a Royal Caribbean ship. Now compare all that a Royal Caribbean cruise offers versus a typical resort and you'll stop pretty quickly. There just is no comparison... A Royal Caribbean cruise ship is a resort of the very first order. Choosing anything less should be your last resort.

The cruise lines combine that sort of aggressive promotion with a hard sell system to retailers. Nearly all cruises in the US market are sold through travel agents who are visited by armies of sales representatives. The commission on sales paid to the agents tends to be higher than that paid for hotel-based holidays. At the same time, the cruise business has been discounting, anxious to fill the berths and so maintain its high occupancy rates. Carnival's pricing strategy is budgeted for an amazing 100 per cent occupancy, which means that prices can be kept down. Caribbean hotels are unable to respond.

While some cruise analysts have pondered the wisdom of the rampant expansion in ships and berths, the big cruise lines continue to report healthy figures. In the third quarter of 2002, for example, Carnival announced profits of US$500.8 million. Increasingly the giant lines are becoming an oligarchy as economies of scale push out the smaller operators. The third largest cruise operator in 2003, P&O Princess Cruises, was discussing a merger in 2002; this would make it the biggest single cruise line overtaking Carnival Cruise Lines – with its 43 ships and five in construction (at an estimated value of US$2.3 billion).

And the passengers, mainly American, keep on coming, and no longer just the old and the rich. The market is changing: the young are being targeted by advertising and are responding. Cruises now attract honeymooners and families, and other 'niche' markets; there are conference cruises, theme cruises around sports, music and education and so on. The populist Carnival Cruise Lines announces in its on-line information that around 30 per cent of its passengers are under 35, with 40 per cent between 35 and 55 and 30 per cent over 55.

The cruise lines argue that they market the Caribbean as well as the ship. A cruise, they say, provides an introduction to the region, a floating showcase for the charms of the Caribbean. One study suggested that up to 25 per cent of stayover tourists had first sampled their holiday choice from the rails of a cruise ship. Another survey indicated that 40 per cent of cruise passengers would like to return to the Caribbean for a land-based holiday.

The Caribbean often misses opportunities to entice cruisers back on to dry-land holidays, say the cruise lines. According to the FCCA's Michelle Paige, destinations do not package themselves as well as they could or advertise their attractions. 'If we don't make the passengers feel comfortable, they are going to get right back on the ship.'[42] The FCCA's 2000 survey also asked the tourists whether they would be likely to return to 10 named destinations on a cruise or on a land-based holiday. The answers showed that the passengers were more likely to return on a cruise. Between 59 per cent (Bahamas) and 90 per cent (USVI) of passengers wanted to return on a cruise. Only Jamaica and the USVI (and Cozumel in Mexico) scored above 60 per cent as places where the passengers would be likely to return as stayover visitors, with only 39 per cent, for example, likely to return to St Kitts.[43] The CTO's strategic plan of 2002 calls for an increase in the conversion of cruise ship tourists to stayover tourists.

Possibilities of partnership, stressed by both the CTO and the FCCA in their more conciliatory moods, have begun to be explored in marketing, employment strategies, sourcing and so on. There is also much talk within the region of a more concerted approach towards the unresolved problems presented by the cruise industry. These more conciliatory tones, perhaps born of desperation, were made official at the end of the Caricom tourism summit in 2001 when a further attempt to ease the tensions between the sea and land industries was launched. A Caribbean cruise committee, co-chaired by the tough-talking Paige and the equally robust figure of Butch Stewart, was formed in an attempt to promote 'effective collaboration' and to maximise benefits to the region.

Yet the introduction of some sort of licensing system for cruise ships in which contracts and guidelines would be observed on both sides, seem far away. In the meantime, the cruise lines are often perceived as using the Caribbean islands as a chain of low-charge parking lots, coming and going as they see fit. The problem is that without them there would be more hardship and less opportunity for those hundreds of thousands of people who watch for the great white whales to appear over the horizon each morning.

Of course, the cruise lines are not the only users of the Caribbean Sea. There is a growing group of tourists who also use the sea as the focus of their holiday for water-skiing, surfing, windsurfing, fishing, sailing, diving or snorkelling. Fishing and sailing, chartered and bareboat, remain the up-market pursuits. Fishing, in particular, has been a sport for tourists from the early days, and it remains particularly popular in the Bahamas where record catches are made in deep-sea game fishing, while in the shallows fishing for barracuda and bonefish is popular.

The British Virgin Islands, one of the region's largest watersport destinations, stresses the attractions of its unspoilt islands and cays. 'One can imagine no better holiday for a fisherman than cruising in a motorboat among the islands, with a tent for shore at nights, with food and conversation enriched from the day's catch,' enthused a circular from the West India Committee in 1921. Then, there was no mention of sailing, but by 1958, McKay's Guide mentioned that the islands had 'wonderful sailing in the waters off their coasts' and advised: 'With time on your hands in St Thomas and a liking for the sea, you couldn't do better than to charter one of the many boats available for the purpose, and cruise among these islands for as many days as you can spare.' Ten years later, another guidebook commented that 'this part of the Caribbean is becoming known as a yachtsman's paradise.'

The British Virgin Islands has forbidden obtrusive development, but encourages marinas and luxury secluded resorts. The main focus of development has been the yacht charter business, which began in 1967. There are now more than 500 yachts for hire out of the British Virgin Islands, which makes it one of the largest bareback charter fleets in the world. Charter yacht tourists outnumber hotel tourists and spend more money than them.[44] Much of the business is in flotillas where beginners in groups of 12 to 15 sail in small dinghies under expert supervision.

Modern-style marinas now dot the Caribbean, hang-outs for a largely young, American clientele, who pay handsomely for a week's charter. For the yachties, the Caribbean is the fashionable place to be in the winter months, when the sailing elite of the world converges on

Martinique after the Route du Rhum transatlantic run or St Lucia for Christmas following the Atlantic Rally for Cruisers. The regatta season then moves on to St Maarten, Puerto Rico and the Virgin Islands before ending in April with Antigua's Sailing Week at English Harbour, where Nicholson's Yachtyard, an expatriate stronghold, was one of the first charter bases in the Caribbean in the 1940s.

Marinas are big business and Jamaica has a new project on hand: a marina at Port Antonio, one of the oldest tourism locations in the Caribbean. Promoted as a 'mega yacht destination', it will, according to the Port Authority of Jamaica, 'compare favourably with any waterfront tourism development in the world.' It will accommodate a range of craft: from 'boutique' cruise ships to the mega yachts of the mega rich. The argument is that Port Antonio will benefit from such up-market visitors. 'The last yacht that came here for a week bought £670 worth of flowers every day,' said Noel Hylton, the president and chief executive of the Port Authority.[45] The opportunities – for linkages into the local economy – are there.

Fishing, sailing and windsurfing tourists are different from the beach-based tourists. They tend to be more up-market, and traditionally were socially and racially select (in an island like Barbados, this is still the case). However, at another level, they are more informal than other tourists. On Bequia, for example, the yachties, who cultivate a lotus-eating manner, hang around St Elizabeth Bay and its bars, owned by barefooted expatriates. While the tourist establishment eyes the boat people with some suspicion (they may be rich but they are scruffy), the yachties themselves appear less affronted by authentic Caribbean life than nervous package tourists. And they can make a significant, and direct, contribution to island economies, depending on local suppliers for provisions. In many cases, farmers supply direct to sailors at the marinas. In the British Virgin Islands two types of trading go on. There is the merchant who supplies the flotillas with fruit and vegetables from the US, shipped in on containers from Florida. The alternative is to buy from individuals who provide Caribbean fruit and vegetables to the more discerning boat captains and owners from a boat-to-boat shop. In Grenada, a small farming cooperative relies on business with sailors for its success and expansion (see Chapter Three) while for the yachties at the uninhabited Tobago Cays in the Grenadines, young men from Union Island arrive by boat to sell whatever service is required.

Much of the ownership of watersports business, however, remains in expatriate hands. This is partly because of the capital expenditure involved and partly because of the ambivalent nature of the relationship of Caribbean peoples to the sea. While the sea is all around them, and while as fishermen and boatbuilders they are linked to it, they have not traditionally seen it as a place to be exploited for sport. Hence, watersport tourism has originally been run by and for white foreigners; with some exceptions this remains largely the case, along with such subsidiary businesses as ships' chandlers and marine supermarkets.

In the watersports business, outsiders dominate both as employers and employees. The yacht charter owners tend to give jobs to other expatriates, often well-connected young men who spend the winter seeking work around Caribbean marinas. So says Jeremy Wright, who owns Boardsailing BVI and is chairman of the Caribbean Windsurfing Association:

> My business employs outsiders due to the skills required in looking after the tourists who arrive with differing abilities. I occasionally employ locals yet find that they generally do not get that excited in the teaching and the beach operation side of things. This is the opposite to the outsider who, of course, loves the chance to work in this environment.'

Diving and snorkelling have also emerged as an important niche market, for the Caribbean has some of the best diving in the world. Islands like Bonaire and the Cayman Islands, for instance, are both long established and have promoted themselves almost exclusively as dive destinations. New destinations, such as Dominica, are also beginning to gain reputations.

Divers, like yachties, are adventurous, relatively wealthy and, most important, conscious of the environment. In the Bahamas, the Exuma National Park, administered by the Bahamas National Trust, has developed a 'support fleet' of yachties, who each contribute US$30 a year to its upkeep. Nick Wardle, of the National Trust, says that the wellbeing of the Park, the first in the Bahamas, relies on goodwill and that the scheme is a strong replenishment exercise. 'The Park is remote; we want to keep it like that. No one is allowed to take anything from it.' The Exuma National Park has become a model of its kind and prompted the Bahamas government to announced the protection of 20 per cent of the Bahamian marine ecosystem in 2000.

The Caribbean Sea is the resource of all who use it. Yet it is under threat from a range of environmental problems, from dumping to sewage disposal and the destruction of reefs (see Chapter Five), and all its users, whether cruise ships or jetskiers, are to some extent to blame. The only way to regulate the operations of cruise ships and to protect the marine environment would be to create regional regulatory bodies embracing every state. The CTO has, on many occasions, appealed to the region 'as a matter of urgency' to put together a joint environmental plan to regulate behaviour, enforce regulations and punish offenders. Other organisations have also called on the region to establish a body to safeguard the marine environment.

Meanwhile, the use of the Caribbean Sea for transporting nuclear waste has made the region even more aware that its waters are a vital component of its patrimony. As Jean Holder points out, the Caribbean has 'few resources left which give us any real bargaining power.'[46] One of those is the Caribbean Sea.

NOTES

1. Caribbean Tourism Organisation, 2002
2. Associated Press, London, 25 December 1994
3. *New York Times*, New York, 15 June 1994
4. Florida-Caribbean Cruise Association, Caribbean Cruising, Second Quarter 2002
5. Caribbean Tourism Organisation, Caribbean Statistical News, Barbados, 2004
6. Ibid
7. Caribbean Tourism Organisation, Caribbean Statistical News, Barbados, 2001
8. Travel Trade News Edition, 7 June 1993
9. Jean Holder, 'Getting the Most from Cruise Tourism for the Caribbean', address to conference at Coopers Lybrand International, Barbados, 1993
10. Ibid
11. *Caribbean Week*, Barbados, 26 June 1993
12. Ibid
13. Holder, op. cit.
14. *Caribbean Insight*, December 1997
15. Ibid
16. IPS agency, November 2000
17. B. Dickinson and A Vladimir, *Selling the Sea: An Inside Look at the Cruise Industry*, Wiley, NY, 1997
18. Florida-Caribbean Cruise Association, Newsletter, July 1994
19. Ibid
20. Ibid
21. Edward G. Bollinger, Vice-President of Purchasing, Properties and Logistics, RCCL, address given to the CTO, San Juan, Puerto Rico, 9 July 1992
22. *Caribbean Week*, 12-25 November 1994
23. Florida-Caribbean Cruise Association, Caribbean Cruising, Second Quarter 2001
24. Caribbean Cruising, Second Quarter 2002
25. Caribbean Cruising, Fourth Quarter 2001
26. *The Democrat for St Kitts*, St Kitts, 26 March 1994

27. *Caribbean Insight*, London, January 1995
28. *Daily Nation*, Barbados, 15 April 2002
29. *Caribbean Travel News Europe*, Summer 1993
30. Robert Wood, 'Caribbean Cruise Tourism: Globalization at Sea', *Annals of Tourism Research*, Vol 27, No 2, 2000
31. Economist Intelligence Unit (EIU), Tourism in the Caribbean, London, 1993
32. *Santo Domingo News*, 25 August 1995
33. Florida-Caribbean Cruise Association, Caribbean Cruising, Second Quarter 2002
34. EIU, op. cit.
35. OAS, op. cit.
36. Caribbean News Agency (CANA), 5 November 1994
37. Holder, op. cit.
38. Robert Dickinson, 'Cruise Industry Outlook in the Caribbean' in Dennis Gayle and Goodrich, Jonathan (eds), *Tourism, Marketing and Management in the Caribbean*, London, 1993, p.118
39. *Caribbean Week*, 12-25 November 1994
40. Dickinson, op. cit.
41. CANA, 26 May 1994
42. Florida-Caribbean Cruise Association, Caribbean Cruising, Second Quarter 2002
43. James W. Lett, 'Ludic and Liminoid Aspects of Charter Yacht Tourism in the Caribbean', *Annals of Tourism Research*, vol 10, 1983, p.35-56
44. Focus on Jamaica, The Times, 6 August 2002
45. Jean Holder, 'Regional Integration, Tourism and Caribbean Sovereignty', mimeo, 1993

8
RECLAIMING THE HERITAGE TRAIL: CULTURE

'Island in the Sun' was the first number featured in the finale of Jubilation, the nightly show at the Crystal Palace Resort and Casino at Nassau's 'fabled' Cable Beach where white America is urged to 'sway to Caribbean rhythms as our Las Vegas-style revue takes on a tropical twist.' The backdrop, which had been changed for the finale, was a stretch of blue sea with a cruise ship on the horizon.

On came the male dancers in striped trousers, one on roller-skates, the prelude to the arrival of a topless female dancer, who was wheeled on to the stage lounging on a large plastic banana and waving merrily. After the gentle melody of 'Island in the Sun', the music changed to the soca number, 'Dollar', and finally to 'Don't Worry, Be Happy', with the dancers in jaunty holiday hats and flowing chiffon scarves. A 'pantomime dame' waddled across the stage dressed as a large-breasted and big-bottomed black woman in a faded cotton frock, sneakers and a curled wig.

The last number was announced as an expression of 'our Bahamian culture' by a blonde-haired singer. Musicians paraded, drumming and blowing cowbells, horns and whistles while dancers appeared in costume in a stage recreation of the Bahamas' great post-Christmas festival, Junkanoo. Meanwhile, for it was December and Junkanoo fever was at its height, a group of waiters came down the aisle also dancing, blowing on whistles, sounding cowbells and beating drums, to great applause.

Like the Crystal Palace Resort itself, Jubilation may be in the Caribbean but it was not of the Caribbean. It was two hours of high-class American kitsch, its gesture to the Bahamas taking place in those final minutes.

The icons of the Caribbean were the songs, labelled 'a medley of island songs'. There was 'Island In the Sun', written by the Jamaican singer Harry Belafonte as the title song of the film of the same name in 1957. It is now an instantly recognisable anthem played to tourists all over the Anglophone Caribbean. The other two songs have different origins: the soca 'Dollar' was a commercial success for the Trinidadian singer Taxi and became a dance favourite all over the region and beyond, while 'Don't Worry, Be Happy' with its calypso rhythms comes, in fact, from the 1988 film 'Cocktail': it was written by Bobby McFerrin, the African-American singer, and sung with a 'Caribbean accent'.

As well as the songs, the finale, with its holiday atmosphere and references to beaches, nudity and fun, used the banana (no joke in the region) and the cruise ship as the emblems of the Caribbean. Of the dancers, more than half were local, including the dancer who introduced 'our Bahamian culture' number and the Junkanoo musicians. One of the male dancers played the 'mammy', the market woman, a comforting black figure of unthreatening fun, with a feeling more of white folk memories of the American south than of the Caribbean.

Into that culturally deracinated programme came the Junkanoo waiters in their working uniforms (appropriately enough because to dress up before Junkanoo violates tradition). As if 'rushing' on the streets of Nassau, their performance was rooted in their own experience and history. They even managed to upstage the main performance.

Jubilation illustrated the two polarities of cultural expression as 'shown' to tourists in the Caribbean. The first is the formal, expensive, foreign-driven performance which is put on to please visitors, to reinforce the tourists' perceptions of the Caribbean and to give them what the Caribbean thinks they want. As the academics express it, the tourism experience is 'typically not authentic, but constructed, commodified and socially comfortable.'[1] The second is the informal (and free) display of local creativity which in form represents the fusion of cultural influences (in this case from Africa and Europe) and in content remains a function of rebellion, of resistance against authority.

Jubilation (and similar representations) threatens, at many levels, to overwhelm the Caribbean with its slick otherness and metropolitan tastes. In many instances, tourism has bred cultural decline despite the efforts of those who are attempting to reclaim control. 'We are busy fighting the mentality that says that if it's not required by tourists or liked by them then it's not needed. Because if we don't stop it, we don't have anything left to give our children,' said Kim Outten of the Pompey Museum, Nassau. The most recent struggle for the Caribbean has been both to nurture its indigenous art forms, to create and perform for its own peoples, amid the demands of tourism, while at the same time finding imaginative ways of 'using' tourists as patrons rather than being used by them. However, there are now significant points at which the interaction between tourism and Caribbean culture has created a new dynamic.

The Intangible Heritage

The genesis and expression of Caribbean culture throughout the region have been shaped by a shared experience of history: of European colonisation, indigenous genocide, slavery, indentureship, struggles for freedom, migration and independence. Those experiences have made for societies where everything and everyone reaching Caribbean shores has been creolised, transformed into being part of a Caribbean identity. That force represents part of the region's creative genius and its strength.

However, most of the Caribbean (with the notable exception of Haiti and, more recently, Cuba) has also suffered from a sense of inferiority. As William Demas, then president of the Caribbean Development Bank, said in a 1973 address to students in Jamaica: 'The deep and disturbing identity problem remains. The problem is... one of not recognising that we as a people have many features of uniqueness – that is to say, a basis upon which a sense of identity can be built. It is fundamentally a typical West Indian problem of lack of self-confidence.'[2]

In the 1970s, awareness of such problems was sharpened by a range of factors: by the recent or imminent independence of most Anglophone countries and a subsequent birth of nationhood, by the civil rights and Black Power movements in the US and the tensions generated by the Cold War. And as the growing tourist industry made increasing claims on the region, there was alarm about cultural dependency, the way in which the region's beliefs and values appeared determined by North America. This process followed on from the long-time cultural conditioning by Europe through colonisation. The Caribbean, it was argued, was not defined by its own peoples, but by tourists and others, according to their own needs and perceptions of sun-baked islands. This cultural standard-setting by metropolitan interests was linked to the Caribbean's political and economic dependence. As Demas said in an address to the University of Guyana in 1970, the 'New Caribbean Man' must 'devise ways and means of reducing the negative aspects of the metropolitan impact on the New Caribbean Society'; this society must be 'selective in its contacts with the metropolis – no less in economics, than in ideology, culture and values.'[3]

The Caribbean was in danger of becoming in thrall to North America and Europe in a recreation of colonialism and the plantation system by other means (largely television). This imitation of the metropole (as described by the Trinidadian V.S. Naipaul in his novel *The Mimic Men*) was what the Bahamian-born actor Sidney Poitier experienced when he returned home one year after the Bahamas gained its independence in 1973. He wrote in his 1980 autobiography, *This Life*:

> It disturbed me deeply that there was no cultural life expressing the history of the people – absolutely none. I did see wood carvings, but they were imported from Haiti to sell to tourists in The Bahamas... It was tourism, so enormously successful over the years, that had contaminated – diluted – debased – the shape of all things cultural in those islands, until there was no longer any real semblance of a Bahamian cultural identity. People even danced to Bahamian musicians playing other people's music – Jamaican music or American artificial calypso music; tunes from the American hit parade or the American 'soul' top ten.[4]

Over a quarter of a century after Demas' warnings and Poitier's lament, much nation-building has been done and achievements in all art forms have been recognised, not just regionally but internationally. There are the visual arts of Jamaica, Haiti, Cuba, Guyana; the great cultural festivals, now known as the festival arts, of Carnival and Junkanoo; the internationally acclaimed music of reggae, calypso, salsa, merengue and zouk; a fine body of literature (including that of St Lucia's Derek Walcott, the Nobel prize-winner); and a vibrant folk culture and customs that are recognised and encouraged. The expression of all this cultural activity has, since 1971, found an outlet in the regional festival, Carifesta, pioneered by Guyana's former president, Forbes Burnham, and held, at intervals, in different countries of the Caribbean. Yet, despite such achievement, the shadow of dependency remains.

Much of what is admired within the Caribbean and is seen to be 'better' remains foreign (usually North American), whether in design, technology, food or the visual arts. And while the tourists continue to flock in, the leaders of the tourist industry, whether local or foreign, have often seemed generally unconcerned to protect the authenticity of Caribbean dance forms, carvings or architectural detail.

A fundamental reason for such neglect is that the Caribbean tourist industry does not depend on castles, ancient buildings, art galleries and museums. The Caribbean's cultural forms are not on display as they are in Venice or Prague, Delhi or Cairo. Such formal, urban environments are not the common currency of the Caribbean tourist industry. The heritage business has been a late arrival and only recently a tool for tourism, although the designation of St Kitts' Brimstone Hill, an 18th-century British military fortress, as a UNESCO world heritage site provides an important opportunity for that island to market something other than its beaches and plantation houses.

Meanwhile the 'people's culture', more vulnerable and diffuse, has been at risk. Sometimes it appears to be flattened into the all-purpose caricature: a smiling guitarist in a Hawaiian shirt crooning 'Jamaica Farewell', with its chorus line 'I Left My Little Girl in Kingston Town' (to be adapted to Nassau town or Castries town or whatever town is relevant). Professor Elliott Parris, of Howard University, noted in 1983: 'If we ignore our history and the cultural legacy that it has left us, we run the risk of developing tourism as an industry which puts the dollar first and our people last. We are saying to ourselves, perhaps unconsciously: we are the field labourers on the modern plantation of the tourist industry.'[5]

A decade later the 'modern plantation' continued. In the 1990s, Reg Samuel was the research officer in Antigua's ministry of culture. His was one of the voices raised against the impact of the tourist industry on his island, blaming it for the loss and degradation of what is unique to Antigua and its history. 'Tourism has impacted on us very seriously,' he said. 'Our total lifestyle – art, food, music, dress, architecture, celebrations – has been altered. We have lost our character.' He argued that Antigua had tried to please tourists by giving them what they know. 'We try to imitate Americans and their ways. We give the impression that what tourists want is what they have and not what we have. Let the tourist know what we have.'

In music, for example, Samuel pointed out that the steel band, which arrived in Antigua with returning oil workers from Trinidad, had been neglected or lost its way, while other musical forms had virtually disappeared. 'We have distinctive forms such as the iron band, which emerged in the 1940s, and is played with hub caps. The tourist should be hearing this particular music that's unique to Antigua.'

Instead, tourists are offered Heritage Quay, a modern duty-free complex of boutiques and souvenir shops, which promotes itself with a poster for 'A night of Antiguan culture' with 'steel band, limbo dancers, gambling, children performing, late evening shopping.' Such entertainment is common in Antigua where, according to Tim Hector, opposition senator and editor of *Outlet* newspaper, young people have been 'ripped from any rootedness in a folk culture.' Instead, wrote Hector, 'Folk culture has become a marketable commodity, readily and monotonously packaged as Yellow Bird, limbo without meaning, except as tourist entertainment, steel bands which now draw no response from the people for whom the music is produced, and a national dish which is really Kentucky Chicken and Fries. A culture has been turned on its head.'[6]

Antigua's disregard for its own identity is perhaps more acute than anywhere else in the Caribbean. This is partly the result of its smallness and the nature of its tourist industry (largely foreign-controlled, dominated by expatriates and investors). Antigua demonstrates the ease with which cultural patrimony becomes threatened.

Antigua is not alone. Other countries, in particular in the Anglophone Caribbean and the Dutch territories, have also failed clearly to define themselves to tourists. As a result, tourists have retained the power to create their own (often uninformed) images of the Caribbean. The whole region thus becomes a homogenised whole, its more subtle contrasts and distinctive heritages either neglected or lost.

The successful export of calypso, salsa and reggae to the US and Europe has meant that those musical forms have become standard-bearers of Caribbean culture. The negative effect of this achievement has been to put at risk the lesser known and more fragile forms of regional music, such as Antigua's iron band and the big drums of Carriacou. On Grenada's tiny sister island, Carriacou, Big Drum, three lapeau cabrit (goat skin) drums, is the traditional musical form. Yet when the cruise ships call, it is a steel band that goes on board to entertain: the steel band rather than the unique Big Drum has become the sound of Carriacou.

Using 'culture' as an ingredient of a tourist industry means work for performers and artists. Much of the entertainment is in hotels which put on musical evenings and floor shows and sometimes buy local paintings and carvings. Once on cruise ships or in hotels, music, dance and art tend to become part of a safe suburban environment.

Like the licensed street vendors, performers who work the hotels have to respond to the requirements of the hoteliers: they shape the tourist experience by deciding who should perform what. 'The people who run the industry are from a different culture and totally disregard our culture,' says one prominent St Lucian. 'They do not breathe down our neck, but there is a reluctance to perform anything that might raise difficulties.' According to one British academic, Jamaican schoolchildren are prepared for a possible career in the tourism industry in their after-school clubs. 'The versions of "traditional" Jamaican culture, which are sanctioned at the school, are sanitised versions that could be seen as contributing to Jamaica's pool of tourist attractiveness.'[7]

Hotel entertainment – along with the welcome committee of local dancers and musicians who often perform in the arrivals' hall of international airports – may well be the only expression of Caribbean culture offered to tourists. Along with 'saloon' reggae, steel band, and sometimes jazz, what the tourist brochures call 'native' floor shows are the most common form of hotel entertainment. These sometimes consist of a fashion show interspersed with 'exotic' dancing which may include fire-eating, limbo dancing and glass-breaking. While there is some evidence that limbo-dancing is a legacy of the Middle Passage (the journey from Africa to the Caribbean), the 'native' show versions have long lost any validity, while fire-eating is usually dismissed as degrading nonsense. A lack of authenticity plagues most tourist shows all over the Third World, and the Caribbean is no exception.

In Barbados, a weekly show called '1627 and All That!' ('a spectacular cultural feast') has been performed nightly for years and takes place in the courtyard of the Museum. In a package which includes a free tour of the Museum, a 'sumptuous Barbadian buffet dinner,' complimentary bar and craft market, the show is a private-sector initiative employing local dance groups. Alissandra Cummins, the Museum's director, had some reservations about the production. It is, she said, 'better than some shows which have no relevance at all to Barbadian culture. However I'm not totally comfortable with what they produce.' There are elements that may come from other Caribbean cultures but are not Barbadian, she added, and while there is 'a generous attribution to Africa' it is non-specific.

The sort of compromises imposed (or allowed) by tourism in the representation of a culture is of concern to those who seek to protect and develop it. Raymond Lawrence, Dominica's chief cultural officer, has observed what has happened to other countries who have lost many of their indigenous forms through pandering to the tourist. Dominica needs to 'learn from the experience of others,' he said. 'We need to strengthen Dominica's folk traditions so that authenticity can be kept when tourism hits us in a big way.' What concerned Lawrence was to continue to 'present ourselves authentically to ourselves.' He hoped that financial rewards would not tempt groups to 'dilute their presentations with dances shortened to become something without value.' Belé, for example, a dance in which the dancer performs to the drummer, cannot, explained Lawrence, be turned into a 'hello' entertainment in which performers play to an audience. 'We want to keep it that way.'

Even more remote from the typical 'floor show' than the intimacy of Dominica's belé are, of course, Haiti's voodoo ceremonies. Before Haiti's tourist industry collapsed in the early 1980s, voodoo performances were put on for them. At one voodoo centre outside Port-au-Prince, for example, two-hour long shows were put on six nights a week. Although voodoo tourism contained all the elements of a staged performance, with an entrance fee, stage and waiters serving drinks, the nature of Haitian culture blurs the edges between 'real' and 'false' and between theatre and religion. The shows were described by an anthropologist, Alan Goldberg:

> The ceremony begins with songs for the particular spirits being called that night. The first episode of spirit possession behaviour occurs about 10.40, usually featuring the sacrifice of a pigeon which is dispatched when the possessed person bites its head off. After the first spirit is sent away another possession may occur or an intermission may mark the end of the first part of the show.[8]

Although performed for tourists (albeit far removed from the typical package tourists), the performers allowed the event to 'become converted into a situation of staged authenticity,' according to Goldberg. The existence of a tourist audience did not in itself invalidate the experience.

Street Culture

If voodoo tourism can fill that grey area between the staged and the authentic, so, in many ways, can the other great cultural set-pieces of the Caribbean, its public street festivals – Carnival, Junkanoo (Bahamas), Crop-Over (Barbados), Christmas Sports (St Kitts). These annual flowerings of music, dance, theatre, language and costume have long histories; most are rooted in the Caribbean's experience of slavery and liberation. To what extent, however, have they flourished or withered at the hands of the marketing departments of tourist boards? Or, indeed, do they and can they ignore tourism?

The best-known, biggest and most visually extravagant of all is the Trinidad Carnival, which takes place on the Monday and Tuesday before Ash Wednesday. The two days of street bacchanal date from emancipation and represent a great outpouring of black dissent and resistance through mockery, satire and display as well as commentary on contemporary life. As Gordon Lewis described it: 'From its opening moment of jour ouvert and the "ole mas" costume bands to its finale, forty-eight hours later, in the dusk of Mardi Carnival, the Trinidadian populace gives itself up to the "jump up", the tempestuous abandon of Carnival.'[9]

Richer, more naturally endowed and diversified than other economies, Trinidad has never bothered much with tourism. So Carnival in Trinidad was neither created for tourists nor has it been recreated for them like Crop-Over in Barbados, or become a distant shadow, as in St Thomas. Trinidad's Carnival has robustly retained its own identity.

Yet it has changed over the years, and it has been influenced by tourism. Indeed, Peter Minshall, one of Trinidad's great mas' designers, articulated his concern when he addressed the Caribbean Tourism Organisation's sustainable tourism conference in 1998: 'The primary value of the Carnival, in my mind, is as food and nurture for the soul – of our own people. If we ignore this essential quality, and concentrate only on packaging carnival according to our misguided options of what foreigners want, then we will be selling our soul, and in the end will have nothing of value at all to sell to anyone.'

Even before the second world war, Carnival organisers had an eye on the tourist market. In 1939, the Carnival Improvement Committee was established, an offshoot of what was called the new Tourist and Exhibitions Board. Its aim was to 'lift Carnival', to make it 'one of the star attractions of the tourist season.' Some calypsonians composed on this theme: Attila, for example, wrote that tourists 'get happy and gay,' finding Trinidad 'a paradise on earth/that is what the tourists say.'[10]

Beneath the welcoming patter, however, there was another issue on the Carnival Improvement Committee's agenda. Its aim was to censor Carnival, to clean it up, to make it more decorous and less wild. In 1951, to the list of annual Carnival don'ts (such as don't dress in an immodest or scanty costume and don't sing any immoral or suggestive tunes) was added: 'Don't forget that visitors are in your midst. Give them the best impression of the festival.'[11] This development, according to Trinidadian writer Lawrence Scott was 'about how organisers wanted Carnival to be presented to the outside world – it was an awareness of what others think of us.'

Middle-class tastes were also behind commercialising trends in the 1950s when company sponsorship first became a significant element of Carnival. The merchants (as in most Caribbean countries, the white and light-skinned elite) sought to take control of Carnival by putting it on Port of Spain's central open space, the Savannah, with expensive seating and big prizes, at the expense of the street calypsonians and road-marchers. The calypsonians retaliated. Sparrow's 'Carnival Boycott' pointed out that it was calypso that was the 'root' of Carnival and steel band the 'foot'.[12]

Forty years on, Carnival has competitions for calypso, pan and thousand-strong costume bands, all sharing in the glory, and all required set-pieces. Television rights, sponsorship from big business, recording opportunities, big prizes, expensive seats, pricey costumes and overseas marketing have contributed to a certain reduction in spontaneity. There is a tricky balance to be achieved: a balance articulated by Peter Minshall. Anxious that Carnival should be properly managed by professionals who know how to mastermind great entertainment with more participants than the Olympic Games, this must be balanced by ensuring that the 'creative soul of the carnival lies with the people, and with its masmen and panmen and calypsonians'. And so Minshall says no to censorship – for that short time when the fool is king and the king the fool. For Carnival remains at the centre of the nation's psyche, an expression of Trinidad's nationhood.

There are other smaller, less known, Lenten Carnivals around the region, mainly in predominantly Catholic islands, such as Martinique and Dominica. Like that in Trinidad's Port of Spain, these carnivals are urban experiences and as such now have a commercial input. Yet although there are those who lament the passing of the 'good old days', regional Carnivals retain their roots and many of their rituals. They are local celebrations in which tourists are welcome to observe or even join in. But as in Trinidad, tourists are peripheral. The village festivals commemorating saints' days, celebrated in Dominica, for example, are entirely local affairs, as are the rural festivals of La Rose and La Marguerite in St Lucia.

In the Bahamas, the equivalent to Carnival is Junkanoo, the Christmas festival. Junkanoo (also known in Jamaica as John Canoe) reaches back to Africa, probably linked to the legendary John Konny, an 18th-century tribal leader from the Gold Coast; and like Carnival it remains an expression of freedom, associated with acts of rebellion and challenge. Its history is also dotted with instances of threats by colonial authorities to ban the 'rush' down Nassau's business centre, Bay Street. Yet the parade of costumes, once made of sacking and sponges and now of cardboard and coloured crepe paper, and the hundreds-strong bands with goat-skin drums, cowbells and trumpets, have flourished and have become a magnificent, home-grown attraction created for and performed by groups of Bahamians for themselves. The groups represent communities with a strong sense of belonging and collective identity; in this way, tourists are almost entirely excluded from participation, their role being to observe, enjoy and spend money among the crowds of Nassau and Freeport, the two main Junkanoo locations.

Yet this spectator role of the tourist has been crucial to the survival of Junkanoo. Gail Saunders, director of the Bahamas archives, believed that without tourism Junkanoo might have died out. She dates the first impact of tourism on Junkanoo from the late 1940s when Sir Stafford Sands, the first head of the Bahamas Development Board, put some money into the festival. The white colonial elite recognised the attractions to tourists of the African Junkanoo festival and provided it with an economic framework which enabled the bands to become organised and more ambitious. In 1958, an American guide book wrote: 'Costumed and masked natives dance ancient rhythms and parade... A real experience – don't miss it.'[13]

In the 1960s, Junkanoo was also given an extra impetus by the involvement of young middle-class Bahamian artists inspired by Black Power and the anti-colonial movement. Jackson Burnside, a Bahamian architect and artist who designs for the Saxons Superstars band, recalled, 'In Junkanoo I found how it had grown from Africa, but beyond Africa – into something that is ours, only ours. In the process, it happens to be the best show on earth.'[14] Through the nexus of community, business and tourism, Junkanoo in the Bahamas has reasserted itself. While it has changed through tourism, it is seen to have done so without compromising its integrity.

On the other side of the Caribbean, the festival of Crop-Over in Barbados is another example of how tourism realigns traditional festivals. Crop-Over evolved from the celebration of the end of the sugar-cane harvest by both planters and slaves. By the end of the 19th century it had developed into a procession of carts, decorated with flowers and coloured material, bearing the last of the canes into the plantation yard. When the labourers had paraded with an effigy of Mr Harding, a figure whom they sometimes burnt, there was dancing and music. However, with the decline in sugar and the arrival of more modern forms of entertainment, Crop-Over was all but dead by the 1940s, only to be revived in 1964 by the Board of Tourism.

According to the authoritative A-Z of Barbadian Heritage, 'the present-day festival is very different from the old-time Crop-Over.'[15] What has happened is that it has become a four-week summer festival (traditionally the low tourist season), transformed by business sponsorship and the marketing machinations of tourism officials into a sequence of organised events such as calpyso, king and queen of the crop competitions and a Carnival-style parade called Kadooment. The ghosts of Crop-Over past are witnessed in the parade of decorated carts. But the parade has become 'commoditised'. 'Corporate Barbados benefits enormously from Crop-Over; it is something that is mutually beneficial,' said the chief cultural officer of the National Cultural Foundation, the organiser of Crop-Over. 'We would like to see corporate Barbados advertising, using for example the decorated cart parade as a medium for advertising.'[16]

Other devices are used to maximise the tourist potential of indigenous local festivals, sometimes with damaging consequences. One is to move traditional celebrations from Christmas to summer. Antigua's Carnival, for example, was deliberately conceived in 1957 to boost tourist arrivals during the slack season (May to July); now it has been moved to July/August (also a slow tourist period) to coincide with the anniversary of Emancipation. Without the Christmas celebrations and parades, the traditional figures, such as John Bull, the clowns and mocojumbies also disappeared.

Festivals are also invented to boost the range of tourist attractions and, by definition, tourist numbers. The Tobago Fest, for example, takes place in September/October, a tourist low season, incorporating Trinidadian Carnival traditions. In the Cayman Islands, Pirates Week was coined at the end of the 1970s to take place at the end of October, again a slow tourist period. This Carnival-style entertainment has become a national event, an excuse for costumes, parades and partying. In the Bahamas, Goombay (probably from a Malian word for festival) was invented by the Tourist Board as a Friday night street dance and then became limited to the summer (again an attraction for the low tourist season), an occasion for performances, food and craft.

Whatever their derivation and history, however deep or shallow their cultural roots, Caribbean festivals have remained, for the most part, a celebration that depends on the participation of local people. As much as anything, this may be a function of their location on the streets. The jump-up in Gros Islet, St Lucia, is an interesting example. Started as a local, small-business initiative, it has become a successful institution in which locals and tourists mix every Friday night on the streets of the village for music, food and drink. Oistins fish fry in Barbados is another successful transition – from one stall frying fish on a Friday night by the docks of Oistins fish market to a popular eating place and weekend outing for locals and tourists that features in all the brochures.

While such events have evolved in an almost casual way, other 'cultural events' have been launched deliberately, masterminded by tourist boards or the equivalent to make the 'product' more diverse (see Chapter Nine) and so boost tourism. These come in two packages: those that are rooted in Caribbean culture and those that are not.

In the first category come festivals from Jamaica and Dominica. From Jamaica, of course, came Sunsplash, the great annual celebration of reggae. It was the pioneer and became a model for festival tourism. It began with a group of Jamaican businessmen who created a company called Synergy Productions: its objectives were to promote reggae, use Jamaican music to develop tourism, especially in the slow summer season in Montego Bay, and to generate employment in the art and craft sector. From 1978, up to 10,000 people, half tourists, half Jamaican, attended the week-long event in Montego Bay, a perfect location for tourists, for Jamaicans who would take their own holiday there and for the reggae industry. Its achievement was to keep the faith of its original function as a showcase for reggae, both homegrown and from overseas. 'The Jamaicans are proud that other countries are interested in playing reggae,' said David Roddigan, the British DJ, who followed the fortunes of Sunsplash for many years. 'It has never compromised itself. The organisers have played it from their hearts – they are committed to the concept of Sunsplash.' Yet despite international acclaim, Sunsplash died. Relying on the box office as the major source of revenue, organisers claimed that the government failed to promote it or invest in it sufficiently and that corporate sponsorship was inadequate. Overall, there was also little value-added activity and the festival itself made no profit. Yet Sunsplash, in its heyday, 'almost single-handedly converted what was a trough in the tourism calendar to a summer season that rivalled the traditional peak season.'[17]

Another attempt to turn a local music sound into an international tourist attraction has been made in Dominica, albeit on a much smaller scale, with its annual World Creole Music Festival. First launched in 1997, the festival has had a difficult task marketing itself for, unlike Jamaica with its worldwide reputation as the home of reggae, Dominica is not known, except by aficionados, as the home of zouk and bouyon, the two modern sounds of the creole musical tradition. As a tourist destination, its distinctions lie not in music but in mountains, not in all-night jammin' but in all-day hikes. To give the festival an international profile, musicians have been flown in from all over the creole world and found an enthusiastic local audience. Whether such an initiative works as a tool to generate foreign exchange remains to be seen.

Such home-grown cultural initiatives take more risks in many ways than the imported ones. On the other hand, the latter depends on having the tourists to attend the event and the locals to be well-disposed towards it. St Lucia's annual Jazz Festival, for example, now attracts big names – both local and international – and has spread to different locations around the island, getting audiences from both home and away. A once resentful local musical fraternity now recognises the benefits and feels included in the process. Other cultural mismatches, such as a blues festival in St Vincent and an opera season and a celtic festival in Barbados, again represent a response to the need to diversify the tourist 'product' – giving the tourists something more than sun, sea and sand (see Chapter Nine).

What then is the economic impact of the Caribbean festival as a tool to promote tourism? An assessment prepared for the Inter-American Development Bank by Keith Nurse of the University of the West Indies draws some interesting conclusions. The main findings are that festivals create a strong 'demand-pull' for tourists and can turn around low season occupancy rates to compare with the best months; they also generate government funds from departure taxes. They support local musical and cultural entrepreneurs and artists and sell cultural-related goods and services. One of the most important advantages was that festivals attracted international media coverage: the St Lucia Tourist Board reckoned that the media value of its jazz festival was in excess of the festival budget. A benefit-to-cost analysis estimated the St Lucia jazz festival with 9.1:1, Trinidad Carnival 7:1 and Barbados Crop-Over at 2.4:1.

Essentially, these festivals are expressions of popular culture. As Rex Nettleford, the Jamaican cultural commentator has said: 'In the absence of ... stone-and-mortar structures are other structures carved in the imagination and intellect of the mass of the population. So songs, stories, music, dance, religious expressions and rituals of the people handed down from generation to generation become central to heritage.'

The Heritage Trail

Jamaica's successful promotion of reggae, nationally, regionally and internationally reflects Jamaica's mature attitude towards its own rich cultural life, looking outwards but staying grounded in local experience. As the proliferation of festivals has shown, the example of the pioneering Sunsplash has been noted and acted on elsewhere in the region. Slowly, the idea of using more than beaches to lure tourists to the region has been attracting interest.

This move to widen the tourist base to include 'cultural' or 'heritage' tourism has partly been caused by increased awareness and pride in Caribbean history within the region. It has also been nudged by the global fashion for re-creating history. More pragmatically, it has also been prompted by concern about falling arrival rates in 'older' tourism destinations. Examples of conservation and restoration for the tourist market come from all over the region, from the Dominican Republic to Bonaire.

One interesting example of official attempts to harness heritage to tourism is the Seville Great House and Heritage Park in St Ann's Bay on the north coast of Jamaica. Seville, now owned and operated by the Jamaica National Heritage Trust, a government agency, was opened in 1994. It was an Arawak settlement before becoming the first Spanish capital of Jamaica and then, under British occupation and slavery, a sugar plantation with a great house and African village. St Ann's Bay was also where Columbus was shipwrecked in 1493, while the town of St Ann's was the birthplace of Marcus Garvey. Speaking at its opening, the minister of education and culture pointed to the value to Jamaicans (as well as to tourists) of such sites. The importance of Seville, he said, lay with its potential to provide 'an interpretation of what is basically a microcosm of Jamaica's history at one location. This is what will empower us to speak with understanding, honesty and truth about who we are as a people.'[18]

Jamaica's Tourism Action Plan (TAP) has also been working on plans to restore and improve not just the great houses, but also towns and villages, recognising the heritage of Jamaica's masons, carpenters and woodworkers in the creation of Jamaica-Georgian architecture. A book, *Jamaica's Heritage – An Untapped Resource*, by three English architects and conservationists (published in 1991 in cooperation with TAP), not only illustrated Jamaica's rich architectural history, but made a proposal for a trail to link the different parts of the island (the Emancipation Trail, the Gingerbread House Trail and the Plantation Trail). From great house to railway station and vernacular cabin, the book was enthusiastic about the potential for visitors to see the other 'remarkable' Jamaica, so that rural Jamaica could generate its own tourist income.[19] Since the publication of the book, the Jamaica Heritage Trail company has been launched to plan a tour for visitors along the lines suggested in the book. The story of the Maroons (the escaped slaves) has also been incorporated into the tourism 'product' with trips to visit their communities.

In Barbados, history has been dusted down, cleaned up and put on display. But it has been more selective than the Jamaica Heritage Trail proposals. The bit of history that Barbados has chosen to market is its plantation houses, the economic epicentres of the sugar industry and slavery. Yet the reconstruction has been partial. Sunbury Plantation House, for example, is described in the 1999 tourist handout, *The Ins and Outs of Barbados*, and suggests that a 'leisurely stroll through Sunbury' will give the visitor 'a very vivid impression of the gracious lifestyle of a bygone era.' Its blurb mentions only the house's magnificent antiques and paintings, while ignoring the role of slavery in its history and the contribution of the slaves to the estate. The Barbados National Trust has tried to introduce the 'folk' side of history at Tyrel Cot, the former home of Sir Grantley Adams, Barbados' first prime minister. It has recreated chattel houses, rum shops, blacksmiths' shops and so on, while artisans are on hand to recreate the story of Adam's life as labour leader in the 1930s to the 'life of the people'.

According to some critics, a problem emerged at the Dows Hill Interpretation Centre in Antigua. Perched on a hillside with a magnificent view of English Harbour, Nelson's old dockyard and once the base of English naval power in the West Indies, the Centre provides in light and sound a Euro-centred version of Antigua's history as narrated by a small boy. Funded and developed by the Canadian government development agency, CIDA, in conjunction with the National Parks Authority, it has alienated Antiguans like cultural officer Reg Samuels. 'We don't relate to it at all,' he says.

On the other hand, those in charge of the restoration of Betty's Hope, also in Antigua, work from a different perspective. Betty's Hope, built in the mid-17th century, was the first large sugar plantation in Antigua. The Betty's Hope Trust, founded in 1990, works towards restoration of the plantation as an open-air museum and interpretation centre. It is hoped that the museum will help all Antiguans and Barbudans, as well as those who visit from off island, to see the strength and human dignity revealed by better understanding of a painful history.' There are indications, however, that such a project does not have the same draw – or the marketing funding – as Antigua's most successful tourist attraction, English Harbour.

English Harbour has been the subject of some criticism, not so much for its careful restoration as for its remoteness from contemporary Antiguan life. Since 1955, Nelson's dockyard and its surrounding buildings have been carefully restored. Now the area is a marina with a ship's chandlery, marine services and yacht club. It also has a museum, restaurants, art gallery, picture framing, boutique, bakery and craft shops, all created for the tourists on a day out from their hotels. It is attractive, tasteful, expensive and very European. Most of the businesses are owned and run by whites for it is the expatriates who are primarily interested in yachting and naval history. For Samuels, 'It is an English colony run by expatriates.'

Slavery and the story of resistance to it usually remain untold in heritage tourism (museums have now become the pioneers in promoting that part of Caribbean history). This is partly because most slave accommodation was built of wood or wattle and daub and has disappeared or been destroyed. Perhaps a more fundamental reason is that until comparatively recently black history has been ignored. Before independence, this was because history was 'organised' by colonial officials; after independence, Caribbean tourist officials were either ignorant of their own history, unskilled in presenting it or controlled by metropolitan tour operators. One result, in contrast to Jamaica's Seville project, is that heritage tourism has become 'for tourists only', at best being ignored by local people, at worst alienating them.

Bonaire, in the Netherlands Antilles, however, has restored an example of its slave huts. These tiny stone houses, whose entrances are only waist-high, were built by and for the slaves who worked on the nearby salt ponds. Dating from 1850, they were restored by the National Parks Foundation of the Netherlands Antilles in a rare commemoration of slavery and vernacular architecture.[20]

Alissandra Cummins of the Barbados Museum drew attention to the process in her description of the impact of Angus Acworth's 1951 colonial survey of the historic buildings of the West Indies, undertaken at the request of the Jamaican Historical Society; this concentrated on European-influenced estate houses and ignored the local. She wrote: 'The lack of popular support for these conservation efforts was hardly surprising and historic preservation remained on the periphery of local cultural consciousness for decades.'[21] Jamaica, Guyana, Cuba and Haiti, were the only exceptions.

The development of museums in the Caribbean in many ways paralleled that of heritage tourism with its concentration on colonial achievement. Museums were the traditional storehouses of knowledge and bearers of the cultural chalice, but their white curators had a largely Eurocentric view of the world. For tourists, a visit to the museum, if there was one, had meant exhibits of Amerindian and colonial relics mixed with natural history. As the Barbados minister of culture said in 1980, the Barbados Museum told the visitor about Barbadian merchants and planters but 'little or nothing about slaves, plantation labourers or peasant farmers.'[22]

Only in the last decade has this changed: a major UNESCO cultural tourism programme on the 'slave route' is now being developed, linking the Caribbean slave sites with those in West Africa. Cummins explained: 'How Caribbean history is presented is largely the result of its institutions – the older the institution, the greater the rigidity of interpretation, which reflects the interests largely of colonials. The new institutions have a totally different perspective.' In these there is less glass and porcelain, fewer portraits of stern white patriarchs and a new emphasis on social history and the Caribbean masses. Under Cummins, the focus of the Barbados Museum has changed, showing black culture and legitimising 'Caribbean culture, making visible what was once a hidden past.' Other Caribbean countries are making similar changes; in the Bahamas, the Pompey Museum in Nassau, the region's first museum on slavery and emancipation (named after the leader of a slave uprising against an absentee landlord in Exuma), opened in 1992. Dominica's museum in Roseau includes a careful documentation of Carib and slave culture as well as colonial history.

While the focus has shifted, the role of museums and historic sites ('the outside child of tourism') has yet to be, according to Cummins, fully recognised or defined: 'For while each country in the region has sought to incorporate a cultural development policy in its overall national development strategy, all too often the policy option has been that of "cultural tourism", as a justification for any activity in this section and certainly as a priority before integration within the Caribbean cultural context.'[23]

There is, however, enormous potential for linking tourism with museums, says Cummins. Yet Caribbean governments have largely underestimated the interests of tourists. 'The tourist comes to the museum to get a clear picture of who Barbadians are,' she says, drawing attention to the comments in the visitors' book. 'The tourist wants a lot more in terms of slavery and the slave trade, particularly the black tourist. Tourists are also intrigued by sports. We need to get out and tell the stories about cricket and racing in Barbados.' Meanwhile, tourists are, on many occasions, 'provided with superficial and contrived experiences… This postmodern task is made all the easier with the realization that playfulness and inautheniticity have long since been acknowledged as marketable commodities.'[24]

It is not only the Anglophone Caribbean which has experienced the difficulties surrounding some heritage tourism. In Cuba, the interests of tourism have threatened to marginalise the poor of colonial Old Havana (population 100,000). This part of the city was declared a UNESCO World Heritage site in 1982. Since then churches, hotels and colonial mansions in the crumbling heart of the city which dates from the 16th century have been restored (part funded by UNESCO), while local housing conditions remain poor.

When the government realised that there was little for tourists to buy in Old Havana, a state agency, Habaguanex SA, was set up in 1994 to provide food and drink, entertainment and souvenirs for tourists and to earn dollars to be ploughed back into the restoration work. Yet tourism and a dollar economy sit uneasily with the peso-earning Cubans crammed into their crumbling and unsanitary accommodation and struggling to eat. The potential for unrest (and so-called 'anti-social' behaviour like begging) forced a compromise, according to the magazine *Cuba Business*, which reported in June 1994 that 10 per cent of the services would be available in pesos. Where this was difficult to implement, 10 per cent of the produce would be distributed to local schools and old people's homes. Other profits from Habaguanex would go to improve housing and infrastructure for Cubans.[25]

The idea that tourists could be interested in a built environment beyond a beach is not restricted to Cuba. Slowly the rest of the region has awakened to the attractions of its own architecture. Yet for decades, with a disregard for its own architectural traditions, the Caribbean tore down its old buildings to promote other people's. Both foreign chains and local developers built (and continue to do so) hotels inappropriate to place and purpose: foreigners because they did not care, locals because they associated old buildings with backwardness and assumed that foreigners required (and liked) the paraphernalia of modern, urban societies. Philistine and desperate-for-investment Caribbean governments sanctioned such developments. As a result, Caribbean resorts often look like somewhere else, usually Florida but perhaps Spain, Mexico or Italy. Hotel brochures boast that their charmless complexes have villas with 'Spanish roofs' and reception halls of 'Italian marble'. Richard Branson's luxurious Necker Island has been 'Balinised' in the sense that the buildings are in traditional Bali style, while the timber came from Brazil, the floor stone from the north of England and the statues, furniture and fabrics from Indonesia. Only the land, the sky and the sea are of the Caribbean.

The rush to build for tourism resulted in many pieces of vandalism. Among the worst was the destruction of the Amerindian caves in St Maarten, discovered during the construction of the Concord Hotel (now the Maho Beach Hotel). Amerindians used caves as places of worship, and petroglyphs and other images have been found there. The site supervisor told the government, which expressed a keen lack of interest, and when building eventually began again parts of the caves were destroyed and one was used as a septic tank. During the months that the caves were exposed, at least three limestone statues were found, one white, one red, painted with dyes, and one black. The red and white statues are thought to date from around 1300AD and to have been carved by the Tainos. Only very few such carvings have ever been found and it is not known what petroglyphs and other statues might have been in the caves now smothered by rubble and sewage.

The new trends in heritage tourism have not only turned plantation houses into museums, but have also transformed them into hotels (such as the up-market examples on Nevis), while parts of the capital of Aruba, Oranjestad, have even been rebuilt in colonial style. There is also more attention paid to vernacular architecture (paralleling the developments in museums), if sometimes only in a post-modernist mode. Sandals resort in Antigua, for instance, is painted in 'Caribbean colours'; Chris Blackwell's new hotel outside Nassau has cottages, vernacular in colours and style; and even parts of downtown Philipsburg, capital of St Maarten, have been restored in 'Caribbean style'. All such appropriations draw attention to a tradition which echoes the homes of ordinary people, outside the tourist zones. Yet, in its rush to modernise, the traditional chattel houses of Barbados, for example, are being created not to live in but as artefacts for the tourist gaze.

> Whilst the local sustainable Caribbean vernacular architectural house form suffers from state, elite and consensual rejection, at the same time, it is both promoted and lauded within the private and tourist sectors. In the grounds of the hotel at Sam Lords Castle, Barbados, for example, chattel houses and rum shops have been built to entertain guests in the grounds. Pretence meets pretension but in a safe, homogenised environment.[26]

This trend has been criticised for encouraging an all-purpose Caribbean architectural 'heritage', which only loosely belongs in time and place. The restored tourist shopping district in Charlotte Amalie, St Thomas, for example, has architectural details which are not specific to St Thomas but rather reproduce general perceptions of gingerbread work, verandahs and hipped roofs. The result, according to the architectural historian William Chapman, was the creation of 'something that is more fantasy than homage and erodes the value of remaining authentic design and fabric.'[27]

Art for Art's Sake?

Art in the Caribbean, once largely shaped by and for colonials (although both Cuba and Haiti had art schools by the beginning of the 19th century), has been indigenised, with both trained artists and 'intuitives' drawing from their own traditions and influences. For those countries, such as Jamaica, with a longer history of artistic achievement than elsewhere in the English-speaking Caribbean, artists have forged new directions sustained by their peers, teachers and a local market. State patronage in Guyana has resulted in another substantial national collection and national gallery, and has been responsible in part for the country's long and buoyant art movement.

Where there has been less of a tradition, little local support and an established tourist industry – as in Barbados – metropolitan tastes have tended to provide a barometer. Alissandra Cummins commented: 'Painters used to paint what the tourist wanted – the hibiscus was everywhere.' Local people and activities were other favourite subjects for artists, who wished to cater for the tourists' taste in the naive, the primitive and the 'exotic'.

Yet patronage has also created a breadth of demand which has encouraged every sort of artist, from street vendors to painters, to aspire to be picked up by overseas dealers. Tourist purchases of paintings by Amos Ferguson, a self-taught artist of the Bahamas, led to his work being shown in the US. Similarly, in Carriacou, another self-taught artist, Canute Calliste, found his work in demand from tourists whose patronage led to international exhibitions. In Barbados, a sizeable community of expatriates with discerning eyes has bought local art, employed local craftsmen and kept works of art in the country. Sales have nourished talent although one commentator on Jamaican art observed some time ago: 'Gaston Tabois once charmed with his fresh, naive, gaily primitive vignettes of country and city life, but he found it hard to recover after Elizabeth Taylor had bought some of his work. Similarly, David Palmer at Falmouth had a rude strength and truthfulness but has produced disappointing work since Sir Winston Churchill dropped by.'[28]

Whatever the truth of that view, the success of Jamaica's art community has spawned hundreds of local carvers and artists who work on the beach or in shacks along the road-side selling their paintings and sculptures like other street vendors. Official tourist board publications, too, endorse artists and sculptures, urging tourists to buy a local piece of art as a souvenir. Jamaica's *Travel News*, for example, pictures Rastafarian wood carvers; underneath a carving, the caption reads: 'Pick up a carving at the Falls.' The 'airport art' of the Caribbean is dominated by the Haitians who hang out their wares, copied a thousand times, on pavements and parking lots from the Dominican Republic to Antigua.

For Roland Richardson, an artist from St Martin, international recognition (through tourism) can raise standards and provide new directions. Richardson believes that tourism can forge links whereby he and other artists can find international expression for their work. His gallery is at Marigot, in his 150-year-old family house, now restored and open to visitors.

Another of Richardson's achievements was *Discover*, a scholarly full-colour magazine with a print run of 100,000 copies which flourished in the mid 1990s. Richardson was its editor-in-chief.

Sustained by ample advertising and distributed free to every hotel room, it celebrated the lives and culture of the two-sided island at every level. Without tourism it would not have existed. As Richardson argued: 'It's late but we need to deal with tourism creatively and intelligently.' Dismissing the negative influences of tourism as 'so common, so stupid to list,' he believes that tourism can be turned around and be used to 'maintain the health of our culture.'

He also sees tourism as a vehicle to heighten the profile of the Caribbean and offers as an example the Dutch airline KLM, which has sponsored art exhibitions in Europe featuring Caribbean work. 'As an artist I am aware that our Caribbean identity is becoming known on an international scale.' The whole tourist package has encouraged the use of art, dance and music, with hotels providing sponsorship and exhibition space, he says. 'Promotion needs to nourish the arts and this will increase the richness of the resource.' His own work is part of a tour for cruise passengers who are offered a package to see the work of four St Martin artists.

Similarly, a mixture of local patronage and international links nourished Haiti's artists. Inspired by the African-based religion voodoo and its loas or spirits, they have long been singled out for the extraordinary quality of their work. Some became rich and famous, embraced by the American art establishment. Taking their cue from the critics, tourists also became consumers of Haitian art, their artistic interests motivating trips to Port-au-Prince.

This process, unsurprisingly, again spawned a multitude of artists of all kinds: painters with their surreal and magical images, sculptors in wood and metal-work, and the 'airport artists' and the small boys who fashion delicate cathedrals out of paper. All suffered when tourism virtually ended during the 1980s. Yet for one metalworker at least, sanctions inspired new creations; the sculptor Gabriel Bien-Aimé turned to using car spare parts when steel drums became scarce.[29]

In contrast, in Cuba it has been argued that the crisis for art has been the arrival, not the departure, of tourists. The Cuban art critic Gerardo Mosquera has described the impact of tourism on Cuban culture as 'unique and troublesome', in particular pointing to the new-wave cottage industry of craft souvenirs made exclusively for tourists and 'usually devoid of any charm or inventive power.' There, Fidel Castro and Che Guevara have been turned from revolutionary heroes into tourist icons; wooden plaques bear slogans such as 'Always Forward to Victory' (available in five languages) and baseball hats with Che's signature, while the symbols of Afro-Cuban religions have also become tourist-friendly.

Yet what Mosquera sees as the trivialisation of a culture has become a theme for contemporary Cuban artists who, for the first time since the Revolution, have to deal with the concept of a commercial market. Exhibiting their work at Havana's Plaza de la Catedral, a street market for independent craft workers, they show copies of known artists' work and the popular images demanded by tourists. (One artist, however, found that his works of social criticism were popular, at US$25 a picture, and he was subsequently offered an exhibition in the US.)

This complex new relationship – art commentating on the tourist industry but at the same time working through it and with it – has been explored by a young Cuban artist, Tania Bruguera. Her work, called 'Postwar Memory', is made up of souvenir paraphernalia of T-shirts, posters, key holders, ashtrays and so on. 'I wanted to show that what we are selling are pieces of our own misery, of our own failure.'[30] The disastrous effect of tourism on the environment has long been the focus of work by Annalee Davis of Barbados, in, for example, her series of prints, 'This Land of Mine, Past, Present and Future!'

The representation of a nation through souvenir knick-knacks is endemic to much of the Caribbean, where shops overflow with rubbishy imported souvenirs. In one major tourist shop in Da Costa mall in Bridgetown, Barbados, there are baseball caps from China, coasters from Hong Kong, spoons from the US, wooden fruit from Venezuela and straw hats from Mexico. In Antigua, you can buy drinking glasses from Korea, carved turtles from Taiwan and even glass snow storms with palm trees from China. The country features only because its name is printed, stamped or woven on to the souvenir.

This lumpen invasion of other people's produce is partly the result of a tourist demand for souvenirs and crafts far greater than local supplies can satisfy. Local craft is also not always of a high quality and supply is not reliable. A study by Caricom indicated that with the exception of Jamaica and Barbados, the craft industry was in stagnation or decline. The problem was caused by a lack of training, government support, financial aid and knowledge about marketing and promotion. There was also the problem of attracting younger people into the craft work: the status is low and so is the pay. Handicrafts was another example of the failure to capitalise on the key issue of linkages (see Chapter Three).

The Bahamas, for instance, has long been famous for its straw work, a tradition that evolved from domestic need into more decorative (with raffia weave) styles. As demand increased and insufficient supplies of plaited straw arrived from the Out Islands of the Bahamas, many of the craft workers gave up weaving to become importers. Although the Out Islands still produce fine straw work in the style of West Africa, many of the 500 vendors at Nassau's straw market now club together to buy Asian straw goods out of Florida.

The popularity of straw work with tourists has, however, had one positive effect. Bahamians who had earlier rejected straw work, identifying it with poverty and thinking it 'unrefined', have now started to buy and enjoy it as a representation of their own culture.

The straw work of the Bahamas is not the only example of this curious interaction between tourism and culture in which traditional craft becomes locally recognised only after its 'approval' by tourists. The pottery of Nevis has had a similar history and transformation. Nevis pottery, which dates back to the 18th century and African traditions, went into decline with migration, the attraction of other work and its low status. Money earned from pottery was known as 'dirty money' and associated, like Bahamaian straw work, with dispossession and poverty.

Yet in the early 1980s attempts to 'upgrade' pottery-making techniques were introduced by a development project. At the same time the old-style pottery was becoming sought after by hotels and visitors (Nevis tends to attract somewhat up-market tourists). Together these two processes changed the perceptions of Nevisians towards their own pottery; it had now become desirable and 'modern'. According to anthropologist Karen Olwig, recognition by tourists for the pottery has helped Nevisians 'to accept an important part of their cultural heritage, which has not otherwise won much recognition in the island society.'[31] A similar thing has occurred in Choiseul, the southern village of St Lucia, where a tradition of making coalpots and furniture has been revived, largely thanks to various 'upgrading' programmes and subsequent sales to neighbouring hotels. The decline of the banana industry in Dominica and an increase in tourism are reasons why Caribs are beginning to turn more to their traditional craft work ('Fig ka fini, kraft ka vini' or 'bananas go, craft comes').

There is inevitably a limit to the extent to which the Caribbean wishes to be exposed to the tourist gaze, whether or not the encounter generates money, encourages authenticity and promotes self-awareness. At a deeper level, there is a reluctance to make public all its traditions and to sell all its myths on the altar of the tourist industry. The thinking is that the most vulnerable and private aspects of Caribbean expression must remain so. In Barbados, Alessandra Cummins took up this point of view. 'I would hesitate, for example, to get the Barbadian Landship movement involved in tourism because of the risk of exploitation and the negation of our culture.' The Landship movement, which never features in guide books or tourist board brochures, is organised like a friendly society dating from the 19th century; its members parade in naval uniform imitating the manouvres of a ship at sea accompanied by a Tuk band of drums and 'penny whistles'. Typically it fuses European and African elements. More recently, however, even the Landship has come out to play performing every Saturday morning in Bridgetown, at Crop-Over festival and in Independence Day parades. The appearance of Tuk bands at tourist-fuelled festivals provides visitors with another clue to Barbadian culture, showing that Barbados has its own indigenous music, which is neither reggae nor calypso.[32]

Even so, a similar point as to the need for cultural fencing is made by Kim Outten of the Pompey Museum in Nassau, who is worried about the new enthusiasm for official endorsement of local festivals, created for tourists by the Tourist Board. 'I'm concerned that it's just as dangerous to shift from an emphasis on sun, sea and sand tourism to putting on local festivals every few months. It implies that that is all Bahamians do, all the time. The bottom line is how much of our culture do we want to sell?'

The Caribbean consciousness, in its many shapes and forms, remains in the rural hinterlands, on urban streets and along the 'trace' or 'gap' where the tourist minibuses never go. Traditions of religious rites, story-telling, fishing festivals, Carnival, bush medicine, pantomime, the oral language and so on, flourish and evolve despite the prescriptions of the tourist industry.

Yet somehow a compatible future must be found for tourism and the Caribbean's cultural identity. Both need each other, rather as tourism and the environment need each other (see Chapter Five). Otherwise, as Professor Parris warned at a Caribbean seminar on cultural patrimony: 'If we ignore our culture... one morning we will wake up and there will be no more visitors. Visitors will simply have ceased to find us interesting, since we would have become just like them and they will opt to get their suntans somewhere closer to home where the airfares and the meals are cheaper.'[33]

NOTES

1. Dennis Conway, Tourism, Agriculture & the Sustainability of Terrestrial Ecosystems in Small Islands, in *Tourism, Sustainable Development and Natural Resource Management: Caribbean, Pacific and Mediterranean Experiences*, Prager/Greenwood, 2002
2. William Demas, 'Change and Renewal in the Caribbean', Challenges in the New Caribbean, no 2, Caribbean Conference of Churches, Barbados, 1975, p.55
3. Ibid., p.3
4. Cited in Philip Cash, Shirley, Gordon and Saunders, Gail, *Sources of Bahamian History*, London, 1991, p.337
5. Elliott Parris, 'Cultural Patrimony and the Tourism Product: Towards a Mutually Beneficial Relationship', OAS regional seminar, 1983
6. *Outlet*, Antigua and Barbuda, 11 March 1994
7. Beth Cross, 'Performances and Privileged Texts Reproducing the Tourism Product in Jamaican Schools', paper prepared for Society of Caribbean Studies conference, 2002
8. Alan Goldberg, 'Identity and Experience in Haitian Voodoo Shows', *Annals of Tourism Research*, vol 10, 1983, pp.479-495
9. Gordon K. Lewis, *The Growth of the Modern West Indies*, New York, 1968, p.30
10. Gordon Roehler, *Calypso and Society in Pre-Independence Trinidad*, Port of Spain, 1990, p.328
11. Ibid., p.403
12. Ibid., p.452
13. *McKay's Guide to Bermuda, the Bahamas and the Caribbean*, New York, 1958, p.48
14. *The Guardian*, London, 30 October 1993
15. Henry Fraser, Carrington, Sean, Forde, Addington and Gilmore, John, *A-Z of Barbadian Heritage*, Jamaica, 1990
16. Cited in Graham Dann and Potter, Robert, 'Tourism and Post-Modernity in a Caribbean Setting', *Les Cahiers du Tourisme*, Aix-en-Provence, April 1994
17. Keith Nurse, 'The Cultural Political Economy of Bacchanal: festivals and tourism in the Caribbean', paper prepared for Society of Caribbean Studies conference, July 2002
18. Caribbean News Agency (CANA), 13 May 1994
19. Marcus Binney, Harris, John and Martin, Kit, *Jamaica's Heritage – An Untapped Resource*, Kingston, 1991
20. *Caribbean Week*, 9-22 January 1993
21. Alissandra Cummins, 'Exhibiting Culture: Museums and National Identity in the Caribbean', *Caribbean Quarterly*, vol 38, no 2, p.33
22. Ibid.
23. Ibid.
24. Graham Dann and Robert Potter, Supplanting the Planters: Hawking Heritage in Barbados, *International Journal of Hospitality & Tourism Administration*, Vol 2, No 3/4, 2001, the Haworth Press, 2001
25. *Cuba Business*, London, June 1994
26. William Chapman, 'A Little More Gingerbread: Tourism, Design and Preservation in the Caribbean', *Places*, London, vol 8, no 1, 1992
27. Ibid.
28. Norma Rae, 'Contemporary Jamaican Art' in *Ian Fleming Introduces Jamaica*, London, 1965, p.169
29. *International Herald Tribune*, Washington DC, 2-3 July 1994
30. Gerardo Mosquera, 'Hustling the Tourist in Cuba', *Poliester*, London, vol 3, no 10, 1994
31. Karen Fog Olwig, 'Cultural Identity and Material Culture: Afro-Caribbean Pottery', *Folk*, vol 32, Copenhagen, 1990
32. Sharon Meredith, 'Tuk Music: Its Role in Defining Barbadian Cultural Identity', paper prepared for Society for Caribbean Studies conference, 1999
33. Parris, op. cit.

9
NEW FOOTPRINTS IN THE SAND:
THE FUTURE

Thirty years ago, young Caribbean radicals trumpeted 'Tourism is Whorism' and a prime minister told an international conference 'To Hell With Paradise'. Those radicals are now professors and the prime minister, James Mitchell of St Vincent and the Grenadines, became a kind of entrepreneur of 'paradise' caught up in the world of foreign investors and plans for resorts, condos and marinas. Nowadays, there are few voices – and none of them organised – raised in protest against tourism. If there is popular protest it is expressed more covertly, in cool welcomes and indifferent service, rather than in political argument.

A generation or more of Caribbean nationals have now grown up in countries where tourism is the currency of everyday life, and where hotels are the repository of an island's expectations and symbols of achievement and modernity. Tourism has brought modern airports, roads and, for some, the amenities of 21st century urban living. It provides jobs and foreign exchange and, with that money, schools and hospitals can be built. The centre-right orthodoxy that has prevailed in most of the Caribbean for the last two decades or so preaches the virtues of tourism and urges people to make it 'everyone's business'. International bodies say that there is no alternative – that tourism is the last resort. Development agencies fund tourism projects while multinationals invest in them. Every shade of politician in the last generation has embraced tourism in feverish competition for more tourists. Tourism is here to stay.

By the beginning of the 21st century, however, there was a new discourse among practitioners and researchers, politicians and advisers and, indeed, among the people of the Caribbean themselves. While there have always been those who have criticised aspects of the tourist industry, its structures and its adverse impacts on people, places and cultures, this time there seemed a greater urgency. The industry itself had become more analytical; thinking in the industry was shifting. A sea change was taking place – certainly in talk and, sometimes, in action.

The Wrong Tourism

So what prompted this new thinking? As this book has tried to explore, the growth of tourism has brought in its wake a host of negative impacts – economic, environmental, social, cultural. These impacts have begun to fracture the confidence of the industry alongside the external constraints that from time to time trigger a collective nervous breakdown.

What has been recognised is the concept of sustainability, which seeks to create economic and social benefit for now without sacrificing the well-being of future generations and the land on which they live. 'In looking at the issue of sustainability, no longer is it possible to view the industry only in terms of arrivals, bed nights and expenditure,' said Karen Forde-Warner, deputy secretary-general of the Caribbean Tourism Organisation in 2002. 'Our indicators of success have to be much broader because issues of sustainability are highly interrelated.' This is by no means the first time that such utterances have come from the heart of the industry (see Chapter One) but such concerns are now central to discussions, rather than lurking on the fringes.

A recent pronouncement from the industry's leadership has come in the form of a regional tourism strategic plan, prepared in 2002 by the CTO for the Caribbean Community (Caricom) heads of government. Its content provides for what it calls 'the re-positioning of the hospitality industry in the Caribbean in the 21st century' and indicates both 'short-term recovery plans and long-term development measures and resource requirements.' It is, of course, predicated on growth, but a growth that is viable and sustainable. Its vision 'speaks to the further development of a Caribbean tourism industry that is fully understood and embraced by the peoples of the region and which, through co-operative action among governments and private sector, makes a significant and sustainable contribution to development in both mature and emerging destinations.'

It is not a particularly radical document, but it does address some of the complaints that have long come from practitioners of tourism within the region. Each section has had its own preoccupations. For example, hoteliers feel they are burdened by high costs of labour and building, a lack of marketing and over-taxation, especially in comparison to the cruise lines (see Chapter Seven). On the other hand, hotel workers think the owners reap the benefits while the best jobs still go to foreigners (see Chapter Four). At a more profound level, there are those, whether hoteliers or workers, taxi drivers or tour guides, who feel that the industry does not belong to them at all. As Antigua's Prime Minister Baldwin Spencer explained: 'Most of the progress has come from tourism, but it is not in our hands. We can't lay a foundation on which we benefit.' Spencer is perhaps suggesting that although tourism has brought Antiguans a recognisably modern, consumer society they are not stakeholders in their own tourist industry. It is an elusive sort of benefit because Antiguans have not made their own investment in tourism and do not control it.

Other critics have taken issue with particular aspects of the way the industry is run. There are, for example, church groups who are concerned about the impact of tourism on morals, sexual and otherwise; they also comment on the way tourism creates social stress in vulnerable communities (see Chapter Four). There are environmentalists who work to stop the degradation, measure the damage and put together protectionist policies and guidelines to make tourism work for the environment and not against it (see Chapter Five). And there are the artists and intellectuals, who try to present the best of Caribbean culture to tourists rather than phoney versions. Calypsonians, too, have made their contributions, with songs such as 'Alien' in St Lucia (see Chapter Four) and 'Jack' in Barbados (see Chapter Three).

A rather broader attack on the region's tourism has come from the historian Hilary Beckles of the University of the West Indies in Barbados. For him, tourism is a kind of new plantocracy reinventing the economic and social relations of slavery. Even so, does he believe tourism could be a tool for sustainable development? Not in the way that it is organised at present. According to Beckles, tourism has been adopted as an easier option than any other path to economic development. 'Society doesn't have to be so disciplined; it can grow by itself.' The region, he says, has failed to become creative and has failed to develop a philosophy of individual initiative and discipline in the workplace. 'Our minds have not been fashioned to create, so instead of creative services, information services, publishing, printing, we have become a dumping ground for low-grade data processing.' This is why the region 'fell back on tourism as the principal agency for growth,' said Beckles. 'Local people are put on the back burners and the taxpayers' money is used so that the elite benefit.'

As we have observed in Chapters Two and Five, the public sector's 'hands off' approach and its lack of ability to plan for the future have been further constraints to sustainable development. This is particularly critical in islands such as Aruba, Antigua, Barbados, the Bahamas and St Maarten with a mass-tourism profile. Such scenarios have prompted some unfavourable verdicts. Writing about Barbados, for instance, the academic Paul Wilkinson concluded: 'It appears that Barbados is an example of the non-sustainability of a fragile island microstate embracing large-scale mass tourism in what is nearly a policy and planning vacuum.'[1]

For Derek Walcott, there is a catastrophe waiting. As he put it, in his Nobel prize-winning lecture in Stockholm, in 1992:

> The Caribbean's peasantry and its fishermen are not there to be loved or even photographed; they are trees who sweat, and whose bark is filmed with salt, but every day on some island, rootless trees in suits are signing favourable tax breaks with entrepreneurs, poisoning the sea almond and the spice laurel of the mountains to their roots. A morning could come in which governments might ask what happened not merely to the forest and the bays but to a whole people.'[2]

Alongside such traditional and known constraints to good practice, both internal and external, now sits the contemporary threat (or promise, as government and industry prefer to see it) of globalisation and its enforcing agency, the General Agreement on Trade and Services (GATS), which provides the rules and obligations for liberalisation. Under the GATS, foreign companies must have access to domestic markets while domestic investors cannot receive any favourable treatment. Host governments will not be able to prevent the 'invasion' of foreign companies nor will they be able to legally protect their own workers or their environments. As in the manufacturing section, so in the service industries, dominated in tourism by the multinationals, the famous 'level playing fields' are absent, say developing countries; it is northern corporations that will benefit, and not local people or local business.

Critics of the GATS, as it relates to tourism, say that powerful tour operators and hotel chains (see Chapter One) are involved in a range of unfair practices – from the foreign control of management and marketing to low pay and discriminatory working conditions (see Chapter Three). This state of affairs is not exclusive to the Caribbean but affects tourism in the whole of the developing world. These inequalities have prompted groups to begin to organise around the concept of fair trade in tourism. While there is a growing acceptance that producers from the south, such as coffee growers or banana farmers, should be able to negotiate a fair wage and conditions of work within a sustainable environment, this concept has only just begun to be considered by the tourist industry. The Fair Trade in Tourism Network, launched by the British campaigning charity, Tourism Concern, believes that host countries should be consulted in the tourism development process – that there should be partnerships and equitable sharing of costs and benefit between the services and purchasers, providers and communities. That, in itself, provides a setting in which a new sort of tourism could flourish – in the Caribbean and elsewhere.

Against this background some sort of new consensus is emerging: that high-density mass tourism and the open economies and closed ecosystems of small islands are not compatible with sustainable development. One contributor to the debate, from the St Lucia Heritage Tourism Programme has written, 'While tourism is a key economic sector in St Lucia, as indeed in most Caribbean islands, it has so far failed to generate substantial benefits to the poor, and there are important concerns about the sustainability and equity of current, dominant forms of tourism development.' That is the challenge.

The Pioneers

Many years before globalisation, when preferences for Caribbean bananas and sugar were still in place and newly minted Caribbean countries were hungrily building up their tourist industries along a mass market line, an alternative path for tourism had already been launched. The concept, the 'new tourism', was coined as long ago as 1972, by the former prime minister of Jamaica, Michael Manley, at the start of his first term of office. That administration made an attempt to change the top-down, white-on-black culture of the industry. Holidays for Jamaican workers were organised in the tourist resorts to break what Manley called the old elitist patterns in which hotels were 'shut away from the local population by psychology as much as by price.'[3]

The term was later associated with the former prime minister of Grenada, Maurice Bishop, in 1979, just eight months after a bloodless coup had brought his People's Revolutionary Government (PRG) to power. Bishop's administration was to end in his murder in October 1983. However, during its short-lived regime, a new tourism began to take shape.

In December 1979, Bishop gave the opening address to a regional conference on the socio-cultural and environmental impacts of tourism

on Caribbean societies. It was held at the Holiday Inn, on Grande Anse
Beach, Grenada, and was an important opportunity for Bishop to
explain his government's policies on tourism in front of what must
have been a somewhat suspicious regional audience. Delegates
included ministers of tourism, the Cuban ambassador to Grenada and
the executive directors of the Caribbean Tourism Research and
Development Centre and the Caribbean Tourism Association, the
precursors of the Caribbean Tourism Organisation.

It is worth paying some attention to Bishop's speech because
Grenada under the PRG and, to some extent, Jamaica are probably the
only Caribbean states to have created a political framework for the
'new tourism' and to have had, if only briefly, the political will to
deliver it.

Bishop began his speech by emphasising the PRG's commitment to
tourism and to its expansion (he depended on the construction of the
international airport at Point Salines, 'in the centre of our main tourist
area'). He said that Grenada's tourism would reflect 'the nature of our
revolution' and that the 'old tourism' would be replaced by a 'new
tourism'.[4] He associated the old tourism with an imperialist age, when
tourism was 'intended as a means of increasing dependence on the
metropole and of providing development for the few and under-
development for the vast majority of the people of our islands.'[5]

He summarised this 'old tourism' in what now appears to be an old-
fashioned style but its content many might still recognise. 'It was
foreign-owned and controlled, it was unrelated to the needs and
development of the Caribbean people, it had no linkages with other
sectors in the economy and it brought with it a number of distinct
socio-cultural and environmental hazards such as the race question
and undesirable social and economic patterns such as drug abuse,
prostitution and consumerism.'[6] He then examined what shape he
thought the new tourism should take. 'We start from the principle...
that Grenadians as all Caribbean people must be recognised as
controllers of their own destiny and developers of their own process.'
He went on to explore the tenets of the new tourism both from an
internal perspective and from a regional and international one.

Tourism was a tool for development, he said, emphasising its
potential for creating linkages with the rest of the economy at many
levels, including food and handicrafts. The government was also
working towards what he called a proper 'internal climate' for tourism:
this included a strong agroindustrial sector, the international airport,
improved water supply and training and cultural programmes. He

also anticipated that ordinary people could help participate 'in the process of defining the type of tourist activity' Grenada wanted.

Looking outwards, Bishop first identified tourism as being an 'instrument of world peace'. If this now appears a dated concept, it should be remembered that such vocabulary was an ingredient of international left-wing thinking during the Cold War. He then talked about diversifying the tourist market into Latin America, the Caribbean itself and Europe, beyond the United Kingdom. 'To break the relationship between tourism, class and colour,' Bishop wanted to encourage non-white visitors and particularly other Caribbean nationals to become tourists. This was linked to another aim of the new tourism that was to support 'regional solutions to problems in tourism as in other sectors.' He urged 'hassle-free' travel among Caribbean nationals. The PRG did not, however, neglect the traditional market; on the marketing side, it formed a separate ministry of tourism, allocated it US$750,000 in funds (far more than ever before) and opened tourism offices in Toronto and New York.[7]

Bishop's hopes for a new tourism, however, were thwarted. Firstly, and crucially, they failed because the external market was against the regime. Hostile propaganda by the US ensured that visitor arrivals slackened (see Chapter Two), while Bishop's ideas about encouraging Caribbean, Third-World and 'study' tourists never really took off. There were not enough of them and they did not spend as much money as the traditional tourist sector.[8]

Internally, the PRG made more progress towards its new tourism goals. Linkages began to be established. Between 1981 and 1982, both the private and public sector grew, in particular the public sector which recorded a 34 per cent growth in gross production. The island's food import bills had also begun to decrease. Entrepreneurs were involved in tourist-linked operations such as furniture making, brewing, soft drinks and basic food products, while the state set up Grenada Agro-Industries (making jams and jellies and so on) and Grencraft, which encouraged craft cottage industries. Such mixed economy initiatives even won the approval of the conservative World Bank which praised the PRG in 1982 for 'laying better foundations for growth within the framework of a mixed economy.'[9]

There were, however, difficulties with this strategy. One constraint on Grenada's brave new world was the financial burden of infrastructural development. The cost of the new airport, although subsidised by the Cubans to a great degree, became a drain on the PRG's finances, as did other public-sector initiatives, especially agricultural reform. Revenue had to be found somewhere and it was the hotel sector that was saddled with new taxes. In turn, this pushed up prices and made Grenada less competitive.

The new tourism experiment never really had time to settle down. Bishop's ideas became clouded by political rhetoric and the PRG finally collapsed on the steps of St George's' Fort Rupert when, along with three of his ministers, Bishop was murdered in the implosion of Grenadian radical politics in October 1983. The end of the PRG saw the end of Grenada's 'new tourism' experiment. No other government has since picked up the torch.

A Niche in the Making

However, both before and after the under-development of the 'new tourism' ideas, there have been other options that reject the equation of more means good and less means bad. The first option was for second-home tourism. This became popular on the small rather chic islands of St Barts, Nevis and Montserrat, before the latter's volcano crisis. On Montserrat, for example, former agricultural land was sold plot by plot mainly to North Americans and Europeans. From the early 1960s until 1995 when the volcano crisis began, a thriving expatriate sub-culture developed, of villas and well-tended lawns. But by 1997, one of the two villa areas had been destroyed by volcanic activity while the other had become, for a time, part of a no-go zone. But for many years, the 'snowbird' market – villa owners who stayed in Montserrat over the northern winter – created jobs in construction, domestic work and retailing. At one point, according to a study, 'only 287 expatriate resident retirees accounted for one-fifth of all visitor expenditures of the other much more numerous stayover segments: hotel, villa and private home guest.'[10] This was a high-spend alternative to conventional mass tourism.

The white-sand beaches of Anguilla, a tiny, flat island just north of St Maarten, saw another sort of tourism: luxury hotels and villas catering for the extremely rich. The emphasis was on 'quality not quantity', according to Chris Carty, chairman of the Anguillian tourist board. Indeed, for much of the 1980s, as tourism developed, the government adopted a moratorium on new hotels which held until 1991. The success of the 'product' stemmed from a policy that aimed at 'an up-scale market niche of discriminating… visitors who favoured a low-key, high-quality, non-urban, small island setting.' Tourism has provided employment for the island's workforce and produced a GDP per capita which, in 1999, stood at US$7,600 – one of the highest in the Caribbean. There is, however, evidence that such growth is unsustainable: resources are too scarce and pressures on the infrastructure too great. Attempts to encourage local participation have been confined largely to the smaller properties; linkages, too, have not made significant progress, while planning and management remains under-developed. Some of the classic criteria for an alternative approach to tourism, such as local control and participation, are also absent, while, more recently, tourism's onward march suggests a return to the conventional emphasis on economic growth.[11]

Anguilla, with its reputation for exquisite cool in the sand, has been a marketing success. It has become a model for marketing gurus who want to see the Caribbean develop 'niche' marketing. The pressure is on to create holidays that appeal to every sort of special interests and needs: the tourist, for example, who wants to switch from canoeing to casinos, from camping to condos all in one holiday; or the demands of the health-conscious for a luxury spa (see Chapter Six).

Such a tourism, which can respond to individual needs, is the new Caribbean chic. Jamaica, for example, now has its 'boutique' hotels, such as Jake's on Treasure Beach; these small-scale hotels are honed to perfection for a sophisticated metropolitan market that wants to chill out – local but safe, with an ambience of primary coloured cottages, tin roofs and hammocks. Such establishments have pitched into what Auliana Poon, the marketing analyst, has advocated: 'Innovation must not only be total, it must all be continuous... Caribbean tourism will have to fall in line with the new tourism best practice – of flexibility, segmentation and diagonal integration – or fade out!'[12] Sports tourism, such as cricket or even dominoes, has the same 'segment' potential, as has music or scuba diving. The key, according to the promoters of 'niche' tourism, is to provide the particular for the increasingly demanding and experienced traveller.

Independent Visions

Between the now doomed era of Maurice Bishop and the new community-tourism led initiatives, there have been the occasional individuals who have also generated something beyond the obvious, often without significant endorsement from the tourist establishment. One guest-house that has demonstrated a sustainable style of local ownership and management, small-scale development and links with the community is Papillote Wilderness Retreat in Dominica. Its long-term commitment to ecotourism was rewarded in 1994 when it won third prize in the *Islands Magazine* ecotourism award behind the well-established Bonaire National Park and the Turks and Caicos National Museum. The citation was 'for combining a small, low-key resort with a programme that highlights local flora and fauna on an island that's already well known for nature tourism.'

In a rainforest setting at the head of the Roseau Valley, surrounded by a magnificent garden with natural hot spring baths, Papillote is owned and managed by Dominican Cuthbert Jno-Baptiste and his American-born wife Anne. According to the Jno-Baptistes, Papillote evolved from the raw materials that existed, using what was there: 'We took a very strong position that we would work with the available resources and build up from there. Papillote is an integrated whole with natural features.'

The result of this philosophy is that almost everything is locally made and supplied. Everything in the rooms – the furniture, the cane or calabash lampshades, the iron work, the bedspreads – except the linen and bathroom fixtures is made in villages, where locals have set up cottage industries to supply Papillote and other outlets. Many of these people had originally learned their skills through a training programme set up by Papillote. A craft shop on the premises sells local sculpture, woodwork and jewellery. The water is tapped from hot and cold springs. All food is locally grown; the only imports are bacon, butter, sugar and flour from other Caricom states.

The young staff come from the nearby village of Trafalgar. They are recruited according to their interests and are sent on training courses. 'We try to add to their skills. Whoever learns teaches. We teach them respect for animals and the environment. We have an extended family here,' said Anne Jno-Baptiste. 'We generate US$350,000 a year, of which the rooms are one-third, and of that one-third ten per cent might go in commission. Apart from that it all stays in Dominica.' The customers at Papillote are not paying for smartness. They pay for an environmentally-friendly guesthouse from which to walk, explore, bird-watch, swim and dive. 'It's a select clientele with money. They are more and more focussed on global environmental issues. Here it allows them to see the possibilities, to focus on the ideal,' commented Anne Jno-Baptiste.

While Cuba's Las Terrazas in Pinar del Rio province, west of Havana, is not an example of individual vision, it has become the island's flagship attempt to move away from mass tourism into ecotourism (see Chapter Five). Las Terrazas evolved out of a resettlement project in the 1960s, becoming a model of post-revolutionary development nurtured by hosts of environmentalists and government officials. Then, in 1994, during what became known as the 'Special Period' following the collapse of the Soviet Union, tourism became a way of ensuring an income for the people of Las Terrazas. A 26-room hotel, Moka, was built between Las Terrazas and a UNESCO biosphere reserve called Sierra del Rosario; it now welcomes 30,000 tourists a year. 'What we've tried [to do] is to incorporate the natural environment and the local community. The idea is that the tourists and the community together participate in all this,' said the former minister of tourism Osmany Cienfuegos, a key figure in the success of the project.[13]

According to Honey, an early visitor to Moka, 40 per cent of profits from the hotel go into community development and 10 per cent into the health clinic, while 60 per cent of profits from tourism-related businesses go into a community development fund. Las Terrazas characterises low-impact technology, community involvement and a harking back to 'solidarity' tourism. It reflects, in a way, Cuban society's need to conserve and recycle in the post-Soviet Special Period. 'Moka,' Honey wrote, 'encapsulates the best of Cuba's efforts in ecotourism.'

Collective Visions

The occasional, isolated example of good practice is, of course, not enough to ensure sustainability. What is beginning to happen, however, are a few collective approaches, which essentially attempt to go back to basics: to analyse the needs of small-island economies and to explore how the broader needs of communities can be addressed. What has come to be known generally as 'community tourism' in many ways reflects the ideas enshrined by Manley and Bishop.

What all these following examples show is that there cannot just be one single strategy for tourism development, there can only be a vision for development within which tourism is one part of the whole. Examples include projects in Belize, Cuba, Dominica, Jamaica and St Lucia. All have different characteristics and histories but try to address – not always successfully – a grass-roots need to participate in and benefit from the industry which consumes the region. Such thinking has also reached the Caribbean establishment and features in the CTO's strategic plan: one of its objectives is 'to maximise the benefits of tourism to the wider community' and within that broad concept to place tourism 'squarely within national policy frameworks and plans for social and economic development, poverty alleviation, sustainability and conservation of the national patrimony.' Now that it has reached the platform of the region, it is the practice that is required: to date, only a few pioneers have embraced it.

Community tourism was pioneered in Jamaica by a former Jamaican minister of tourism, Desmond Henry (who also spoke at the 1979 Holiday Inn conference in Grenada). It was then defined as a 'from-the-bottom-up concept designed to stimulate community cooperation, pride and a sense of value; to utilise local resources, provide local income and encourage the training of new hospitality skills.'[14] Designed for areas of Jamaica outside the mass tourism enclaves, it was to be locally planned, locally controlled and maintained and small-scale.

One modest contemporary example of community tourism exists at Jack's Hill, a community on the edge of the Blue Mountain/John Crow Mountain National Park, Jamaica's first national park. The 200,000-acre park developed a range of recreational and educational activities to provide attractions for tourism and employment for local people. At Jack's Hill, tourists who stay at Maya Lodge, the headquarters of the Jamaican Alternative Tourism, Camping and Hiking Association, use the Blue Mountains for various sporting activities and spend time with local farmers and residents. Maya Lodge is also a model demonstration site for a community reforestation and environmental education programme and provides support, research and training for other ecotourism operations.

The centre of community tourism in Jamaica, however, is in and around Mandeville, the capital of the parish of Manchester, where it was pioneered by Diana McIntyre-Pike, founder of the Central and South Jamaica Tourism Committee and, more recently, co-founder of the Sustainable Communities Foundation (SCF) through tourism. McIntyre-Pike describes community tourism as a process in which 'everyone is involved from the beginning in the planning and development – from the "big guys" to the man on the street.' The committee, formed in the early 1990s, encouraged a new perspective on local involvement in tourism; it was something quite new for the Caribbean. Among a whole range of activities, it offered visitors a chance to visit a private orchid garden, pepper factory, spa, schools, crocodile farm research station and to have a 'Jamaica chit-chat session' while staying in local homes.

From such beginnings, which saw a role for local institutions and 'ordinary' Jamaicans in tourism, McIntyre-Pike has extended her vision of community tourism and its potential as a tool for development. She sees it as a 'demand product' for communities and visitors because it 'promotes the culture, heritage and way of life whilst protecting the natural environment.' She argues that it can be embraced by all sectors of the industry – large and small hotels, all-inclusives, cruise ships, Caribbean nationals – as the way forward 'to improve the quality of life of communities as it assists in promoting economic growth through tourism for everyone.' The key aspect, says the SCF, is that communities 'are educated in all aspects of managing the business of tourism to ensure complete visitor satisfaction' so they can take charge of their own development. Community tourism, according McIntyre-Pike, is an 'integrated approach which embraces all aspects of a community and should not be as seen as an alternative type of tourism as it also works closely with the traditional resort products.' The SCF focuses on training and education to build up the capacities of local communities to realise their potential.

In southern Belize, a centre of the country's ecotourism industry, community tourism initiatives have been based on a similar philosophy: the idea that villagers who have little training or understanding of the tourist industry can remain in control of their businesses and earn money from services such as guiding and accommodation. The Toledo Ecotourism Association (TEA), for example, was formed to allow local Mayan communities directly to plan, control and profit from ecotourism.

Ten different villages, each with a guesthouse, participate in the TEA; within each village, the provision of guides, food and entertainment rotates among up to nine families. The organisation is communally managed with each village providing an elected representative; profits go to a general fund that contributes to village health and education, rainforest conservation and administration. More than 80 per cent of all funds stay in the individual village that is visited, and villagers have benefited from training schemes and participating in ideas about tourism development.

The TEA is widely considered to be a success story. Inevitably, however, there have been threats to its success, from both external and internal sources. There have been proposals from foreign investors and travel agents to set up other village programmes in competition with the TEA. There have been fears that the outsiders would use their money and marketing expertise to weaken the local movement and, as the TEA said in a letter to the US-based Center for Responsible Tourism, 'to control tourism in the villages that we have painstakingly developed.' This threat has not materialised, but there have been other problems. Some villages, for example, have attracted more visitors than others because of their location or because they are more developed than others.

More fundamentally, the development of ecotourism in the area has become caught up with the issues around Mayan rights. The Kekchi Council for Belize, for example, does not want Maya communities to become dependent on ecotourism but to diversify into sustainable logging and farming. Within the context of Mayan rights, there is also the charge that its culture is commodified and its craft bastardised (see Chapter Eight) by ecotourism. This, in turn, fuels the flames for the appeal for a Maya homeland, a position opposed by the government. Rosaleen Duffy, in her book *A Trip Too Far*, concluded that the constraints working against the success of community tourism were 'inextricably linked to the very processes that ensure these communities have remained relatively impoverished.'[15] Involved in these processes were interest groups ranging from the tourism establishment to road builders, international financial institutions and even dealers in illegal wildlife and timber.

Community tourism projects, such as the TEA, are grounded in the idea, promoted by national and international institutions, that the poor, too, can benefit from tourism. The experience of Belize shows how precarious and complex is its practice. The experience of one village in Dominica, Vielle Case on the north coast, shows how expectations are raised and then hopes dimmed when the conditions for community tourism are not quite in place.

This village has yet to see any tourists although some of the villagers will know about mass tourism from their own holidays, perhaps in St Maarten, or from working in Antigua or Guadeloupe. But for the moment they are not waiters, receptionists, hair-braiders or taxi drivers; they do not sell duty-free Colombian emeralds or T-shirts with 'Vielle Case Jammin' printed on them. Despite its beauty, few outsiders visit the village, which sits on cliffs high above the Atlantic along a twisting road that leads only to one other, even more remote, settlement.

Yet Vielle Case has been gearing itself up for tourists for at least a decade. The trouble is that they have taken a long time to arrive. The village's search for the tourist dollar began in 1994 when a tourist board representative held a meeting about tourism with the village council saying that the board was visiting communities all over the island to 'dialogue with the people' and to explain the potential for tourism. The village council was enthusiastic. It had drawn up a list of potential attractions in and around the village: a waterfall, a pond 'like a bath tub', an underwater cave and the fishermen's cove, old trails, views across the sea to Marie Galante and Les Saintes, a church, where the first mass on the island was held, Carib artefacts and so on.

The next stage was to draw up a plan of action. There was, he said, a small development fund to help finance the programme. Eight years on, however, Vielle Case was still waiting. There has been some institutional development, said Vernice Bellony, the former MP of the area. Committees had been set up in many of the villages of the north and the northeast to 'sensitise' villagers to the concept of tourism and to develop attractions. 'We want to tell people about the importance of tourism and how they can all benefit, all of us together, not just one set of people,' said Bellony. 'There have been talks in schools and we are looking at beautifying what we have to offer and developing facilities.'

The communities have prepared themselves the best they know how. But finance that had been promised, from the EU, had not arrived. There has also been a lack of strategic thinking, skills and technical support. The community has been told that when a new road is completed it will bring buses – laden with cruise ship tourists – through the village. But is cruise tourism something that the village can respond to? How will it be involved in the decision-making? 'All this brings a sense of frustration,' said Bellony. 'We've been talking for so many years but with no tangible results.' Bellony also commented that local people were reluctant to put money into tourism projects until they saw that tourists would actually come to Vielle Case. 'It is a chicken and egg situation,' she said. Within this piecemeal framework, it will be hard to reach the laudable objectives first targeted by the village council of Vielle Case.

As Good as it Gets

While St Lucia's Jalousie Hilton Resort characterises the sort of mass market tourism that typifies the region (see Chapter One), St Lucia is also the home of a radical community tourism initiative. The St Lucia Heritage Tourism Programme (SLHTP) is an attempt to avoid the sort of problems that have plagued the experiences, for example, of the people of Toledo and Vielle Case.

St Lucia has grown fast as a mass tourism destination with many all-inclusive hotels popular for weddings and honeymoons. Beyond the tourist enclave in the northwest of the island, however, is an island of banana farmers with pockets of serious poverty. The SLHTP is not an attempt to oppose mass tourism but to direct its opportunities into more and smaller tributaries. It aims to build on what exists in an attempt to 'shift an entire sector, as quickly and as effectively as can reasonably be expected so that it becomes more sustainable, more equitable, and more focussed on the needs of poor people.'

From the start, the SLHTP was aware of the difficulties and of the need for a holistic approach. As a paper on its programme emphasised: 'The nature of international tourism and its development in St Lucia and other Caribbean countries is extremely complex. Due to the failure of previous isolated efforts to affect change, it was felt that only a concerted programme operating simultaneously with complementary initiatives in policy, capacity building, marketing, product development and public awareness, could have a significant impact.'

The SLHTP was launched in 1998, an initiative of the government of St Lucia, funded by the government and the European Union with a budget of around US$1.5 million. Its mission was 'to establish heritage tourism as a viable and sustainable component of St Lucia's tourism product by facilitating a process of education, capacity building, product development, marketing, credit access and the promotion of environmental and cultural protection for the benefit of host communities and St Lucians.' Its aim was to broaden the benefits of the existing tourism sector by developing 'unique and authentic' visitor attractions in rural communities and thus promote 'a sense of participation in and ownership of the industry.'

In 2001, the programme could point to its achievements: it had provided loans and technical assistance to a range of initiatives, including a turtle-watching venture, a community-managed mangrove forest and a seafood night. It had developed marketing initiatives – in particular, the packaging of the attractions to sell as a 'heritage tourism product' and a publicity programme. The branding of 'heritage tourism' had not only helped in the sale of heritage tours but had also raised its profile within the island as a whole. The SLHTP had also supported and thus strengthened relevant local organisations to enable capacity building. Lastly it had worked on developing policy and planning in a participatory framework. Each was part of the integrated whole.

The village of Anse La Raye is one community helped by the SLHTP. One of the poorest villages in St Lucia, on the coast south of the capital Castries, it has traditionally had two privately-owned tourism sites, but through its connections with the SLHTP it has begun to mobilise the whole village to tourism-oriented activities by using its natural resources – waterfalls, sea and scenery. One of its most successful initiatives is its weekly 'seafood night' which supports 40 vendors, most of whom are women, providing food and drink to both visitors and locals. Its success is in generating revenue – sustainably – while creating linkages; it spreads economic gain throughout the community while retaining an authentic cultural flavour. Fundamentally, it 'shows how participatory planning and community ownership can encourage community pride and generate support for the product.'

A different sort of SLHTP initiative is at Fond Latisab in the north of the island. There, two local entrepreneurs have developed a small family farm into a 'truly kweyol experience, which provides a two-hour tour of local cultural skills – sawing lumber accompanied by drumming and chanting, catching crayfish and processing cassava. Although it is a private initiative its cultural emphasis has raised awareness and given pride to the whole of the local community. Most of its customers are cruise ship passengers; St Lucia's programme aims to incorporate customers from the traditional markets into its activities.

This is only a beginning, but these and other features of the SLHTP have begun to make what the writer of a paper on pro-poor tourism in St Lucia calls 'cracks in the fortress'. The main achievement, according to the writer, has been to demonstrate to most stakeholders that the need and opportunity exist to transform the tourism product. Its careful and considered approach has shown that there is a demand for an island's cultural and natural assets, and that these assets need to be protected and managed. Furthermore, it has illustrated the link between social capital and the ability to stimulate economic development. In such a way has it been able to create some of the conditions to make change possible.

However, the programme has inevitably revealed many constraints, some internal, some external. Such problems are typical of experiences found in other projects on other islands. What the SLHTP found was that while those involved in the programme had a clear vision, there was no policy framework at a national level to guide its development;

nor was there sufficient political support for the programme. These findings are not surprising given the deficiencies of the public sector (see Chapters One, Four and Five). At another level, it was also recognised that the 'product' had to meet international standards: to achieve this, with marketing skills and support in place, it was necessary for local communities to understand the workings of the tourist industry and to acquire the capacity to turn an idea into that viable tourist 'product'.

These are all demanding goals, yet fundamental for the wellbeing of the industry. The crisis that the region's leaders are facing at the start of the 21st century is more profound than it was a decade earlier. The Jamaican commentators, Dunn & Dunn, found from opinion polls and focus groups that tinkering on the margins with, for example, media and educational campaigns 'could not adequately address [the] problems.' Such approaches, they concluded, would be 'futile unless there was fundamental industry restructuring in line with many of these legitimate concerns.' Grass-roots disillusion and ambivalence (see Chapters Three and Four) are likely to continue if governments cling on to the old-fashioned tourism concepts – while the pressures on the people of the Caribbean will increase.

Major political decisions are needed to re-shape tourism in order for it to become more democratic. Local people need to participate in the decision-making process and share in the benefits and responsibilities. Countless workshops have been held to examine the new approaches and the need for the reform and realignment of the tourist industry. Indeed, as this book has tried to show, plenty of people have also pointed out that strategies such as rational long-term planning, environmental protection, diversification, improved linkages and so on need to be addressed with some urgency. Yet the theory remains more in place than the practice.

If tourism in the Caribbean continues to grow as predicted, more and more corners of the region will be touched by the industry. Caricom's strategic plan, for example, is projecting a 'high case' scenario in which by 2012 the industry will have delivered, a total stayover arrival count of 33 million (an increase of 64 per cent over 2000). Visitor expenditure will by then have increased by 77 per cent over the same period to US$35 billion. Those many communities on distant hillsides now undisturbed by tourism will inevitably be drawn into its orbit in the hope that it will ease their hardship. The transformation of much of the Caribbean, from the Bahamas to Belize, has been fast and would have been unimaginable a generation ago.

St Lucia, for example, has been one of those countries whose tourism development has been swift. It has, as we have seen, experienced both mass and alternative tourism. It is not a question of one or the other, it is a matter of broadening the industry's economic and social base. As the SLHTP pioneers wrote: 'We propose to describe a tourism that provides an avenue for environmental protection, social and economic development, and financial viability regardless of product type. What is important is the process of tourism development that achieves the objectives of environmental sustainability, economic empowerment of host communities and national development.' Those who have most to gain from a sustainable tourist industry are often those furthest away from being able to effect change. The strategies to achieve that are gradually being put in place. If that happens, tourism, the engine of growth for the modern Caribbean, will become an effective instrument to take the people of the Caribbean forward in the 21st century.

NOTES

1. Graham Dann and Potter, Robert, 'Tourism in Barbados: Rejuvenation or Decline?', in D.G. Lockhart and Drakakis-Smith, D. (eds), *Island Tourism*, London, forthcoming
2. 'The Antilles: Fragments of Epic Memory', Nobel Prize lecture by Derek Walcott, December 7, 1992
3. Michael Manley, *Jamaica: Struggle in the Periphery*, London, n.d., p.94
4. Maurice Bishop, Address to Regional Conference on the Socio-Cultural and Environmental Impact of Tourism on Caribbean Societies, Grenada, December 1979
5. Ibid.
6. Ibid.
7. Marcus Stephenson, Tourism is Everyone's Business, MA Dissertation, Manchester Metropolitan University, 1990
8. Tony Thorndike, *Grenada: Politics, Economics and Society*, London, 1985, p.100
9. James Ferguson, *Grenada: Revolution in Reverse*, London, 1990, p.94
10. Jerome McElroy and De Albuquerque, Klaus, 'The Economic Impact of Retirement Tourism in Montserrat: Some Provisional Evidence', *Social and Economic Studies*, vol 41, 1992, pp. 127-152
11. 'Tourism Development in Anguilla' by Paul Wilkinson, *Tourism Recreation Research*, vol 26(32), 2001
12. Auliana Poon, 'Competitive Strategies for Caribbean Tourism: the New versus the Old', *Caribbean Affairs*, Trinidad, vol 2, no 2, 1989
13. Martha Honey, *Ecotourism and Sustainable Development: Who Owns Paradise?*, Washington 1999
14. Desmond Henry, untitled paper given at Regional Conference, Grenada, 1979
15. Rosaleen Duffy, *A Trip Too Far: Ecotourism, Politics and Exploitation*, London 2002

PHOTOGRAPHS
by Philip Wolmuth

1 ST. LUCIA: A teenager watches as a tourist cruiser leaves Soufrière.

2 CUBA: Construction of a new hotel in the Vedado district of Havana.

3 ST. LUCIA: A tourist is served drinks on the beach at the controversial Jalousie resort near the town of Soufrière.

4 ST. LUCIA: A security guard watches as a local man pulls his boat onto the public beach.

5 DOMINICAN REPUBLIC: American tourists play golf at the Altos de Chavón hotel complex.

6 ANTIGUA: Tourists from a cruise ship shop for souvenirs in St. John.

7 DOMINICA: A cruise ship leaves Roseau after a few hours' stopover.

8 TRINIDAD: Carnival in Port-of-Spain.

9 BARBADOS: Bar owner on the outskirts of Bridgetown.

SELECT BIBLIOGRAPHY

For a general coverage of the issues around tourism in the South, two of the best (if somewhat out of date) books are Emanuel de Kadt (ed.), *Tourism: Passport to Development? Perspectives on the Social and Cultural Effects of Tourism in Developing Countries* (1978); and L. Turn and J. Ash, *The Golden Hordes: International Tourism and the Pleasure Periphery* (1975). A more recent set of essays is David Harrison (ed.), *Tourism and the Less Developed Countries* (1992) while *Tourism and Sustainability: New Tourism in the Third World* (1998) by Martin Mowforth and Ian Munt examines some alternatives for the future of tourism.

For books specifically about the region, the most up to date (albeit pricey) is *Tourism and the Caribbean: Trends, Developments, Prospects* (2004), edited by David Duval. There is also *Tourism Planning and Policy: Case Studies from the Commonwealth Caribbean* by Paul Wilkinson (1997) and the multi-disciplinary approach of *Island Tourism and Sustainable Development: Caribbean, Pacific and Mediterranean Experiences* (2002), edited by Yorghos Apostolopoulos and Dennis Gayle. Now somewhat out of date is *Tourism, Marketing and Management in the Caribbean* (1975) edited by Dennis Gayle and Jonathan Godrich, a collection of essays.

The West Indian Commission's 'Time for Action: Overview of the Report of the West Indian Commission' (1992) is a sober look at the issues that faced the region in the early 1990s.

There are few country-specific books. An exception is Frank Fonda Taylor, *To Hell with Paradise: A History of the Jamaican Tourist Industry* (1993). More recent, and very welcome, is *People and Tourism* by Hopeton S Dunn and Leith L Dunn (2000), a rare piece of research into what Jamaicans feel about the tourist industry that surrounds them.

Other important books which have sections on aspects of the tourist industry in the Caribbean or have views on tourism in particular countries include 'Sun, Sex and Gold, Fantasy Islands' by Julia O'Connell Davidson and Jacqueline Sanchez Taylor, edited by Kamala Kempiadoo (1999) about the sex tourism industry. There are sections on tourism in Anguilla, Antigua, Barbados and Belize in *A Reader in Caribbean Geography* edited by David Barker, Carol Newby and Mike Morrissey (1998); *Sources of Bahamian History* (1991) by Philip Cash, Shirley Gordon and Gail Saunders includes well-researched material on the Bahamas. *The Urban Caribbean in an Era of Global Change* (2000), by Robert B Potter includes an interesting chapter on Barbados. *Behind the Smile: The Working Lives of Caribbean Tourism* (2003) explores the views of Barbadian workers in the tourism industry.

In a class of their own are Jamaica Kincaid's excoriating essay on tourism in Antigua *A Small Place* (1988) and Derek Walcott's lecture on receiving the Nobel prize, 'The Antilles, Fragments of Epic Memory' (1992).

The following books are on the Caribbean in general, with passing references to tourism. The two classics are *The Growth of the Modern West Indies* (1968) by Gordon Lewis and *West Indian Societies* (1972) by David Lowenthal. Others are Tom Barry, Beth Wood and Deb Preusch, *The Other Side of Paradise: Foreign Control in the Caribbean* (1984); Jean Besson and Janet Momsen, *Land and Development in the Caribbean* (1987) Kathy McAfee, *Storm Signals: Structural Adjustment and Development Alternatives in the Caribbean* (1991); Janet Momsen (ed.), *Women and Change in the Caribbean* (1993).

One useful and questioning book on ecotourism is *Ecotourism and Sustainable Development* by Martha Honey (1999), which includes an extensive chapter on Cuba. Rosaleen Dufy's *A Trip Too Far, Ecotourism, Politics and Exploitation* (2002) is an uncompromising analysis of tourism in Belize. Island Resources Foundation has produced an important look at the environment, *Tourism and Coastal Resources Degradation in the Wider Caribbean* (1996).

Some Caribbean travelogues include observations on tourism. The classic, first published in the 1950s and never bettered (if a trifle patrician) is Patrick Leigh Fermor's *The Traveller's Tree: A Journey Through the Caribbean Islands* (re-published 1984). A more recent batch includes Quentin Crewe, *Touch the Happy Isles: A Journey Through the Caribbean* (1987); Zenga Longmore, *Tap-Taps to Trinidad: A Caribbean Journey* (1989); and Lucretia Stewart, *The Weather Prophet* (1995). Henry Shukman's *Travels with my Trombone* (1992), contains interesting accounts of the islands' musical scene. Martha Gellhorn's *Travels with Myself and Another* (1983), has a wonderful chapter on her Caribbean experiences during the Second World War.

Travel guides sometimes include useful background information on tourism: the *Caribbean Islands Handbook*; the Insight Guides, Lonely Planet and Rough Guides. All have a considered approach to tourism and provide good background information over and above details on accommodation. Old travel guides tell it how it was.

Statistical information: the Caribbean Tourism Organisation provides statistical information about tourist arrivals and expenditure country by country; its statistics also show useful comparisons over the years. National tourist boards and/or ministries of tourism will also supply statistics and, of course, brochures. The World Tourism Organisation also has a section on the Caribbean, and provides comparative information worldwide.

Journals: *The Annals of Tourism Research* publishes academic papers on all aspects of tourism and features the Caribbean from time to time; Malcolm Crick, 'Representations of International Tourism in the Social Sciences: Sun, Sex, Sights, Savings and Servility', *Annual Review of Anthropology*, vol 18, 1989, sets out an overview of the academic material up to the late 1980s.

Periodicals: the subscription-only, on-line weekly magazine *Caribbean Insight* provides some coverage and occasional statistics: insight@caribbean-council.org

Local Caribbean papers often carry stories about tourism, particularly in those countries with a developed tourist industry. Look out for *Outlet* (Antigua); the *Gleaner* (Jamaica); *Barbados Advocate* and *Barbados Sun*, and the Nassau *Tribune* (Bahamas).

Tourism Concern (www.tourismconcern.org.uk) is an excellent resource and membership organisation which campaigns for fair and ethically traded tourism. The best online site on ecotourism is www.planeta.com, a global journal of practical ecotourism with serious discussion groups and excellent information. Also see the Caribbean Ecotourism Information Network: contact cangonet@yorku.ca. Reponsibletravel.com provides information about how and where to take "responsible" holidays.

Many of the views and quotations that appear in this book were supplied by people in the Caribbean and elsewhere whom I interviewed in the course of my research. Their quotations are not referenced in the end-notes.

INDEX

agriculture 9, 42, 51-59, 63, 66, 69, 73, 77, 141, 157, 159, 160
Air Jamaica 22, 23
Airlines 23-7, 30, 32, 33, 37, 73, 118, 158, 182, 183
Airtours 25-6, 147-8, 178
Albuquerque, Klaus de 140
all-inclusives 19, 29, 58, 69, 70, 95-6, 98, 101, 124, 146, 148, 175, 177, 180, 188
American Airlines 22, 23, 167
Amerindians 161-3, 174, 177, 236
Amis, Martin 105
Anguilla 252, 253, 263
Antigua 107, 119, 130, 133-4, 140-2, 147, 164, 170, 178, 181, 194, 196, 221-2, 232-3, 236, 238, 240, 248, 258
Aristide, Jean-Bertrand 38
Aruba 9, 11, 17, 19, 53, 65, 68, 116, 117, 119, 196, 236, 253, 248

Bahamas 248, 262
Barbados 5, 11, 13-19, 23, 25, 26, 28, 31-3, 40, 42, 45-7, 49, 50, 54, 56, 67, 70-4, 76-7, 80, 82-5, 89, 90, 104, 108, 111, 112, 119, 120-3, 129, 130, 132, 133, 135-6, 167, 169, 170-2, 178, 180-7, 198, 200, 212, 223-9, 230, 233, 234, 237, 238, 240, 242, 247, 248
beaches, access 105
Beckles, Hilary 82, 206, 247
Belize 5, 17, 18, 39, 136, 143, 144, 149, 151-4, 156, 160, 163, 165, 196, 255, 257, 258, 262
Bequia 62, 69, 82, 94, 95, 98, 112, 126, 136, 212
Bird, Lester 102
Bishop, Maurice 81, 171, 249, 253
Black Power movement 15
Bonaire 26, 61, 119, 151, 155, 177, 213, 231, 233, 254,
British Airways 22, 23, 146, 147, 167,
British Virgin Islands 61, 129, 131, 211, 212,
Burnham, Forbes 161, 220
Butler model 11
BWIA 22-4

calypso 76, 90, 101, 104, 124, 176, 177, 218, 220, 222, 226, 243,
Canada 110, 169
Caribbean
    history 53, 62, 81, 82, 91, 99, 107, 126, 133, 167, 169, 174, 175, 177, 218, 219, 220, 221, 227, 229, 231-4, 237, 241, 243
    population 249
Caribbean Agricultural Research and Development Institute 59

Caribbean Community (Caricom) 6-9, 12-13, 21, 23, 48, 52, 134, 184-5, 197-8, 201, 210, 248, 254
Caribbean Conference of Churches 110, 182, 243
Caribbean Conservation Association 131, 133
Caribbean Development Bank 15, 219
Caribbean Ecotourism Conference 149, 154
Caribbean Hotel Association 10, 12, 31, 40, 45, 52, 80, 86, 145, 182, 198, 209
Caribbean Hospitality Training Institute (CHTI) 86
Caribbean Tourism Association 182, 250
Caribbean Tourism Organization (CTO) 8, 12, 70, 92, 246, 250
Caribbean Tourism Research and Development Centre 250
Caribbean Week 79, 208
Carnival 220, 224-8, 242
Carnival Cruise Lines 197, 202, 204, 208-10
Carriacou 222, 238
Casinos 10, 44, 65, 73, 116-9, 120, 194, 199, 253
Castro, Fidel 60, 239
Cater, Erlet 163
Cayman Islands 26, 61, 109, 136-7, 151, 177, 184, 207, 213, 228
Center for Marine Conservation Organization 138
Center for Responsible Tourism 258
Charles, Eugenia 46, 55, 155
Chastenet, Allen 30, 33, 88, 198
Cohen, Erik 40
Columbus, Christopher 129
Compton, John 197
Connolly, Mark 114
Conway, Dennis 51
Coppola, Francis Ford 154
Coward, Noel 14, 171
crime – see *also* casinos, drugs 110, 116, 117-9, 120-3, 180
Crop-over 224, 225, 227, 228, 230, 242
Cruise ships see Chapter Seven
    arrivals 7, 9, 16, 17, 18, 22, 39, 40, 41, 48, 61, 78, 119, 120, 121, 143, 150, 152, 155, 169, 170, 184,
        185, 195, 196, 202, 223, 228,
    destinations 7, 9, 10, 11, 12, 14, 15 to 17, 19, 20, 21, 23, 25, 26, 29, 33, 40, 41, 47, 49, 58, 73, 95,
        124, 140, 142, 152, 155, 157, 158, 159, 162, 163, 167, 169, 170, 181, 182, 185, 186, 187, 188,
        194 to 197, 202-6, 208, 210-13, 230, 231, 246, 260
    dumping 132, 137, 138, 213, 247
    employment 1, 2, 5, 31, 58, 60, 65-75, 77, 79, 80, 81, 83, 85, 87, 89, 91, 93, 94-5, 97, 99, 119, 124,
        162, 163, 199, 210, 229, 253, 256
    passenger expenditure 206
Cuba 5, 7, 9, 13-17, 22, 23, 25, 29, 32, 33, 35, 38, 39, 40, 44, 54, 60, 63, 67, 70, 71, 73, 81, 98, 105,
    107, 109, 113, 114, 116, 120, 126, 133, 136, 149, 151, 152, 159, 170, 171, 172, 182, 186, 187, 219,
    220, 234-7, 239, 240, 243, 250, 251, 253, 254, 255
culture, see Chapter Eight
    as entertainment 222, 223
    festival arts 220
    'heritage tourism' 150-1, 231, 233-6, 249, 259, 260
    museums 221, 233-6, 243
    souvenirs 235, 239, 240
    visual arts 220

Cumberbatch, Edward 50, 110
Cummins, Alissandra 223, 224, 238
Curaçao 13, 30, 116, 119, 196

Dear, Jack 76, 104
Demas, William 15, 219
Derrick, Foster 141
diversification 8, 47, 53, 63, 186, 262
Dominica 9, 11, 26, 41, 49, 53, 55, 68, 78, 79, 80, 90, 105, 120, 124, 150, 152, 154, 155-9, 160, 163, 176-7, 184, 196, 200-2, 207-8, 213, 224, 226, 229, 230, 241, 254-5, 258
Dominican Republic 5, 6, 16, 17, 18, 23, 25, 26, 29, 33, 34, 40, 41, 61, 67, 73, 75, 76, 99, 109, 113, 114, 119, 126, 131, 147, 169, 170, 172, 177, 181, 184, 187, 196, 231, 238
drugs 9, 78, 111, 114, 115, 116, 118, 121, 172
   cartels 116, 117
   money laundering 116, 118
   trafficking 115, 116
Durant, Orville 123

ecotourism 5, 10, 34, 129, 131, 133, 135, 137, 139, 141, 143, 145, 147-155, 157, 159-165, 186, 254-8, 263
Ecumenical Coalition for Third World Tourism 110
employment – see Chapter Three
   demand 16, 42, 52, 66, 68, 72, 106, 120, 130, 148, 149, 172, 186, 230, 238, 240, 241, 257, 261
   informal sector 65, 73, 76, 96
   job satisfaction 69, 70
   training 30, 45, 51, 67-70, 75, 79, 82-89, 91, 99, 122, 145, 148, 162, 183, 189, 240, 250, 254, 256, 256, 257
   working conditions 82, 173, 200, 248
environment – see Chapter Five
   coastal erosion 132, 135, 136, 164
   coral reefs 131 to 133, 135, 136, 139, 143, 144, 203
   sand mining 132, 135
   waste 132, 134, 137, 138, 139, 143, 147, 148, 184, 198, 214
   wetlands 131 to 133, 137, 138, 164
European Union 8, 183, 260
Evans, Robert 44

Fanon, Frantz 82
fantasy 28, 106, 115, 138, 155, 174, 177, 199, 204, 205, 237
Fleming, Ian 14
Florida-Caribbean Cruise Association (FCCA) 214, 215
Flynn, Errol 14
Foster, Drew 48, 171, 182

Garvey, Marcus 231
Gellhorn, Martha 129-130

Grenada 9, 11, 16, 18, 23, 39, 41, 42, 44, 47, 56, 57, 65, 66, 72, 74, 77, 81, 106, 119, 122, 135-6, 171, 176-7, 181, 194, 208, 212, 249, 250-2, 256
Groves, Wallace 44
Guadeloupe 17, 27, 33, 87, 108, 119, 170, 196, 258

Guyana 49, 67, 160 to 163, 165, 177, 219, 220
    Amerindians 161 to 163, 174, 177, 236

Haiti 5, 9, 38, 39, 114, 119, 121, 171, 182, 196, 204, 219, 220, 224, 234, 237, 239
harassment 51, 69, 75, 104, 122-4, 126, 180, 181, 203
Hector, Tim 83, 107, 222
Hemingway, Ernest 14
Henry, Desmond 256
Henry, Edward 135
Hiller, Herbert 37
Holder, Jean 12, 17, 48, 52, 56, 65, 81, 88, 123, 131, 139, 149, 184, 197, 199, 201, 207, 214
Hopkin, Royston 45, 198
hotels see also Caribbean Hotel Association
    6, 11, 12, 14, 15, 19, 21-34, 37, 38, 39, 42 to 46, 52, 53, 54, 57-61, 65-74, 76, 77, 81, 86,
    87, 89, 93-99, 101-3, 105, 107, 114-5, 118, 119, 120, 122, 131, 133-6 145-7, 153, 155, 161, 162,
    168, 170, 172, 175, 176, 180, 182, 185-8, 199, 209, 222, 223, 233, 235, 236, 239, 241, 245, 249,
    252, 253, 257, 260
    occupancy rates 17, 18, 19, 28, 30, 41, 45, 46, 68, 209, 230
    ownership 28, 30, 31, 32, 59
Howell, Calvin 131
Hoyte, Desmond 161
Humphries, Hilroy 141
hurricanes 38, 39, 132, 203

informal economy 107, 207
Ingraham, Hubert 31, 109
International Monetary Fund (IMF) 6, 31
Issa, John 29, 31

Jalousie Plantation Resort 1-15, 29, 33, 259
Jamaica 6, 9, 10, 12-9, 20, 22, 23, 26, 28-9, 30-3, 38, 39, 40, 44, 49, 50-3, 56-8, 61, 62, 67, 68, 70, 74,
    75, 81, 82, 84-5, 89, 91, 94-5, 97-8, 106, 108, 111, 115-7, 120, 121, 122, 131, 136, 145, 147, 169,
    170-2, 176-8, 180, 181, 185-9, 195-7, 200, 203, 210, 212, 219, 220-1, 227, 229, 230-4, 237, 240,
    249, 250, 253, 255-7
Junkanoo 217, 218, 220, 224, 227

KLM 22, 239
Korzner, Sol 27, 118

'leakages', see Chapter Three
Les Saintes 259
Lewis, Gordon 68, 225
LIAT 23-4
'linkages', see Chapter Three
Lomé Convention 6

M Group Corporation 3
Manley, Michael 12, 57, 249
Marpol Convention 137
Martinique 13, 27, 41, 87, 108, 119, 170, 193, 196, 212, 226
migration 8, 66, 68, 177, 219, 241

Mitchell, James 245
Montserrat 11, 17, 252
Morgan, Peter 31, 80, 104, 182
Mosquera, Gerardo 107, 239
Moyne Commission 7
Mustique 3, 15, 170

Naipaul, V.S. 82, 220
Nevis, see also St Kitts-Nevis 59, 236, 241, 252
Nibbs, Shirlene 85, 92
North American Free Trade Agreement (NAFTA) 8

Odle, Peter 26, 54, 89, 198
Organisation for Economic Co-operation and Development (OECD) 6
Organization of American States 2, 52
Organization of Eastern Caribbean States 55, 131, 183, 196, 198

Paradise Island, Bahamas 27, 28, 91, 118
Papillote Wilderness Retreat 155, 254
Pavarotti, Luciano 168
Peoples' Revolutionary Government, Grenada 57
Pindling, Lynden 31, 117, 118
Pitons, the 1, 2, 3, 154, 177
Poitier, Sidney 220
Poon, Auliana 253
prostitution 107, 109, 110, 111, 113-5, 250
Puerto Rico 15, 23, 40, 119, 138, 143, 169, 172, 184, 186, 195, 202, 205, 212

racism 15, 71, 174
Rastafarians 110, 139
reggae 177, 189, 220, 222, 223, 229, 231, 242
Reid, Lionel 57
Richards, Le Vere 72, 89
Richards, Viv 178
Richardson, Roland 238
Rider, Barry 116

Saba 5, 17, 196
St Barthélémy 196, 252
St Kitts see also Nevis 17, 57, 68, 75, 79, 108, 142, 194, 196, 201, 202, 210, 221, 224
St Lucia 1, 4, 9, 10, 17, 18, 22, 23, 26, 29, 30, 33, 57, 58, 61, 70, 88, 91, 92, 95, 96, 101, 105, 119, 130, 136, 144, 146, 147, 151, 176-8, 185, 188, 196-8, 200, 212, 226, 229, 230, 241, 247, 249, 155, 259, 260, 261, 263
St Maarten 11, 18, 19, 33, 40, 68, 74, 92, 116, 119, 194, 195, 196, 212, 236, 237, 248, 252, 258
St Martin 107, 108, 238, 239
St Vincent 9, 11, 15, 41, 182, 185, 193, 203, 205, 208, 230, 245
Samuel, Reg 241
Sandals Resorts 22, 57, 58, 69, 96, 120, 146
Sandiford, Erskine 50
Sands, Stafford 44, 117, 227
Scott, Lawrence 226

sex tourism 108, 109, 111, 113-5
slavery 5, 53, 81-3, 107, 129, 177, 219, 225, 231-5, 247
Soufrière 1, 2, 3, 144, 159
Stewart, Butch 22, 29, 31, 43, 80, 120, 122, 188, 210
Stone, Carl 69, 70, 93
Super Clubs 29, 32
Suriname 9

Tennant, Colin 3, 15
Thomas, Mark 53, 63
Toledo Ecotourism Association 153, 257
tour operators 14, 21, 23-6, 30, 32, 33, 37, 38, 48, 114, 155, 158, 167, 171, 173, 182-4, 187, 207, 233, 248
tourism industry
  advertising 12, 13, 30, 44, 108, 110, 182, 184, 185, 188, 189, 207-9, 228, 239
  arrivals 7, 18, 39, 61, 78, 119, 143, 150, 153, 228
  'community tourism' 152, 160, 253, 255-9
  economic dependency 12, 15, 38, 65, 69, 220
  employment 67, 69, 70, 73-4, 87, 94, 95, 97, 162, 199, 229, 253, 256
  expatriates 3, 79, 87, 88, 91, 206, 212-3, 222, 233, 238
  foreign investment 33, 43-5, 154, 161
  government role 161, 162, 187, 235, 246, 250, 252, 260
  history of 13-16, 37, 81, 107-8, 169, 174, 177, 221
  imported food 54-56
  infrastructure 7, 38, 40, 42, 86, 131, 148, 152, 154, 155, 156, 161, 202, 235, 253
  land prices 42, 44
  manufacturing 8, 52, 57, 59, 60, 74, 248
  marketing 23, 30, 37, 49, 51, 53, 73, 95, 150, 155, 158-9, 181-6, 188, 201, 205, 207, 210, 225, 226, 228, 230, 238, 240, 246, 251, 253, 258, 260, 262
  'new' 253
  political stability and 38, 39, 117,
  social impact see Chapter Four
  tax revenue 43, 196, 199, 246
  'tourism awareness' 89, 90
  trade shows 155, 186, 201
  training 30, 67-8, 70, 75, 79, 82-9, 91, 145, 162, 189, 240, 250, 254, 256-7

Tourists, see Chapter Six
  attitudes 81, 125, 171-3
  spending 11, 18, 97, 158, 205, 206, 208
  weddings and honeymoons 176, 260
trade unions 71, 73
travel agents 21, 24, 38, 153, 173, 177, 183, 186, 187, 209, 257
Trinidad and Tobago 18, 19, 26, 32, 84, 85, 200
Turks and Caicos Islands 18, 26, 29, 155, 254

United Fruit Company 20, 21
United Nations 6, 7, 132, 164
UNESCO 2, 143, 143, 154, 158, 221, 234, 235, 255
United States 7, 44, 185, 188, 199
  Agency for International Development (USAID) 55, 60, 142, 145

Department of Commerce 25
Department of State Bureau of International Narcotics Matters 116
State Department 116
US Virgin Islands 11, 15, 17, 18, 68, 117, 136, 138, 149, 194, 195, 203, 205

vendors 38, 57, 74, 75-8, 90, 93, 94-6, 98, 103, 105, 122, 123, 136, 156, 180, 208, 223, 238, 241, 261
Venezuela 5, 183, 200, 240
Vielle Case, Dominica 258-260

Walcott, Derek 2, 68, 130, 220
watersports 29, 68, 132, 207, 212, 213
West India Committee 211
· West Indian Commission 6
Williams, Patrick 142
World Bank 6, 31, 32, 198, 251
World Tourism Organisation 7, 149
World Wildlife Fund 143